Spanish for Travelers

FODOR'S SPANISH FOR TRAVELERS

Travel information copyright © 2002 by Fodors LLC

Fodor's is a registered trademark of Random House, Inc.

Copyright © 1989 by Living Language, A Random House Company

Living Language and colophon are registered trademarks of Random House, Inc.

Published in the United States by Living Language, A Random House Company

www.livinglanguage.com

Editor: Nina Rubin
Production Editor: Jacinta O'Halloran
Production Manager: Heather Lanigan
Interior Design: Sophie Ye Chin
Third Edition

ISBN 1–4000–1492–1

ISSN 1538–6031

PRINTED IN THE UNITED STATES OF AMERICA

10 9 8 7 6 5 4 3 2 1

Fodor's LIVING LANGUAGE®

Spanish
for
Travelers

Fodor's Travel Publications New York, Toronto, London, Sydney, Auckland

CONTENTS

PREFACE   **xii**

CARPE HISPANIA   **1**

PRONUNCIATION GUIDE   **3**

Pronunciation Chart   3

1 APPROACHING PEOPLE   **6**

Courtesy   6

Greetings   6   Asking for Help   7

Question Words   7   Emergencies   8

2 THE BASICS   **10**

Colors   10   Age   18

Numbers and Quantities   10   Telling Time and Expressions of Time   18

Days, Months, and Seasons 13

The Date   14   Temperature Conversions   22

Holidays   15   Weather   23

     Abbreviations   23

3 AT THE AIRPORT   **25**

Dialogue: Customs and Immigration   25   At the Airline Counter   28

Clearing Customs   26   Airport Services and Transportation   29

Luggage and Porters   28   Common Airport Terms and Signs   29

4 MONEY MATTERS   **31**

About the Currency   31   Paying the Bill   33

Changing Money   31   Tipping   33

5 GETTING AROUND 34

Exploring on Foot 34

Taking a Taxi 35

Dialogue: Talking to the
Driver 36

On the Bus 37

Using the Metro 39

Going by Train 39

Common Public Signs 42

6 ACCOMMODATIONS 44

Dialogue: At the Front Desk
45

Hotel Arrangements and
Services 45

Using the Hotel Telephone
49

7 DINING OUT 51

Dialogue: At the Restaurant
52

Going to a Restaurant 53

Condiments and Utensils 55

The Bill 56

About Spanish Food 57

Spanish Restaurants 58

Typical Spanish Dishes 59

About Mexican Food 62

Mexican Restaurants 64

Typical Mexican Dishes 65

General Food Categories 68

8 SOCIALIZING 73

Dialogue: Meeting Someone
New 73

Introductions 74

Where Are You From? 75

Countries and Nationalities
77

What Do You Do? 79

Jobs and Occupations 80

Making Friends 81

The Family 83

In the Home 85

Talking About Language 86

9 PERSONAL CARE 88

Dialogue: Getting a Haircut
88

At the Barbershop 88

At the Beauty Parlor 89

Laundry and Dry Cleaning
91

10 HEALTH CARE 93

Dialogue: Finding a Doctor 94

Finding a Doctor 94

Talking to the Doctor 95

At the Hospital 101

The Dentist 103

The Optician 104

At the Pharmacy 105

11 ON THE ROAD 108

Car Rentals 108

Dialogue: At the Car-Rental Agency 108

Distances and Liquid Measures 110

The Service Station 111

Driving 111

Emergencies and Car Problems 113

Road Signs 117

12 COMMUNICATIONS 121

Telephones 121

The Post Office 123

E-mail and the Internet 125

Faxes and Telegrams 125

The Media 126

13 SIGHTSEEING 128

Dialogue: Touring the City 128

Finding the Sights 129

At the Museum 130

In the Old Part of Town 130

In the Business District 131

In the Country 132

Places to See in Spain 133

Places to See Around Mexico City 135

14 SHOPPING 139

Shopping in Spain 139

Shopping in Mexico 139

Dialogue: At the Gift Shop 140

Types of Folk Art 141

Bargaining 142

General Shopping List 144

Types of Stores 144

Clothing 145

Women's Clothing Sizes 147

Men's Clothing Sizes 148

The Jewelry Store 148

The Photo Shop 149

Music 150

Books, Magazines, and Paper Goods 151

Toiletries 152

Food Shopping 153

Weights and Measures 154

15 ENTERTAINMENT 155

Dialogue: Swimming 155

Camping 157

Movies 157

Theater, Concerts, Opera, and Ballet 158

Clubs, Discos, and Cabarets 161

Sports 162

Bullfights 163

16 GRAMMAR IN BRIEF 166

Definite and Indefinite Articles 166

Nouns 167

Adjectives 168

Adverbs 169

Comparisons with Adjectives and Adverbs 170

Pronouns 171

Prepositions 173

Negative Sentences 174

Questions 175

Verbs 175

ENGLISH-SPANISH DICTIONARY 181

SPANISH-ENGLISH DICTIONARY 218

SPAIN

La Coruña
Santiago
Vigo
Orense
CANTABRIAN MTS.
Gijón
Oviedo
PICOS DE EUROPA
León
Bay of Biscay
Santander
Bilbao
Seba
Burgos
Valladolid
Duero
Salamanca
Ávila
Segovia
SIERRA DE GUADARR
Guadal
MADRID
T
PORTUGAL
SIERRA DE GREDOS
Toledo
Tajo
Cáceres
Guadiana
Badajoz
SIERRA MORENA
Córdoba
Guadalquivir
Seville
Granada
SIERRA NEV
Gulf of Cadiz
COSTA DE LA LUZ
Jerez
Cádiz
Málaga
Marbella
Gibraltar
COSTA DEL SOL
CO
ATLANTIC OCEAN
Strait of Gibraltar
Tangiers
MOROCCO
TO CANARY ISLANDS
↓

Ensenada

BAJA

Golfo

de

California

CALIFORNIA

Nogales

Hermosillo

Ciudad
Juárez

Chihuahua

N
La

La Paz

Culiacán

Torreón

Durango
Mazatlán

Cabo
San Lucas

San José
del Cabo

Zacatecas

Aguascalientes

Puerto Vallarta

León

Guadalajara

Colima

Morelia

Cuernav

GUERRERO
Ixtapa
Zihuatanejo

Acapulco

PACIFIC OCEAN

N

| 0 | 200 miles |
| 0 | 300 km |

PREFACE

You don't need to know Spanish to get along in the Spanish-speaking world. The hundreds of Spanish phrases in this guide will see you through almost every situation you encounter as a tourist, from asking for directions at the start of your trip to conversing in a bar at the end. To make yourself understood, all you have to do is read the phonetics that appear after each expression, just as you would any English sentence. You'll come closer to approximating Spanish sounds if you study the pronunciation guide at the beginning of the book, and you can really polish your speech with the *Fodor's Spanish for Travelers* CDs, on which native speakers pronounce the guide's key Spanish dialogues. The words and phrases that are boldfaced in this book are recorded on the CDs. You will hear most of these expressions first in English, then in Spanish. If you are more likely to encounter an expression in Spanish first—an item on a menu, or questions such as "Are you here on vacation?"—you will hear the expression first in Spanish, then in English.

If you want to understand the structure of the language and begin to learn it on your own, check out the grammar chapter, Chapter 16. Additionally, a two-way 1,600-word dictionary at the end references all the key words in the book.

To help you get the most out of your trip, read the travel tips and cultural information covering Mexico and Spain interspersed throughout the chapters. You'll find, among other things, traditional Mexican and Spanish menu items, bank and store hours, metric conversion tables, and federal holidays, all gathered by Fodor's expert resident-writers.

Before you start chatting away, be sure to familiarize yourself with the table of contents on the previous pages, so that you know where to quickly find phrases and information when you need them.

¡Buen viaje! [bwehn VYAH-heh] Have a good trip!

CARPE HISPANIA

A vivir que son dos días—"live it up, life's only a couple of days"—is the Spanish version of Horace's *carpe diem,* and indeed it often seems that Spaniards are trying for two at a time. Few corners of the globe embrace pleasure and living for the moment more wholeheartedly than Iberia. Since 1975, the end of the 40-year military dictatorship that followed the 1936–39 Spanish Civil War, Spain has emerged as one of the most vibrant democracies in the world, a constitutional monarchy in which an essentially two-party system has shared power smoothly through over half a dozen elections. National elections regularly draw an astronomically high 80% rate of voter participation and result in conclusive mandates. In October 2001, Spain hosted the Conference on Democratic Transition and Consolidation, a global seminar on the problems and lessons resulting from the shift from a totalitarian to a democratic government. Thus, the country that James Michener described in the 1960s as "incapable of governing herself in the responsible French-English-American manner" is, forty years later, teaching the world how to do just that.

The Spanish language, spoken by some 360 million people around the globe, stemmed from Castilian, one of the six variants of Latin origin spoken on the Iberian peninsula in the 10th century. The others were Gallego, Leonés, Navarro-Aragonés, Catalán, and Mozárabe. (Euskera, the Basque language, is a non–Indo-European tongue thought to have been the aboriginal language of the Iberian tribes that inhabited the peninsula prior to the arrival of the Greeks, Phoenicians, Carthaginians, Romans, and Moors.)

Castile, originally a thin strip of territory running from Santander on the northern Atlantic coast south through Burgos, Palencia, Valladolid, and Avila, swelled in size and power, and by the 13th century, most of central Spain, through Andalucía to the Strait of Gibraltar, spoke Castilian Spanish. The Spanish humanist Elio Antonio de Nebrija (1441–1522) published the first Castilian grammar book, *Arte de la lengua castellana,* in 1492 for the express purpose of codifying Spanish and providing the means to spread the language to the lands Columbus was about to conquer. Today Spanish is the world's fourth most-spoken language—you will hear it in Spain, Mexico, Central America, the Caribbean, South America (except, largely, Brazil) and many parts of the United States.

In Spain, the diffusion (and in some cases, the forcible imposition) of Castilian Spanish has become the focus of a political debate, especially in the peripheral areas of the Iberian Peninsula struggling to preserve their cultural identities. First suppressed by the Bourbons, who took the Spanish throne in 1714, and later by the Franco regime from 1939 to 1975, Spain's other languages, especially Catalán, Gallego and Euskera, are recognized today by the Spanish monarchy and government; they are, a thousand years later, regaining ground lost to "the language of Cervantes," which remains Spain's common tongue and the one taught in this book.

Latin American Spanish developed as a direct result of the grammar books by Antonio de Nebrija. Spanish explorers and colonists arrived on the continent armed with Nebrija's texts and his famous maxim: *"Siempre la lengua fue compañera del imperio"*—Language has always been the companion of the empire.

Latin American Spanish is closer to the kind of Spanish spoken in Andalucía and southern Spain than it is to that of Castile. The most important phonetic difference is the sibilant *s* sound used instead of the *th* sound. *Cerveza* in Mexico, Andalucía (and, in fact, most of the Spanish-speaking world outside Castile) is pronounced sehr-BAY-sah. In Castile, you say thehr-BAY-thah. Despite all the different stories about the *th*, it probably came not from a lisping monarch, but from the Arabic that is such an important part of Castilian Spanish, a direct result of nearly eight centuries of Moorish domination. Since then, the language has also borrowed words from the indigenous languages of Central and South America, and more recently from English.

Latin American Spanish also includes many idiomatic expressions foreign to Spain, some of which have potentially embarrassing import. *Coger,* to catch or take, as in *coger un taxi* in Castilian Spanish, would mean to (attempt to) have sexual relations with a taxi in Mexico. There are long lists of these "false friends," or idiomatic idiosyncrasies. In this book, we've used words and phrases acceptable in all Spanish-speaking countries. Despite the occasional pitfall, there's no doubt that knowing the mother tongue has a way of opening doors. So, memorize some of the basic phrases in this book, and keep it handy to dip into when you need it. Most of the people you meet will welcome even your most halting attempts to use their language.

PRONUNCIATION GUIDE

Each English word and phrase in this book is presented with a Spanish equivalent. An easy-to-follow sound key (transcription) helps you achieve the correct pronunciation of the Spanish word. Simply read the sound key as you would in English. Although English and Spanish sounds are often not identical, the result should be fairly comprehensible to most Spanish speakers. To sharpen up your pronunciation, use the accompanying CD, which contains dialogues by native speakers. Listen and repeat what you hear on the recording and try to imitate their pronunciation as best you can.

PRONUNCIATION CHART

The chart below will be your guide to transcriptions used in this book. Review the chart to see how Spanish sounds are properly pronounced. As you use this book, you will become more familiar with the spelling of Spanish words and the sound key. Eventually you may be able to read the words without referring to the guide at all.

Four points should be stressed about pronouncing Spanish: First, since the Spanish spelling system is much more phonetic than English spelling, it is easier to tell, by reading it, how a word should be pronounced. Second, pay special attention to vowels since they affect the overall pronunciation of a word and are crucial to making yourself understood. Third, note that vowels in Spanish are generally more flat than in English. The long *o* sound in particular does not carry the *w* sound that usually accompanies it in English. Fourth, in the chart below—and throughout the book—note that the syllable stressed in a word appears in capital letters in the phonetic transcription, as in *taco* (TAH-koh), the first example below.

Vowels

Spanish Spelling	Approximate Sound in English	Phonetic Symbol	Example-Transcription
a	(f<u>a</u>ther)	ah	**taco** (<u>TAH</u>-koh)
e	(m<u>e</u>t)	eh	**cerca** (<u>SEHR</u>-kah) or **donde** (DOHN-d<u>eh</u>)
i	(b<u>ee</u>t)	ee	**día** (<u>DEE</u>-ah)
o	(b<u>o</u>th)	oh	**foto** (<u>FOH</u>-toh)
u	(b<u>oo</u>th)	oo	**mucho** (<u>MOO</u>-choh)
y	(f<u>ee</u>t)	ee	**y** (only a vowel when standing alone)

Frequent Vowel Combinations (Diphthongs)

Spanish Spelling	Approximate Sound in English	Phonetic Symbol	Example-Transcription
au	n<u>ow</u>	ow	**auto** (<u>OW</u>-toh)
ai/ay	r<u>i</u>pe	ahy	**bailar** (b<u>ahy</u>-LAHR) **hay** (<u>ahy</u>)
ei	(m<u>ay</u>)	ay	**peine** (<u>PAY</u>-neh)
ia	(<u>ya</u>rn)	yah	**gracias** (GRAH-s<u>yah</u>s)
ie	(<u>ye</u>t)	yeh	**siempre** (S<u>YEH</u>M-preh)
io	(<u>yo</u>del)	yoh	**adiós** (ah-D<u>YOH</u>S)
iu	(<u>you</u>)	yoo	**ciudad** (s<u>yoo</u>-DAHD)
oy	(s<u>oy</u> sauce)	oy	**estoy** (ehs-T<u>OY</u>)
ua	(<u>wa</u>nd)	wah	**cuando** (K<u>WAH</u>N-doh)
ue	(<u>we</u>t)	weh	**bueno** (B<u>WEH</u>-noh)
ui/uy	(s<u>wee</u>t)	wee	**ruido** (R<u>WEE</u>-doh) or **muy** (m<u>wee</u>)

Consonants

Spanish Spelling		Approximate Sound in English	
b/d/k/l/m/n/p/s/t		similar to English	

Spanish Spelling	Approximate Sound in English	Phonetic Symbol	Example-Transcription
c* (before e/i)	s (<u>c</u>ertain)	s	cine (<u>S</u>EE-neh)
c (before a/o/u)	k (<u>c</u>atch)	k	como (<u>K</u>OH-moh)
cc	cks (a<u>cc</u>ent)	k-s	lección (lehk-<u>S</u>YOHN)
ch	ch (<u>ch</u>amp)	ch	mucho (MOO-<u>ch</u>oh)
g (before a/o/u)	hard g (<u>g</u>o)	g	gato (<u>G</u>AH-toh)
g (before e/i)	hard h (<u>h</u>at)	h	gente (<u>H</u>EN-teh)
h	always silent	—	hasta (AHS-tah)
j	hard h (<u>h</u>at)	h	jefe (<u>H</u>EH-feh)
ll	y (<u>y</u>ard)	y	silla (SEE-<u>y</u>ah)
ñ	ny (ca<u>ny</u>on)	ny	señor (seh-<u>NY</u>OHR)
qu	k (<u>k</u>ite)	k	qué (<u>k</u>eh)
r	[single trill] (th<u>r</u>ow)	r	pero (PEH-<u>r</u>oh)
r	[double trill]	rr	rosa (<u>RR</u>OH-sah)
rr	[double trill]	rr	arroz (ah-<u>RR</u>OHS)
v	v (like <u>b</u>)	v	vaca (<u>B</u>AH-kah)
x	cks (ro<u>ck</u>s)	ks	taxi (TAH<u>K</u>-see)
z*	s	s	zona (<u>S</u>OH-nah)

*In parts of Spain, z—and also c before e or i—is pronounced like English *th*. Examples: *zona* (THON-nah), *cera* (THEH-rah), *cinco* (THEEN-koh). In this book, however, Latin American pronunciation is used throughout, as described in the chart above.

1 APPROACHING PEOPLE

COURTESY

Please.	Por favor.*	pohr fah-BOHR
Thank you.	Gracias.	GRAH-syahs
You're welcome.	De nada.	deh NAH-dah
Sorry (excuse me).	Disculpe.	dees-KOOL-peh
Excuse me.	Con permiso/	kohn pehr-MEE-soh/
	Perdón.	pehr-DOHN
It doesn't matter.	No importa.	noh eem-POHR-tah

GREETINGS

Good morning.	Buenos días.	BWEHN-nohs DEE-ahs
Good afternoon.	Buenas tardes.	BWEHN-nahs TAHR-dehs
Good evening.	Buenas noches.[†]	BWEHN-nahs NOH-chehs
Good night.	Buenas noches.[†]	BWEHN-nas NOH-chehs
Hello.	Hola.	OH-lah
Good-bye.	Adiós.	ah-DYOHS
See you soon.	Hasta pronto.	AHS-tah PROHN-tah
See you later.	Hasta luego/	AHS-tah LWEH-goh/
	Hasta la vista/	AHS-tah lah BEES-tah/
	Te veo más tarde.	teh BEH-oh mahs TAHR-deh
See you tomorrow.	Hasta mañana.	AHS-tah mah-NYAH-nah

* Boldface indicates phrases that are recorded on the audio cassette and CD.
† In Spanish, *buenas noches* is used both when arriving and when leaving, after around 6:00 P.M.

QUESTION WORDS

Who?	¿Quién?	kyehn?
Who? (plural)	¿Quiénes?	KYEH-nehs?
What?	¿Qué?	keh?
Why?	¿Por qué?	pohr KEH?
When?	¿Cuándo?	KWAHN-doh?
Where?	¿Dónde?	DOHN-deh?
Where from?	¿De dónde?	deh DOHN-deh?
Where to?	¿Adónde?	ah-DOHN-deh?
How?	¿Cómo?	KOH-moh?
How much?	¿Cuánto?	KWAHN-toh?

ASKING FOR HELP

Excuse me,	Perdón,	pehr-DOHN
_sir.	_señor.	_seh-NYOHR
_ma'am.	_señora.	_seh-NYOH-rah
_miss/ms.	_señorita.	_seh-nyoh-REE-tah
Do you speak English?	¿Habla usted inglés?	AH-blah oos-TEHD een-GLEHS?
Do you understand English?	¿Comprende inglés?	kohm-PREN-deh een-GLEHS?
Yes./No.	Sí./No.	see/noh
I'm sorry.	Lo siento.	loh SYEHN-toh
I'm a tourist.	Soy turista.	soy too-REES-tah
I don't speak Spanish.	No hablo español.	noh AH-bloh ehs-pah-NYOHL
I speak very little Spanish.	Hablo muy poco español.	AH-bloh mwee POH-koh ehs-pah-NYOHL
I don't understand.	No comprendo.	noh kohm-PREHN-doh
I understand a little.	Comprendo un poco.	kohm-PREHN-doh oon POH-koh
Please speak more slowly.	Hable más despacio, por favor.	AH-bleh mahs des-PAH-syoh, pohr fah-BOHR

7

Please repeat.	Repita, por favor.	rreh-PEE-tah, pohr fah-BOHR
May I ask a question?	Una pregunta, por favor.	OO-nah preh-GOON-tah, pohr fah-BOHR
Could you please help me?	¿Podría ayudarme?	poh-DREE-ah ah-yoo-DAHR-meh?
Where is the bathroom?	¿Dónde está el baño?	DOHN-deh ehs-TAH ehl BAH-nyoh?
Thank you very much.	Muchas gracias.	MOO-chas GRAH-syahs*

*Note: In Spanish, although there are some exceptions (*turista,* for example), most nouns and adjectives end in *-o* for males and *-a* for females, with the corresponding plurals *-os* and *-as.* Use *-os* when including both males and females. So, if you're an American male, you'd say, *Soy norteamericano.* If you're an American female, you'd say, *Soy norteamericana.* A group of females might say, *Somos norteamericanas,* and a mixed group would say, *Somos norteamericanos.*

EMERGENCIES

Look!	¡Mire!	MEE-reh!
Listen!	¡Escuche!	ehs-KOO-cheh!
Watch out!	¡Cuidado!	kuee-DAH-doh!
Fire!	¡Fuego!	FWEH-goh!
Help!	¡Ayuda!	ah-YOO-dah!
Help me!	¡Socorro!	soh-KOH-rroh!
Hurry!	¡Dése prisa!	DEH-seh PREE-sah!
Stop!	¡Alto!	AHL-toh!
I need help quick!	¡Necesito ayuda, pronto!	neh-seh-SEE-toh ah-YOO-dah, PROHN-toh!
Can you help me?	¿Puede ayudarme?	PWEH-deh ah-yoo-DAHR-meh?
Police!	¡Policía!	poh-lee-SEE-ah!
I need a policeman!	¡Necesito un policía!	neh-seh-SEE-toh oon poh-lee-SEE-ah!
It's an emergency!	¡Es una emergencia!	ehs OO-nah eh-mehr-HEHN-syah!

Leave me alone!	¡Déjeme en paz!	DEH-heh-meh ehn pahs!
That man's a thief!	¡Ese hombre es un ladrón!	EH-seh OHM-breh ehs oon-lah-DROHN!
Stop him!	¡Deténganlo!	deh-TEHN-gahn-loh!
He's stolen my	Me ha robado	meh ah rroh-BAH-doh
_pocketbook.	_la cartera.	_lah kahr-TEH-rah
_wallet.	_la billetera.	_lah bee-yeh-TEH-rah
_passport.	_el pasaporte.	_ehl pah-sah-POHR-teh
_watch.	_el reloj.	_ehl rreh-LOH
I've lost my	He perdido	eh pehr-DEE-doh
_suitcase.	_mi maleta.	_mee mah-LEH-tah
_money.	_mi dinero.	_mee dee-NEH-roh
_glasses.	_los anteojos.	_lohs ahn-teh-OH-hohs
car keys.	_las llaves de mi automóvil.	_lahs YAH-behs deh mee ow-toh-MOH-beel

2 THE BASICS

COLORS

red	rojo	RROH-hoh
yellow	amarillo	ah-mah-REE-yoh
green	verde	BEHR-deh
blue	azul	ah-SOOL
white	blanco	BLAHN-koh
brown	café/ marrón	kah-FEH/ mah-RROHN
orange	anaranjado	ah-nah-rahn-HAH-doh
purple	morado	moh-RAH-doh
black	negro	NEH-groh
gold	dorado	doh-RAH-doh
silver	plateado	plah-teh-AH-doh

NUMBERS AND QUANTITIES

Take the time to learn how to count in Spanish. You'll find that knowing the numbers will make everything easier during your trip.

Cardinal Numbers

zero	cero	SEH-roh
one	uno	OO-noh
two	dos	dohs
three	tres	trehs
four	cuatro	KWAH-troh
five	cinco	SEEN-koh
six	seis	says
seven	siete	SYEH-teh
eight	ocho	OH-choh
nine	nueve	NWEH-beh

ten	diez	dyes
eleven	once	OHN-seh
twelve	doce	DOH-seh
thirteen	trece	TREH-seh
fourteen	catorce	kah-TOHR-seh
fifteen	quince	KEEN-seh
sixteen	dieciséis	dyeh-see-says
seventeen	diecisiete	dyeh-see-SYEH-teh
eighteen	dieciocho	dyeh-see-OH-choh
nineteen	diecinueve	dyeh-see-NWEH-beh
twenty	veinte	BAYN-teh
twenty-one	veintiuno	bayn-tee-OO-noh
twenty-two	veintidós	bayn-tee-DOHS
twenty-three . . .	veintitrés . . .	bayn-tee-TREHS
thirty	treinta	TRAYN-tah
forty	cuarenta	kwah-REHN-tah
fifty	cincuenta	seen-KWEN-tah
sixty	sesenta	seh-SEHN-tah
seventy	setenta	seh-TEHN-tah
eighty	ochenta	oh-CHEHN-tah
ninety	noventa	noh-BEHN-tah
one hundred	cien	SYEHN
one hundred one	ciento uno	SYEHN-toh OO-noh
one hundred two . . .	ciento dos . . .	SYEHN-toh dohs
one hundred twenty . . .	ciento veinte . . .	SYEHN-toh BAYN-teh
one hundred thirty . . .	ciento treinta . . .	SYEHN-toh TRAYN-tah
two hundred	doscientos(-as)	dohs-SYEHN-tohs (-tahs)
three hundred	trescientos(-as)	trehs-SYEHN-tohs (-tahs)

11

four hundred	cuatrocientos(-as)	kwah-troh-SYEHN-tohs (-tahs)
five hundred	quinientos(-as)	kee-NYEHN-tohs (-tahs)
six hundred	seiscientos(-as)	says-SYEHN-tohs (-tahs)
seven hundred	setecientos(-as)	seh-teh-SYEHN-tohs (-tahs)
eight hundred	ochocientos(-as)	oh-choh-SYEHN-tohs (-tahs)
nine hundred	novecientos(-as)	noh-beh-SYEHN-tohs (-tas)
one thousand	mil	meel
two thousand	dos mil	dohs meel
three thousand . . .	tres mil . . .	trehs meel
one million	un millón	oon mee-YOHN
two million . . .	dos millones . . .	dohs mee-YOH-nehs

Ordinal Numbers

first	primero	pree-MEH-roh
	primer(-a)	pree-MEHR (MEHR-ah)
second	segundo(-a)	seh-GOON-doh(-dah)
third	tercero	tehr-SEH-roh
	tercer(-a)	tehr-SEHR (-SEH-rah)
fourth	cuarto(-a)	KWAHR-toh(-tah)
fifth	quinto(-a)	KEEN-toh(-tah)
sixth	sexto(-a)	SEHKS-toh(-tah)
seventh	séptimo(-a)	SEHP-tee-moh(-mah)
eighth	octavo(-a)	ohk-TAH-boh(-vah)
ninth	noveno(-a)	noh-BEH-noh(-nah)
tenth	décimo(-a)	DEH-see-moh(-mah)

Quantities

once	una vez	OO-nah behs
twice	dos veces	dohs BEH-sehs
last	último	OOL-tee-moh
half	medio	MEH-dyoh
a half	una mitad	OO-nah mee-TAHD
one-third	un tercio	oon TEHR-syoh
one-quarter	un cuarto	oon KWAHR-toh
percent	por ciento	pohr-SYEN-toh

Note: In Spanish, decimal points are indicated by commas. For example, 6.5 would be written 6,5 and pronounced "says KOH-mah SEEN-koh."

DAYS, MONTHS, AND SEASONS

Days of the Week	Días de la semana	DEE-ahs deh lah seh-MAH-nah
What day is it?	¿Qué día es hoy?	keh DEE-ah ehs oy?
Today is	Hoy es	oy ehs
_Monday.	_lunes.	_LOO-nehs
_Tuesday.	_martes.	_MAHR-tehs
_Wednesday.	_miércoles.	_MYEHR-koh-lehs
_Thursday.	_jueves.	_HWEH-behs
_Friday.	_viernes.	_BYEHR-nehs
_Saturday.	_sábado.	_SAH-bah-doh
_Sunday.	_domingo.	_doh-MEEN-goh

Months of the Year	Meses del año	MEH-sehs dehl AH-nyoh
January	enero	eh-NEH-roh
February	febrero	feh-BREH-roh
March	marzo	MAHR-soh
April	abril	ah-BREEL
May	mayo	MAH-yoh
June	junio	HOO-nyoh
July	julio	HOO-lyoh

August	agosto	ah-GOHS-toh
September	septiembre	sehp-TYEHM-breh
October	octubre	ohk-TOO-breh
November	noviembre	noh-BYEHM-breh
December	diciembre	dee-SYEHM-breh
Seasons	Estaciones	ehs-tah-SYOH-nehs
spring	la primavera	lah pree-mah-BEHR-rah
summer	el verano	ehl beh-RAH-noh
autumn	el otoño	ehl oh-TOH-nyoh
winter	el invierno	ehl een-BYEHR-noh

THE DATE

What is today's date?	¿Cuál es la fecha de hoy?	kwahl ehs lah FEH-chah deh oy?
Today is	Hoy es	oy ehs
_June 1, 2005	_el primero* de junio, de dos mil cinco	_ehl pree-MEH-roh deh HOO-nyoh deh dohs MEEL SEEN-ko
_April 12, 2005	_el doce de abril, de dos mil cinco.	_ehl DOH-seh deh ah-BREEL, deh dohs MEEL SEEN-ko
Her birthday is December 2, 1956.	Su cumpleaños es el dos de diciembre de mil novecientos cincuenta y seis.	soo coom-pleh-AH-nyohs ehs ehl dohs deh dee-SYEHM-breh deh mil noh-beh-SYEHN-tohs seen-KWEHN-tah ee says

*El primero ("the first") is used for the first day of each month. Otherwise, regular cardinal numbers are used for dates.

HOLIDAYS

In addition to celebrating familiar holidays like Christmas and New Year's, Spain and Latin America celebrate many holidays that are unique to specific areas. Most of these holidays are religious or national in origin. Small towns often hold celebrations to honor their patron saint or namesake (San José, San Luis, etc.). Keep holidays in mind when planning your trip, because most public offices and banks, and some museums, will be closed on these dates.

The following holidays are generally celebrated throughout the Spanish-speaking world.

Año Nuevo (AH-nyoh NWEH-boh)	New Year's Day	January 1
Día de los Reyes (DEE-ah deh lohs RREH-yehs) (or) Epifanía (eh-pee-fah-NEE-ah)	Epiphany	January 6
San José (sahn hoh-SEH).	St. Joseph's Day	March 19
Día del Trabajo (DEE-ah dehl trah-BAH-hoh)	Labor Day	May 1
San Juan Bautista	St. John the Baptist's Day	June 24
San Pedro y San Pablo (sahn PEH-droh ee sahn PAH-bloh)	Saint Peter's and Saint Paul's Day	June 29
Santiago (sahn-TYAH-goh)	Saint James' Day	July 25
Asunción (ah-soon-SYOHN)	Assumption Day	August 15
Día de la Raza (DEE-ah deh lah RRAH-sah)	Columbus Day	October 12
Todos los Santos (TOH-dohs lohs SAHN-tohs)	All Saints' Day	November 1

| Inmaculada Concepción (een-mah-koo-LAH-dah kohn-sehp-SYOHN) | Immaculate Conception | December 8 |
| Navidad (nah-bee-DAHD) | Christmas | December 25 |

Some religious holidays change dates according to the calendar. These include:

Viernes Santo (BYER-nehs SAHN-toh)	Good Friday
Pascua Florida (PAHS-kwah floh-REE-dah) or Pascua de Resurrección (PAHS-kwah deh rreh-soo-rrehk-SYOHN)	Easter
Corpus Christi (KOHR-poos KREES-tee)	Corpus Christi

Other holidays which have different dates in accordance with the country are:

Día de la Madre (DEE-ah deh lah MAH-dreh)	Mother's Day
Día del Padre (DEE-ah dehl PAH-dreh)	Father's Day
Día del Maestro (DEE-ah dehl mah-EHS-troh)	Teacher's Day

In Mexico

Most businesses in Mexico close on the following holidays as well as those listed above.

Día de la Constitución (DEE-ah deh lah kohns-tee-too-SYOHN)	Constitution Day (marks the signing of the constitutions of 1917 and 1957)	February 5
Benito Juárez (beh-NEE-toh HWAH-rehs)	Birthday of Benito Juárez (former President of Mexico)	March 21
Cinco de Mayo (SEEN-koh deh MAH-yoh)	Fifth of May (commemorates Mexico's victory over the French at the Battle of Puebla in 1862)	May 5
Apertura del Congreso (ah-pehr-TOO-rah dehl kohn-GREH-soh)	Opening Session of Congress (President's State of the Union Address)	September 1
Día de la Independencia (DEE-ah deh lah een-deh-pehn-DEHN-syah)	Independence Day (officially begins at 11:00 P.M. the night before, with El Grito (ehl GREE-toh), re-enacting Father Hidalgo's cry for independence from Spain in 1810)	September 16
Día de la Revolución (DEE-ah deh lah rreh-boh-loo-SYOHN)	Anniversary of the Revolution (parades and fireworks mark the anniversary of the Mexican Revolution of 1910)	November 20
Toma de posesión del Presidente (TOH-mah de poh-seh-SYOHN)	President's inauguration (held every six years)	December 1

Nuestra Señora de Guadalupe (NWEHS-trah seh-NYOH-rah deh gwah-dah-LOO-peh)	Our Lady of Guadalupe (day of the patron saint of Mexico; colorful processions and parades are held, especially at the Basilica in Mexico City)	December 12

AGE

How old are you?	¿Cuantos años tiene usted?	KWAHN-tohs AH-nyohs TYEH-neh oo-STEHD?
I'm 36.	Tengo treinta y seis años.	TEHN-goh TRAYHN-tah ee seh-EES AH-nyohs

TELLING TIME AND EXPRESSIONS OF TIME

What time is it?	¿Qué hora es?	keh OH-rah ehs?
At what time?	¿A qué hora?	ah keh OH-rah?
It's	Es	ehs
_one o'clock.	_la una.	_lah OO-nah
_1:15.	_la una y cuarto.	_lah OO-nah ee KWAHR-toh
_1:30.	_la una y media.	_lah OO-nah ee MEH-dyah
It's	Son las	sohn lahs
_1:45.*	_dos menos cuarto.	_dohs MEH-nos KWAHR-toh
_two o'clock.	_dos.	_dohs
_two o'clock in the morning.	_dos de la mañana.	_dohs deh lah mah-NYAH-nah
_two o'clock in the afternoon.	_dos de la tarde.	_dohs deh lah TAHR-deh

*In Spain, after the half hour on the clock, minutes are subtracted from the next hour. The literal translation of the Spanish for 1:45 is "two minus a quarter" (of an hour).

18

_2:10.	_dos y diez.	_dohs ee dyehs
_2:50.	_tres menos diez.	_trehs MEH-nohs dyehs
_three o'clock.	_tres.	_trehs
_four o'clock.	_cuatro.	_KWAH-troh
_five o'clock.	_cinco.	_SEEN-koh
_six o'clock.	_seis.	_says
_seven o'clock.	_siete.	_SYEH-teh
_eight o'clock.	_ocho.	_OO-choh
_nine o'clock.	_nueve.	_NWEH-beh
_ten o'clock.	_diez.	_dyehs
_eleven o'clock.	_once.	_OHN-seh
_twelve o'clock.	_doce.	_DOH-seh
It's midnight	**Es media noche**	ehs MEH-dyah NOH-cheh
It's noon	**Es mediodía**	ehs meh-dyoh-DEE-ah
Five minutes ago	**Hace cinco minutos**	AH-seh SEEN-koh mee-NOO-tohs
In a half hour	**En media hora**	ehn MEH-dyah OH-rah
After 8 P.M.	**Después de las ocho de la noche**	dehs-PWEHS deh lahs OH-choh deh lah NOH-cheh
Before 9 A.M.	**Antes de las nueve de la mañana**	AHN-tehs deh lahs NWEH-beh deh lah mah-NYAH-nah
When does it begin?	**¿Cuándo empieza?**	KWAHN-doh ehm-PYEH-sah?
He came.	**Él llegó.**	ehl yeh-GOH
_on time.	_a tiempo.	_ah TYEHM-poh
_early.	_temprano.	_tehm-PRAH-noh
_late.	_tarde.	_TAHR-deh

In Spanish-speaking countries, the 24-hour system, familiar in the United States as "military time," is often used in official listings, such as transportation schedules and theater times (3:00 P.M. is 12 plus 3, or 15:00, and so on, until 24:00, which is midnight). Midnight is also expressed as 00:00, and minutes past midnight are expressed as 00:01, and so forth, until 01:00.

You can use the following chart for quick reference.

The 24-Hour System

1 A.M.	01:00	la una	lah OO-nah
2 A.M.	02:00	las dos	lahs dohs
3 A.M.	03:00	las tres	lahs trehs
4 A.M.	04:00	las cuatro	lahs KWAH-troh
5 A.M.	05:00	las cinco	lahs SEEN-koh
6 A.M.	06:00	las seis	lahs says
7 A.M.	07:00	las siete	lahs SYEH-teh
8 A.M.	08:00	las ocho	lahs OH-choh
9 A.M.	09:00	las nueve	lahs NWEH-beh
10 A.M.	10:00	las diez	lahs dyehs
11 A.M.	11:00	las once	lahs OHN-seh
12 noon	12:00	las doce	lahs DOH-seh
1 P.M.	13:00*	las trece	lahs TREH-seh
2 P.M.	14:00*	las catorce	lahs kah-TOHR-seh
3 P.M.	15:00*	las quince	lahs KEEN-seh
4 P.M.	16:00*	las dieciséis	lahs dyeh-see-SAYS
5 P.M.	17:00*	las diecisiete	lahs dyeh-see-SYE-teh
6 P.M.	18:00*	las dieciocho	lahs dyeh-see-OH-choh
7 P.M.	19:00*	las diecinueve	lahs dyeh-see-NWEH-beh
8 P.M.	20:00*	las veinte	lahs BAYN-teh
9 P.M.	21:00*	las veintiuno	lahs bayn-tee-OO-noh
10 P.M.	22:00*	las veintidós	lahs bayn-tee-DOHS
11 P.M.	23:00*	las veintitrés	lahs bayn-tee-TREHS
12 midnight	24:00*	las veinticuatro	lahs vayn-tee-KWAH-troh

*Starting with 13:00 it's common to add the word **horas**: *Son las trece horas.*

The show you're planning to see might start at 7:30 P.M. or 19:30 (*las diecinueve horas y treinta minutos*).

Expressions of Time

now	*ahora*	ah-OH-rah
earlier	*más temprano*	mahs tehm-PRAH-noh

later	más tarde	mahs TAHR-deh
before	antes	AHN-tehs
after/afterward	después	dehs-PWEHS
soon	pronto	PROHN-toh
morning	mañana	mah-NYAH-nah
afternoon	tarde	TAHR-deh
night	noche	NOH-cheh
in the morning	por la mañana	pohr lah mah-NYAH-nah
in the afternoon	por la tarde	pohr lah TAHR-deh
at night	por la noche	pohr lah NOH-cheh
tomorrow morning	mañana por la mañana	mah-NYAH-nah por lah mah-NYAH-nah
the day after tomorrow	pasado mañana	pah-SAH-doh mah-NYAH-nah
yesterday	ayer	ah-YER
the day before yesterday	anteayer	ahn-teh-ah-YEHR
in a week	en una semana	ehn OO-nah seh-MAH-nah
next week	la semana próxima	lah seh-MAH-nah PROHK-see-mah
last week	la semana pasada	lah seh-MAH-nah pah-SAH-dah
next month	el mes próximo	ehl mehs PROHK-see-moh
last month	el mes pasado	ehl mehs pah-SAH-doh
next year	el año próximo	ehl AH-nyoh PROHK-see-moh
last year	el año pasado	ehl AH-nyoh pah-SAH-doh
five years ago	hace cinco años	AH-seh SEEN-koh AH-nyohs
during the eighties	durante los años ochenta	doo-RAHN-teh los AH-nyohs oh-CHEHN-tah

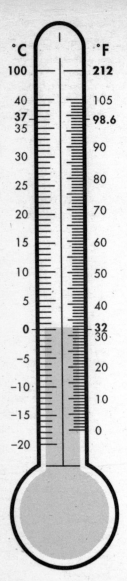

°C
100
40
37
35
30
25
20
15
10
5
0
-5
-10
-15
-20

°F
212
105
98.6
90
80
70
60
50
40
32
30
20
10
0

TEMPERATURE CONVERSIONS

In both Spain and Mexico, temperature is measured in degrees Celsius, or centigrade. To convert degrees Celsius into degrees Fahrenheit, use this formula:

To convert centigrade to Fahrenheit

$$\left(\frac{9}{5}\right)C° + 32 = F°$$

1. Divide by 5
2. Multiply by 9
3. Add 32

To convert Fahrenheit to centigrade

$$(F° - 32)\frac{5}{9} = C°$$

1. Subtract 32
2. Divide by 9
3. Multiply by 5

WEATHER

In Spain, summers are hot and winters are mild and rainy along the coast and bitterly cold elsewhere, with snow in the mountains. In Mexico, coasts and low-lying sections of the interior are often hot if not actually tropical in winter, even steamier in summer. But the high central plateau on which Mexico City and many colonial cities are located is springlike year-round. October and May are generally the driest months, but even during rainy season, June through September, it usually only rains for a few hours every day.

What's the weather like?	¿Qué tiempo hace?	keh TYEHM-poh AH-seh?
It's nice today.	Hace buen tiempo hoy.	AH-seh bwehn TYEHM-poh oy
The day's not too nice.	El día no está muy bueno.	ehl DEE-ah noh ehs-TAH muee BWEH-noh
It's	Hace	AH-seh
_windy.	_viento.	_BYEHN-toh
_hot.	_calor.	_kah-LOHR
_cold	_frío.	_FREE-oh
_sunny.	_sol.	_sohl
It's cloudy.	Está nublado.	ehs-TAH noo-BLAH-doh
It's rainy.	Llueve.	YWEH-beh
It's not snowing now.	No nieva ahora.	noh NYEH-bah ah-OH-rah

ABBREVIATIONS

Sr.	señor	Mr.
Sra.	señora	Mrs.
Srta.	señorita	Miss/Ms.
Dr.	Doctor	Dr. (Doctor)
Prof.	Profesor	Prof. (Professor)
Ud.	usted	you
Uds.	ustedes	you (plural)
Tel.	teléfono	Tel. (telephone)

Apdo.	Apartado de correos	P.O. Box
Avda.	Avenida	Ave. (Avenue)
c/	Calle	St. (Street)
Edo.	Estado	State
EE.UU.	Estados Unidos	U.S. (United States)
Cía.	Compañía	Co. (Company)
S.A.	Sociedad Anónima	Inc. (Incorporated)
Ltda.	Limitada	Ltd. (Limited)
FF.CC.	Ferrocarriles	Railroads
RENFE	Red Nacional de Ferrocarriles Españoles	National Railroad Network (*Spain*)

As a tourist, you should pass through customs smoothly and as rapidly as airport security measures and the number of arriving passengers will allow. Most personal belongings are duty-free, however tobacco products, alcohol, and perfume above certain amounts are taxed. In Mexico, you will have to itemize what you are bringing into the country. Officials may check that you still have those items when you leave—proof that they weren't resold in Mexico.

When leaving Spain or Mexico, remember that you may bring up to $800 worth of souvenirs duty-free back to the U.S. Residents 21 and over may bring back 1 liter of alcohol duty-free. Regardless of your age, you may return with 200 cigarettes and 100 non-Cuban cigars.

Canadian residents who have been out of Canada for more than seven days may return with C$750 worth of goods duty-free, or C$200 worth of goods if they've been away less than seven days.

Residents of the U.K. usually don't pass through customs when returning from a trip spent wholly in the European Union. When returning from Mexico (or another country outside the EU), U.K. residents may bring home 136 pounds worth of souvenirs, and limited amounts of tobacco and alcohol. Prohibited items include meat products, seeds, plants, and fruits.

Australian residents 18 and older may bring home A$400 worth of souvenirs duty-free, and New Zealanders 17 and older may bring home $700 worth of souvenirs duty-free.

DIALOGUE
Customs and Immigration (Aduana e inmigración)

Empleado de inmigración:	Buenos días. ¿Puedo ver su pasaporte?	BWEH-nohs DEE-ahs. PWEH-doh behr soo pah-sah-POHR-teh?
Turista:	Sí, aquí lo tiene.	see, ah-KEE loh TYEH-neh

Empleado:	¿Es usted norteamericano(-a)?	ehs oos-TEHD nohr-teh-ah-meh-ree KAH-noh (-nah)?
Turista:	Sí, lo soy.	see, loh soy
Empleado:	¿Cuánto tiempo va a estar en el país?	KWAHN-toh TYEHM-poh bah ah ehs-TAHR ehn ehl PAH-ees?
Turista:	Voy a estar aquí por tres semanas.	boy ah ehs-TAHR ah-KEE pohr trehs seh-MAH-nahs

....

Officer:	Hello. May I see your passport?
Tourist:	Yes, here it is.
Officer:	Are you American?
Tourist:	Yes, I am.
Officer:	How long will you stay in the country?
Tourist:	I'll be here for three weeks.

CLEARING CUSTOMS

What nationality are you?	¿Qué nacionalidad tiene?	Keh nah-syoh-nah-lee-DAHD TYEHN-eh?
I'm	Soy	soy
_American.	_norteamericano (-a).	_nohr-teh-ah-meh-ree-KAH-noh(-nah)
_Canadian.	_canadiense.	_kah-nah-DYEHN-seh
_English.	_inglés(-a).	_een-GLEHS(-GLEH-sah)
What's your name?	**¿Cómo se llama?**	**KOH-moh seh YAH-mah?**
My name is . . .	**Me llamo . . .**	**Meh YAH-moh . . .**
Where will you be staying?	¿Dónde va a hospedarse?	DOHN-deh bah ah ohs-peh-DAHR-seh?
I am staying at the Rex hotel.	**Estoy en el hotel Rex.**	**ehs-TOY ehn ehl oh-TEHL rrehks**

Are you here on vacation?	¿Está de vacaciones?	ehs-TAH deh bah-kah-SYOH-nehs?
I'm just passing through.	Estoy de paso.	ehs-TOY deh PAH-soh
I'm here on a business trip.	Estoy aquí en viaje de negocios.	ehs-TOY ah-KEE ehn BYAH-heh deh neh-GOH-syohs
I'll be here for	Voy a estar aquí por	boy ah ehs-TAHR ah-KEE pohr
_a few days.	_unos días.	_OO-nohs DEE-ahs
_a week.	_una semana.	_OO-nah seh-MAH-nah
_several weeks.	_unas semanas.	_OO-nahs seh-MAH-nahs
_a month.	_un mes.	_oon mehs
Your passport, please.	Su pasaporte, por favor.	soo pah-sah-POHR-teh, pohr fah-BOHR
Do you have anything to declare?	¿Tiene algo para declarar?	TYEH-neh AHL-goh pah-rah deh-klah-RAHR?
No, I have nothing to declare.	No, no tengo nada para declarar.	noh, noh THEN-goh NAH-dah pah-rah deh-klah-RAHR
Can you open the bag?	¿Puede abrir la maleta?	PWEH-deh ah-BREER lah mah-LEH-tah?
Of course.	Por supuesto.	pohr soo-PWEHS-toh
What are these?	¿Qué son éstos?	keh sohn EHS-tohs?
They're _personal effects.	Son _efectos personales.	sohn _eh-FEHK-tohs pehr-soh-NAH-lehs
_gifts.	_regalos.	_rreh-GAH-lohs
Do I have to pay duty?	¿Tengo que pagar impuestos?	TEHN-goh keh pah-GAHR eem-PWEHS-tohs?
Yes./No.	Sí./No.	see/noh
Have a nice stay.	¡Buena estadía!	BWEH-nah ehs-tah-DEE-ah!

LUGGAGE AND PORTERS

Porters are usually available at major airports and train stations. Some places may provide baggage carts to help you move your luggage to ground transportation. Be wary of bystanders who are not official employees.

I need	Necesito	neh-seh-SEE-toh
_a porter.	_un maletero.	_oon mah-leh-TEH-roh
_a baggage cart.	_un carrito para maletas.	_oon kah-RREE-toh PAH-rah mah-LEH-tahs
Here is my luggage.	Aquí están mis maletas.	ah-KEE ehs-TAHN mees mah-LEH-tahs
Take my bags	Lleve mis maletas	YEH-beh mees mah-LEH-tahs
_to the taxi.	_al taxi.	_ahl TAHK-see
_to the bus.	_al autobús.	_ahl ow-toh-BOOS
_to the sidewalk.	_a la acera/banqueta (Mexico).	_ah lah ah-SEH-rah/bahn-KEH-tah
Please be careful!	¡Cuidado, por favor!	kwee-DAH-doh, pohr fah-BOHR!
How much is it?	¿Cuánto es?	KWAHN-toh ehs?

AT THE AIRLINE COUNTER

Do you know where . . . is?	¿Sabe dónde está	SAH-beh DOHN-deh ehs-TAH
_the airline	_la aerolínea?	lah ah-eh-roh-LEE-neh-ah
_Iberia	_Iberia?	_ee-BEHR-ee-ah?
_Mexicana	_Mexicana?	_meh-hee-KAH-nah?
Where is	¿Dónde está	DOHN-deh ehs-TAH
_the information booth?	_el mostrador de información?	_ehl mohs-trah-DOHR deh een-fohr-mah-SYON?
_the ticket counter?	_el despacho de billetes?	_ehl dehs-PAH-choh deh bee-YE-tehs?
_luggage check-in?	_la entrega de equipaje?	_lah en-TREH-gah deh eh-kee-PAH-heh?

28

| _the place to pay the airport tax? | _el lugar para pagar el impuesto de salida? | _ehl loo-GAHR pah-rah pah-GAHR ehl eem-PWEHS-toh deh sah-LEE-dah? |

AIRPORT SERVICES AND TRANSPORTATION

In Spain, you'll find taxi stands and bus stops directly outside of the airports.

In Mexico, you should purchase taxi vouchers sold at stands inside or just outside the terminal. Fares generally vary by zones.

Taxis colectivos take two to three passengers and let them off in order of their destination on the route. Private taxis will cost you more.

Where is	**¿Dónde está**	**DOHN-deh ehs-TAH**
_the lost-baggage office?	_la sección de equipaje perdido?	_lah sehk-SYOHN deh eh-kee-PAH-heh pehr-DEE-doh?
_the duty-free shop?	_la tienda libre de impuestos?	_lah TYEHN-dah lee-BREH deh eem-PWEHS-tohs?
_the money exchange?	_la casa de cambio?	_lah KAH-sah deh KAHM-byoh?
_the car rental agency?	_la agencia de alquiler de autos?	_lah ah-HEHN-syah deh ahl-kee-LEHR deh ow-tohs?
_the bus stop?	_la parada de autobuses?	_lah pah-RAH-dah deh ow-toh-BOO-sehs?
_the taxi stand?	_la parada de taxis?	_lah pah-RAH-dah deh TAHK-sees?

COMMON AIRPORT TERMS AND SIGNS

vuelo directo	BWEH-loh dee-REHK-toh	direct flight (non-stop)
vuelo con escalas	BWEH-loh kohn ehs-KAH-lahs	direct flight (with stops)

número de vuelo	NOO-meh-roh deh BWEH-loh	flight number
viaje de ida	BYAH-heh deh EE-dah	one-way flight
viaje de ida y vuelta	**BYAH-heh deh EE-dah ee BWEHL-tah**	**round trip**
primera clase	**pree-MEH-rah KLAH-seh**	**first class**
clase turística	KLAH-seh too-REES-tee-kah	tourist class
asiento de ventanilla	ah-SYEHN-toh deh vehn-tah-NEE-yah	window seat
asiento de pasillo	ah-SYEHN-to deh pah-SEE-yoh	aisle seat
número de asiento	NOO-meh-roh deh ah-SYEHN-toh	seat number
sección de fumar	sehk-SYOHN deh foo-MAHR	smoking section
equipaje de mano	**eh-kee-PAH-heh deh MAH-noh**	**carry-on luggage**
etiquetas	eh-tee-KEH-tahs	luggage tags
LÍNEAS NACIONALES	LEE-neh-ahs nah-syoh-NAH-lehs	National Airlines
LÍNEAS INTERNACIONALES	LEE-neh-ahs een-tehr-nah-syoh-NAH-lehs	International Airlines
VUELOS NACIONALES	BWEH-lohs nah-syoh-NAH-lehs	National Flights
VUELOS INTERNACIONALES	BWEH-lohs een-ter-nah-syoh-NAH-lehs	International Flights
SALIDAS	sah-LEE-dahs	Departures
LLEGADAS	yeh-GAH-dahs	Arrivals
NO FUMAR	noh foo-MAHR	No Smoking
PUERTA DE SALIDA	PWEHR-tah deh sah-LEE-dah	Departure Gate

30

ABOUT THE CURRENCY

In Mexico, the currency is the *peso* (PEH-soh) which contains 100 *centavos* (sen-TAH-bos).

Coins: 5, 10, 20, and 50 centavos; 5, 10, and 20 pesos. Banknotes: 10, 20, 50, 100, 200, 500, and 1,000 pesos.

Many of the coins and bills are very similar, so check carefully. Some vendors accept dollars.

The official currency in Spain, as in the rest of the European Monetary Union, is the *euro* [EH-oo-roh], which replaced the *peseta* in January 2002. The euro is divided into 100 cents, or *céntimes* [sehn-TEE-mehss], and is symbolized as €.

Coins: 1, 2, 5, 10, 20, and 50 céntimes; 1 and 2 euros. Banknotes: 5, 10, 20, 50, 100, 200, and 500 euros.

Banks in Mexico are generally open weekdays 9 to 3—but later and on Saturdays in some large cities. In Spain, banks are open in summer on weekdays 8:30 to 1 PM and the rest of the year, weekdays 8:30 to 2 and Saturdays 8:30 to 1. Rates are usually best at banks and at ATMs. Remember that at banks, you usually need your passport to change money. At ATMs in both Spain and Mexico, you can use only four-digit PIN numbers; note that transaction fees may be higher than at home. Credit cards must be programmed for use at ATMs if you want cash advances.

CHANGING MONEY

Where can I change	¿Dónde puedo cambiar	DOHN-deh PWEH-doh kahm-BYAHR
_some money?	_algún dinero?	_ahl-GOON dee-NEH-roh?
_dollars?	_dólares?	_DOH-lah-rehs?
_this check?	_este cheque?	_EHS-teh CHEH-keh?
_traveler's checks?	_cheques de viajero?	_CHEH-kehs deh byah-HEH-roh?
Is the bank open?	¿El banco está abierto?	ehl BAHN-koh ehs-TAH ah-BYEHR-toh?

No, it's closed.	No, está cerrado.	noh ehs-TAH seh-RRAH-doh
But the currency exchange is open.	Pero la oficina de cambio está abierta.	PEH-roh lah oh-fee-SEE-nah deh KAHM-byoh ehs-TAH ah-BYEHR-tah
Do you accept	¿Acepta	ah-SEHP-tah
_personal checks?	_cheques personales?	_CHEH-kehs pehr-soh-NAH-lehs?
_a bank draft (cashier's check)?	_un giro bancario?	_oon HEE-roh bahn-KAH-ryoh?
_a money order?	_una orden de pago?	_OO-nah OHR-dehn deh PAH-goh?
How much is the . . . worth?	**¿A cómo está**	**ah KOH-moh ehs-TAH**
_dollar	_el dólar?	_ehl DOH-lahr?
_peso	_el peso?	_ehl PEH-soh?
_euro	_el euro?	_ehl eh-OO-roh?
Do you need _identification?	**¿Necesita _identificación?**	**neh-seh-SEE-tah _ee-dehn-tee-fee-kah-SYOHN?**
_my passport?	_mi pasaporte?	_mee pah-sah-POHR-teh?
_other documents?	_otros documentos?	_OH-trohs doh-koo-MEHN-tohs?
Where do I sign?	**¿Dónde firmo?**	**DOHN-deh FEER-moh?**
May I have _small bills?	**¿Puede darme _billetes pequeños?**	**PWEH-deh DAHR-meh _bee-YEH-tehs peh-KEH-nyos?**
_large bills?	_billetes grandes?	_bee-YEH-tehs GRAHN-dehs?
_some large and small bills?	**_billetes grandes y pequeños?**	**_bee-YEH-tehs GRAHN-dehs ee peh-KEH-nyos?**
_some coins?	_algunas monedas?	_ahl-GOO-nahs moh-NEH-dahs?
_the rest in change?	**_el resto en cambio?**	**_ehl RREHS-toh ehn KAHM-byoh?**

PAYING THE BILL

How much does it cost?	¿Cuánto cuesta?	KWAHN-toh KWEHS-tah?
The bill, please.	La cuenta, por favor.	lah-KWEN-tah pohr fah-BOHR
How much do I owe you?	¿Cuánto le debo?	KWAN-toh leh DEH-boh?
Is service included?	¿La propina está incluida?	Lah proh-PEE-nah ehs-TAH een-kloo-EE-dah?
This is for you.	Esto es para usted.	EHS-toh ehs pah-rah oos-TEHD

TIPPING

Service charges are fairly common in the more expensive restaurants and hotels in both Spain and Mexico. This may amount to about 10% to 15%. A tip may be added to the service charge in accordance with the level of service provided. It is customary to round up the bill or leave small change for the waiter. However, when no service charge is added to the bill, you should leave at least 15% tip in better restaurants and 10% in less expensive restaurants and in smaller towns. Tip cocktail servers and bartenders €.30 to €.50 per drink in Spain, about 10%–15% of the bill in Mexico.

In hotels, tip porters and bellboys about €.50 per suitcase in Spain, and 10 pesos to 20 pesos per suitcase in Mexico. Leave room-cleaning staff €.50 per night in Spain and about 10 pesos per night in Mexico. Tip the concierge if he or she has provided any special services. Give a doorman who calls a taxi for you about €.50 in Spain, 10 pesos in Mexico.

Tipping taxi drivers is optional in Mexico, but in Spain you should tip about 10% of the total fare, plus some for a long ride or help with suitcases.

Tip tour guides €2 in Spain and 50 pesos per half day in Mexico. Ushers should get €.50 or about 5 pesos. Hairdressers expect at least €1 in Spain and at least 30 pesos in Mexico.

5 GETTING AROUND

EXPLORING ON FOOT

It is hard to dispute the old saying that the best way to see a city is to explore it on foot. Many guidebooks provide self-guided walking tours of the most interesting landmarks and areas in major cities. Since most European cities are characterized by their twisty, charming, but maze-like streets, you will need a map (available at visitor information centers, newsstands, hotels, and bus stops) and, most likely, you will need to ask for directions. In Spain and Mexico, people use the metric system, so you'll hear people refer to distances in meters, *metros* [MEH-trohs], or they may point out landmarks such as traffic lights, *semaforos* [seh-MAH-foh-rohs].

Do you have a map of the city?	¿Tiene usted un mapa de la ciudad?	TYEH-neh oos-TEHD oon MAH-pah deh lah syoo-DAHD?
Could you show me on the map?	¿Puede usted indicármelo en el mapa?	PWEH-deh oo-STEHD een-dee-KAHR-meh-loh ehn ehl MAH-pah?
Can I get there on foot?	¿Puedo llegar allí a pie?	PWEH-doh yeh-GAHR ah-YEE ah pyeh?
How far is it?	¿A qué distancia està?	ah keh dees-TAHN-syah ehs-tah?
I'm lost.	Estoy perdido(-a).	ehs-TOY pehr-DEE-doh(-dah)
Where is	¿Dónde está	DOHN-deh ehs-TAH
_the Rex hotel?	_el hotel Rex?	_ehl oh-TEHL rreks?
_. . . Street?	_la calle . . . ?	_lah KAH-yeh . . . ?
_. . . Avenue?	_la avenida . . . ?	_lah ah-beh-NEE-dah . . . ?
How can I get to	¿Cómo puedo ir a	KOH-moh PWEH-doh eer ah
_the train station?	_la estación de ferrocarril?	_lah ehs-tah-SYON deh feh-rroh-cah-RREEL?
_the bus stop?	_la parada de autobuses?	_lah pah-RAH-dah deh ow-toh-BOO-ses?

_the ticket office?	_la taquilla?	_lah tah-KEE-yah?
_the subway entrance?	_la entrada del metro?	_lah ehn-TRAH-dah dehl MEH-troh?
_the airport?	_el aeropuerto?	_ehl ah-eh-roh-PWEHR-toh?
straight ahead	derecho	deh-REH-choh
to the right	a la derecha	ah lah deh-REH-chah
to the left	a la izquierda	ah lah ees-KYEHR-dah
a block away	a una cuadra	ah OO-nah KWAH-drah
on the corner	en la esquina	ehn lah ehs-KEE-nah
on the square	en la plaza	ehn lah PLAH-sah
facing, opposite	enfrente	ehn-FREHN-teh
across	al frente	ahl FREHN-teh
next to	al lado	ahl LAH-doh
near	cerca	SEHR-kah
far	lejos	LEH-hohs

TAKING A TAXI

Taxis in Spain are usually easy to identify; most display a logo on the door or have a light on top. Taxis are normally easy to find at airports near the baggage-claim areas. From your hotel, taxis taken at a taxi stop (*una parada de taxis* [OO-nah pah-RAH-dah deh TAHK-sees]) or just outside the hotel may sometimes be a little more expensive than those you can hail along the street. Some taxis charge by zones and should display a map showing the fares by zone. Others charge whatever appears on the meter. If there is no meter, you should settle on the fare before getting in. Do *not* hail taxis on the street in Mexico City. Many foreigners have been mugged in pirate taxis. This is generally not a problem in any other Mexican city or town. Also watch for any special regulations applying to charges for bags or supplemental fees after certain hours. In Mexico, a small tip may be given, usually by rounding off the fare. A 10% tip is customary in Spain.

DIALOGUE
Talking to the Driver (Conversación con el taxista)

Turista:	**Buenos días. ¿Está libre?**	BWEH-nohs DEE-ahs, ehs-tah LEE-breh?
Chofer:	**Sí, ¿adónde va?**	see, ah-DOHN-deh bah?
Turista:	**A la estación de autobuses.**	ah lah ehs-tah-SYOHN deh ow-toh-BOO-sehs
Chofer:	**Está bien.**	ehs-TAH byehn
Turista:	**¿Cuánto tarda?**	KWAHN-toh TAHR-dah?
Chofer:	**Unos veinte minutos.**	OO-nohs BAYN-teh mee-NOO-tohs
Turista:	**Está bien. Muchas gracias.**	ehs-TAH byehn. MOO-chas GRAH-syahs

....

Tourist:	Good day. Is this taxi free?
Driver:	Yes, where are you going?
Tourist:	To the bus station.
Driver:	Fine.
Tourist:	How long does it take?
Driver:	About twenty minutes.
Tourist:	That's fine. Thank you.

Is this taxi	¿Está	ehs-TAH
_free?	_libre?	_LEE-breh?
_occupied?	_ocupado?	_oh-koo-PAH-doh?
Do you know this address?	**¿Conoce usted esta dirección?**	koh-NOH-seh oos-TEHD EHS-tah dee-rehk-SYOHN?
Please take me	**Lléveme, por favor,**	YEH-beh-meh, pohr fah-BOHR,
_to the Rex hotel.	_al hotel Rex.	_ahl oh-TEHL rrehks
_to the station.	_a la estación.	_ah lah ehs-tah-SYOHN

_to the main square.	_a la plaza principal.	_ah lah PLAH-sah preen-see-PAHL
_to the center (of town).	_al centro.	_ahl SEHN-troh
_to Calle Blanca	_a la calle Blanca	_ah lah KAH-yeh BLAHN-kah
_to Avenida Real	_a la avenida Real	_ah lah ah-beh-NEE-dah reh-AHL
Slower, please.	**Más despacio, por favor.**	**mahs des-PAH-syoh, pohr fah-BOHR**
Stop over there.	**Pare allí**	**PAH-reh ah-YEE**
meter	el taxímetro	el tahk-SEE-meh-troh
fare	la tarifa	lah tah-REE-fah
fixed rate	la tarifa fija	lah tah-REE-fah FEE-hah
tip	la propina	lah proh-PEE-nah

ON THE BUS

The bus networks in Spain and Mexico are extensive and efficient. In both countries, inter-city buses go where trains do not, service is frequent, and tickets can usually be purchased on the spot. First-class buses have televisions and, in Mexico, even hostess service. There are often several bus stations (*las terminales de autobuses* [lahs tehr-mee-NAH-lehs deh ow-toh-BOO-sehs]) in different parts of the city; which you use depends on your destination.

Most other Latin American cities have extensive urban bus systems; however, buses do tend to be overcrowded.

Although it is usually easiest and fastest to take a taxi to your destination, there are good reasons to take a bus. It's inexpensive and you can sightsee at the same time. In Mexico City, another transportation option is the *pesero* or *combi*, usually a taxi or small van that follows a fixed route and charges a fixed fare. Although they pick up and drop off passengers along the way, they are faster than the larger city buses.

| I'm looking for the bus stop. | Estoy buscando la parada de autobuses. | ehs-TOY boos-KAHN-doh lah pah-RAH-dah deh ow-toh-BOO-sehs |

What bus line goes	¿Qué línea va	keh LEE-neh-ah bah
_north?	_al norte?	_ahl NOHR-teh?
_south?	_al sur?	_ahl soor?
_east?	_al este?	_ahl EHS-teh?
_west?	_al oeste?	_ahl oh-EHS-teh?
What bus do I take to go to	¿Qué autobús tomo para ir a	keh ow-toh-BOOS TOH-moh PAH-rah eer ah
_Madrid?	_Madrid?	_mah-DREED?
_Mexico City?	_la ciudad de México?	_lah syoo-DAHD deh MEH-hee-koh?
How many stops until the Museum of Modern Art?	¿Cuántas paradas hasta el Museo de Arte Moderno?	KWAHN-tahs pah-RAH-dahs AHS-tah ehl moo-SEH-oh deh AHR-teh moh-DEHR-noh?
How long does it take to get to Seville?	¿Cuánto demora para ir hasta Sevilla?	KWAHN-toh deh-MOH-rah PAH-rah eer AHS-tah seh-BEE-yah?
Can you tell me when to get off?	¿Podría decirme cuándo debo bajarme?	poh-DREE-ah deh-SEER-meh KWAN-doh DEH-boh bah-HAHR-meh?
How much is the fare?	¿Cuánto es el billete?	KWAHN-toh ehs ehl bee-YEH-teh?
Should I pay when I get on?	¿Debo pagar al subir?	DEH-boh pah-GAHR ahl soo-BEER?
Where do I take the bus to return?	¿Dónde se toma el autobús para regresar?	DOHN-deh seh TOH-mah ehl ow-toh-BOOS PAH-rah rreh-greh-SAHR?
How often do the return buses run?	¿Cada cuánto hay autobuses de regreso?	KAH-dah KWAHN-toh ahy ow-toh-BOO-sehs deh rreh-GREH-soh?
Which is the closest stop to the park?	¿Cuál es la parada más cercana al parque?	KWAHL ehs lah pah-RAH-dah mahs sehr-KAH-nah ahl PAHR-keh?
I would like	Quisiera	kee-SYEH-rah
_a ticket.	_un billete.	_oon bee-YEH-teh

38

_a receipt.	_un recibo.	_oon reh-SEE-boh
_a reserved seat.	_un asiento numerado.	_oon ah-SYEHN-toh noo-meh-RAH-doh
_first class.	_primera clase.	_pree-MEH-rah KLAH-seh
_second class.	_segunda clase.	_seh-GOON-dah KLAH-seh
_a direct bus.	_un autobús directo.	_oon ow-toh-BOOS dee-REHK-toh
_an express bus.	_un autobús directo.	_oon ow-toh-BOOS ehks-PREH-soh
_ticketed luggage.	_equipaje facturado.	_eh-kee-PAH-heh fahk-too-RAH-doh

USING THE METRO

Metros, or subway systems, in Madrid, Barcelona, Mexico City, Caracas, and Buenos Aires are all quite efficient, and Mexico City's is especially fast and spacious. All will save you time and get you to all of the most important places. Like subways anywhere, they tend to be crowded, especially at rush hour.

Where can I buy a token?	¿Dónde puedo comprar una ficha?	DOHN-deh PWEH-doh kohm-PRAHR OO-nah FEE-chah?
Where can I buy a ticket?	¿Dónde puedo comprar un billete?	DOHN-deh PWEH-doh kohm-PRAHR oon bee-YEH-teh?
How much are they?	¿Cuánto cuestan?	KWAHN-toh KWEHS-tahn?
Is there a map for the metro?	¿Hay un mapa del metro?	ahy oon MAH-pah dehl MEH-troh?
Which train do I take to go to . . . ?	¿Qué tren tomo para ir a . . . ?	keh trehn TOH-moh PAH-rah eer ah . . . ?
Can you tell me when we arrive at . . . ?	¿Me avisa cuando lleguemos a . . . ?	meh ah-BEE-sah KWAHN-doh yeh-GEH-mohs ah . . . ?

GOING BY TRAIN

Traveling by train in Spain is not only convenient, but also a great way to see the countryside if you travel by day, and a comfortable way to go overnight on a long stretch. Discounts

39

are available for trips in accordance with the kilometers you travel. It's a good idea to make reservations, which can be done at travel agencies or at the railway station.

Sadly, passenger trains in Mexico have been phased out, with the exception of the spectacular ride through the Copper Canyon.

Train services in Spain are classified in several ways:

Expreso (ehks-PREH-soh)	A long-distance night train with few stops.
Rápido (RAH-pee-doh)	A fast train, but not nearly as fast as the Expreso, which makes more stops.
Talgo (TAHL-goh)	Deluxe accommodations, reclining seats, and air conditioning. Travels between major cities, such as Madrid, Barcelona, Valencia, Sevilla, Cádiz, Málaga, and Bilbao.
Ave (AH-beh)	High speed deluxe train with service between Madrid and Sevilla.
Electrotren (eh-LEHK-troh-trehn)	A luxury train, not as fast as the Talgo, with more stops, and also more economical.
TER (teh eh eh-reh)	A luxury diesel express, like the Talgo, but with more stops.
TAF (te ah eh-feh)	A second-class diesel train.
Ferrobuses (feh-rroh-BOO-sehs)	Local trains.

When does the train leave for Madrid?	¿Cuándo sale el tren para Madrid?	KWAN-doh SAH-leh ehl trehn PAH-rah mah-DREED?
Is it a . . . train?	¿Es un tren	ehs oon trehn
_local	_local?	_loh-KAHL?
_express	_expreso?	_eks-PREH-soh?
_through	_directo?	_dee-REHK-toh?
When does the train . . .	¿Cuándo . . . el tren?	KWAHN-doh . . . ehl trehn?
_leave?	_sale	_SAH-leh
_arrive?	_llega	_YEH-gah

Is the train	¿Está el tren	ehs-TAH ehl trehn
_on time?	_en hora? a tiempo?	_ehn OH-rah? ah TYEHM-poh?
_late?	_retrasado?	_rreh-trah-SAH-doh?
From what platform does it leave?	¿De qué andén sale?	deh keh ahn-DEHN SAH-leh?
Does this train stop at	¿Este tren para en	ES-teh trehn PAH-rah ehn
_Córdoba?	_Córdoba?	_KOHR-doh-bah?
_Toledo?	_Toledo?	_toh-LEH-doh?
_Jerez?	_Jerez?	_heh-REHS?
Is there time to	¿Hay tiempo para	ahy TYEHM-poh PAH-rah
_eat something?	_comer algo?	_koh-MEHR AHL-goh?
_drink something?	_tomar algo?	_toh-MAHR AHL-goh?
_buy something?	_comprar algo?	_kohm-PRAHR AHL-goh?
_take pictures?	_tomar fotografías?	_toh-MAHR foh-toh-grah-FEE-ahs?
Is there a dining car?	¿Hay un coche-comedor?	ahy oon KOH-cheh koh-meh-DOHR?
Is there a sleeping car?	¿Hay un coche-cama?	ahy oon KOH-cheh KAH-mah?
I'd like a . . . ticket.	Quisiera un billete de	kee-SYEH-rah oon bee-YEH-teh deh
_round-trip	_ida y vuelta.	_EE-dah ee BWEHL-tah
_one-way	_ida.	_EE-dah
Is this seat taken?	¿Está ocupado este asiento?	ehs-TAH oh-koo-PAH-doh EHS-teh ah-SYEHN-toh?
Excuse me, I believe this is my seat.	Perdón, creo que éste es mi asiento.	pehr-DOHN, KREH-oh keh EHS-teh ehs mee ah-SYEHN-toh
Sorry, this seat is occupied.	Perdón, este asiento está ocupado.	pehr-DOHN, EHS-teh ah-SYEHN-toh ehs-TAH oh-koo-PAH-doh
No, it's not occupied.	No, no está ocupado.	noh, noh ehs-TAH oh-koo-PAH-doh

| I would like a no-smoking compartment. | Quisiera un compartimiento de no fumadores | kee-SYEH-rah oon cohm-pahr-tih-MYEHN-toh deh noh foo-mah-DOH-rehs |

COMMON PUBLIC SIGNS

ABIERTO	ah-BYEHR-toh	Open
AGUA NO POTABLE	AH-gwah noh poh-po-TAH-bleh	Do Not Drink the Water
ALTO	AHL-toh	Stop
ASCENSOR	ah-sehn-SOHR	Elevator
BAJADA	bah-HAH-dah	Down
BAÑOS	BAH-nyohs	Bathrooms
BIENVENIDOS	byen-beh-NEE-dohs	Welcome
CABALLEROS	kah-bah-YEH-rohs	Gentlemen
CAJA	KAH-hah	Cashier
CALIENTE (C)	kah-LYEHN-teh	Hot
CAMBIO	KAHM-byoh	Exchange
CERRADO	seh-RRAH-doh	Closed
COMPLETO	kohm-PLEH-toh	Full
CUIDADO	kwee-DAH-doh	Watch Out
DAMAS	DAH-mahs	Ladies
EMPUJE	ehm-POO-heh	Push
ENTRADA	ehn-TRAH-dah	Entrance
FRÍO (F)	FREE-oh	Cold
JALE (Mexico) (or) TIRE	HAH-leh TEE-reh	Pull
LAVABO	lah-BAH-boh	Sink
LIBRE	LEE-breh	Vacant
LIQUIDACIÓN	lee-kee-dah-SYOHN	Close-Out Sale
NO FUMAR	Noh foo-MAHR	No Smoking
NO HAY PASO	noh ahy PAH-soh	Do Not Enter
NO PASE	noh PAH-seh	Do Not Enter
NO PISAR EL CÉSPED	noh pee-SAHR ehl SEHS-pehd	Keep Off The Grass

NO PISAR EL ZACATE (Mexico)	noh pee-SAHR ehl sah-KAH-teh	Keep Off The Grass
NO TOCAR	noh toh-KAHR	Do Not Touch
OCUPADO	oh-koo-PAH-doh	Busy, Occupied
PARADA	pah-RAH-dah	(Bus) Stop
PASE	PAH-seh	Walk, Cross
PELIGRO	peh-LEE-groh	Danger
PRIVADO	pree-BAH-doh	Private
PROHIBIDO	proh-ee-BEE-doh	Forbidden
PROHIBIDO EL PASO	proh-ee-BEE-doh ehl PAH-soh	No Entrance, Keep Out
PROHIBIDO FUMAR	proh-ee-BEE-doh foo-MAHR	No Smoking
PROHIBIDO TOMAR (SACAR) FOTOGRAFÍAS	proh-ee-BEE-doh toh-MAHR (sah-KAHR) foh-toh-graf-FEE-ahs	No Photographs
PROHIBIDO TIRAR OBJETOS POR LA VENTANA	proh-ee-BEE-doh tee-RAHR ohb-HEH-tohs pohr lah behn-TAH-nah	Do Not Throw Objects Out of the Window
REBAJAS	rreh-BAH-hahs	Sale
REMATE	rreh-MAH-teh	Auction
RESERVADO	rreh-sehr-BAH-doh	Reserved
SALIDA	sah-LEE-dah	Exit
SALIDA DE EMERGENCIA	sah-LEE-dah deh eh-mehr-HEHN-syah	Emergency Exit
SE ALQUILA	seh ahl-KEE-lah	For Rent
SEÑORAS	seh-NYOH-rahs	Women
SEÑORES	seh-NYOH-rehs	Men
SERVICIOS (Spain)	sehr-BEE-syohs	Toilets
SE VENDE	seh BEHN-deh	For Sale
SUBIDA	soo-BEE-dah	Up
TIRE	TEE-reh	Pull
VENENO	beh-NEH-noh	Poison
VENTA	BEHN-tah	Sale

6 ACCOMMODATIONS

In most cases, it's best to make hotel reservations in advance, especially if an important holiday or celebration is taking place where you are going. In Spain, hotels include both new high-rises and lovely *paradors* (inns installed in castles, monasteries, and convents). You will find complete hotel information in the *Guía de Hoteles* (Hotel Guide), available at any branch of the Spanish National Tourist Office.

In Mexico, accommodations range from simple budget properties to modern high-rise hotels. You will also find restored estates, haciendas, or monasteries dating from the 16th and 17th centuries but with modern amenities. All the better hotels have air-conditioning; the simpler ones have showers but not bathtubs.

In both Spain and Mexico, the government rates properties with one to five stars. Ratings reflect the number of facilities and amenities rather than the quality of the property.

hotel	hotel	oh-TEHL
pension (usually with meals)	pensión	pehn-SYOHN
hostel	hostal	oh-STAHL
small hotel	albergue	ahl-BEHR-geh
top-quality government hotel (*Spain*)	parador	pah-rah-DOHR
inn (usually in the countryside)	refugio	rreh-FOO-hyoh
inn	posada	poh-SAH-dah
student residence	residencia estudiantil	rreh-see-DEHN-syah ehs-too-dyahn-TEEL

DIALOGUE
At the Front Desk (En la recepción)

Turista:	Quisiera una habitación doble, por favor.	kee-SYEH-rah OO-nah ah-bee-tah-SYOHN DOH-bleh, pohr fah-VOHR
Recepcionista:	¿Por cuánto tiempo?	pohr KWAHN-toh TYEHM-poh?
Turista:	Por cuatro noches.	pohr KWAH-troh NOH-chehs
	¿Cuánto cuesta por noche?	KWAHN-toh KWEHS-tah pohr NOH-cheh?
Recepcionista:	Cuesta 35.000 pesos por noche.	KWEHS-tah trayn-tee-SEEN-koh meel PEH-sohs pohr NOH-cheh
Turista:	Está bien. ¿Puedo registrarme?	ehs-TAH byehn. PWEH-doh rreh-he-STRAR-meh?
Recepcionista:	Sí. Llene este formulario, por favor.	see. YEH-neh EHS-teh fohr-moo-LAH-ryoh, pohr fah-VOHR
Turista:	¡Cómo no! Gracias.	KOH-moh noh! GRAH-syahs

Tourist:	I'd like a double room, please.
Clerk:	For how long?
Tourist:	For four nights. How much is it per night?
Clerk:	It's 35,000 pesos per night.
Tourist:	Fine. May I register?
Clerk:	Yes. Please fill out this form.
Tourist:	Of course. Thank you.

HOTEL ARRANGEMENTS AND SERVICES

I have a reservation.	Tengo una reservación./ una reserva. (Spain)	TEHN-goh OO-nah rreh-sehr-vah-SYOHN/ . . . OO-nah rre-SEHR-vah

I would like a room for	Quisiera una habitación por	kee-SYEH-rah OO-nah ah-bee-tah-SYOHN pohr
_one night.	_una noche.	_OO-nah NOH-cheh
_two nights.	_dos noches.	_dohs NOH-chehs
_a week.	**_una semana.**	**_OO-nah seh-MAH-nah**
_two weeks.	_dos semanas.	_dohs seh-MAH-nahs
How much is it	**¿Cuánto es**	**KWAHN-toh ehs**
_for a day?	_por día?	_pohr DEE-ah?
_for a week?	_por una semana?	_pohr OO-nah seh-MAH-nah?
Does that include tax?	¿Incluye impuestos?	een-KLOO-yeh eem-PWEHS-tohs?
Do you have a room with	**¿Tiene una habitación con**	**TYEH-neh OO-nah ah-bee-tah-SYOHN kohn**
_a private bath?	_baño privado?	_BAH-nyoh pree-BAH-doh?
_a shower?	_una ducha?	_OO-nah DOO-chah?
_air-conditioning?	_aire acondicionado?	_AY-reh ah-kohn-dee-syoh-NAH-doh?
_heat?	_calefacción?	_kah-leh-fak-SYOHN?
_television?	_televisor?	_teh-leh-bee-SOHR?
_hot water?	_agua caliente?	_AH-gwah kah-LYEHN-teh?
_a balcony?	_balcón?	_bahl-KOHN?
_a view facing the street?	_vista a la calle?	_BEES-tah ah lah KAH-yeh?
_a view facing the ocean?	_vista al mar?	_BEES-tah ahl mahr?
Does the hotel have	**¿Tiene el hotel . . . ?**	**TYEH-neh ehl oh-TEHL . . . ?**
_a restaurant?	_un restaurante?	_oon rrehs-tow-RAHN-teh?
_a bar?	_un bar?	_oon bahr?
_a swimming pool?	_una piscina/ alberca (Mexico)?	_OO-nah pee-SEE-nah/ahl-BEHR-kah?

46

_room service?	_servicio de habitación?	_sehr-BEE-syoh deh ah-bee-tah-SYOHN?
_a garage?	_un garaje?	_oon gah-RAH-heh?
_a safe-deposit box?	_una caja de valores/ seguridad? (Mexico)	_OO-nah KAH-hah deh bah-LOH-rehs/ seh-goo-ree-DAHD?
_laundry service?	_servicio de lavandería?	_sehr-BEE-syoh deh lah-vahn-deh-REE-ah?
I would like	**Quisiera**	**kee-SYE-rah**
_meals included.	_con las comidas incluidas.	_kohn lahs koh-MEE-dahs een-KLUEE-dahs
_breakfast only.	_solamente con desayuno.	_soh-lah-MEN-teh kohn deh-sah-YOO-noh
_no meals included.	_sin comidas.	_seen koh-MEE-dahs
_an extra bed.	_una cama más.	_OO-nah KAH-mah mahs
_a baby crib.	_una cuna	_OO-nah KOO-nah
_another towel.	_otra toalla.	_OH-trah TWAH-yah
_soap.	_jabón.	_hah-BOHN
_clothes hangers.	_ganchos de ropa.	_GAHN-chohs deh RROH-pah
_another blanket.	_otra manta.	_OH-trah MAHN-tah
_drinking water.	_agua para beber.	_AH-gwah PAH-rah beh-BEHR
_toilet paper.	_papel higiénico.	_pah-PEHL ee-HYE-nee-koh
This room is very	**Esta habitación es muy**	**EHS-tah ah-bee-tah-SYOHN ehs muee**
_small.	_pequeña.	_peh-KEH-nyah
_cold.	_fría.	_FREE-ah
_hot.	_caliente.	_kah-LYEHN-teh
_dark.	_oscura.	_ohs-KOO-rah
_noisy.	_ruidosa.	_rruee-DOH-sah

The . . . does not work.	No funciona . . .	noh foon-SYOH-nah
_light	_la luz.	_lah loos
_heat	_la calefacción.	_lah kah-leh-fahk-SYOHN
_toilet	_el baño.	_ehl BAH-nyoh
_the air conditioner	_el aire acondicionado.	_ehl AY-reh ah-kohn-dee-syo-NAH-doh
_key	_la llave.	_lah YAH-beh
_lock	_la cerradura	_lah seh-rah DOO-rah
_fan	_el ventilador.	_ehl BEHN-tee-lah-DOHR
_outlet	_el enchufe.	_ehl ehn-CHOO-feh
_television	_el televisor.	_ehl teh-leh-bee-SOHR
May I change to another room?	¿Podría cambiar de habitación?	poh-DREE-ah kahm-BYAR deh ah-bee-tah-SYOHN?
Is there . . .	¿Hay . . .	ahy
_room service?	_servicio de habitación?	_sehr-BEE-syoh deh ah-bee-tah-SYOHN?
_laundry service?	_servicio de lavandería?	_sehr-BEE-syoh deh lah-vahn-deh-REE-ah?
_a beauty parlor?	_un salón de belleza?	_oon sah-LOHN deh beh-YEH-sah?
_a barber shop?	_una barbería?	_OO-nah bahr-beh-REE-yah?
_a babysitter?	_una niñera?	_OO-nah nee-NYEH-rah?
_a gift shop?	_una tienda de regalos?	_OO-nah TYEHN-dah deh rreh-GAH-lohs?
I would like to place an order for room number four.	Quisiera hacer un pedido para la habitación número cuatro.	kee-SYEH-rah ah-SEHR oon peh-DEE-doh PAH-rah lah ah-bee-tah-SYOHN NOO-meh-roh KWAH-troh

Can you recommend a babysitter for my child?	¿Puede recomendarme una niñera para cuidar a mi hijo(a)?	PWEH-deh rreh-koh-mehn-DAHR-me OO-nah nee-NYEH-rah PAH-rah KUEE-dahr ah mee EE-hoh(-hah)?
How much do you charge?	¿Cuánto cobra?	KWAHN-toh KOH-brah?
Can you stay until midnight?	¿Puede quedarse hasta la medianoche?	PWEH-deh keh-DAHR-seh AHS-tah lah meh-dyah-NOH-cheh?

USING THE HOTEL TELEPHONE

operator	operadora	oh-peh-rah-DOH-rah
May I have an outside line, please?	**¿Me da la línea, por favor?**	**meh dah lah LEE-neh-ah, pohr fah-BOHR?**
I would like to make	Quisiera hacer	kee-SYEH-rah ah-SEHR
_a long-distance call.	_una llamada de larga distancia.	_OO-nah yah-MAH-dah deh LAHR-gah dees-TAHN-syah
_a collect call.	_una llamada a cobro revertido.	_OO-nah yah-MAH-dah ah KOH-broh reh-behr-TEE-doh
_a person-to-person call.	_una llamada de persona a persona.	_OO-nah yah-MAH-dah deh pehr-SOH-nah ah pehr-SOH-nah
_a credit-card call.	_una llamada con tarjeta de crédito.	_OO-nah yah-MAH-dah kohn tahr-HEH-tah deh KREH-dee-toh
Please connect me with	**Me comunica con**	**meh koh-moo-NEE-kah kohn**
_room 203.	_la habitación doscientos tres.	_lah ah-bee-tah-SYOHN doh-SYEHN-tohs trehs
_the reception desk.	_la recepción.	_lah rreh-sehp-SYOHN
_the dining room.	_el restaurante.	_ehl rehs-tow-RAHN-teh

49

_telephone number . . .	_el teléfono número . . .	_ehl teh-LEH-foh-noh NOO-meh-roh . . .
_room service.	_el servicio de habitación.	_ehl ser-BEE-syoh deh ah-bee-tah-SYOHN
_the bell captain.	_el jefe de botones.	_ehl HEH-feh deh boh-TOH-nehs
We're leaving now.	Salimos ahora.	sah-LEE-mohs ah-OH-rah
We need a porter for the luggage.	Necesitamos un botones para las maletas.	neh-seh-see-TAH-mohs oon boh-TOH-nehs PAH-rah lahs mah-LEH-tahs
The bill, please.	La cuenta, por favor.	lah KWEHN-tah, pohr fah-BOHR
Could you call us a taxi, please?	¿Podría lla-marnos un taxi, por favor?	poh-DREE-ah yah-MAHR-nohs oon TAHK-see, pohr fah-BOHR?

DINING OUT

Spain and Mexico—as well as other areas in Latin America—offer rich and varied cuisines. Spanish cuisine spread throughout Latin America, where it often mixed with native dishes, resulting in many exotic combinations.

Can you recommend a good restaurant?	¿Puede recomendarme un buen restaurante?	PWEH-deh rreh-koh-mehn-DAHR-me oon bwehn rrehs-tow-RAHN-teh?
I want a(n) . . . restaurant.	Quiero un restaurante	KYEH-roh oon rrehs-tow-RAHN-teh
_typical	_típico.	_TEE-pee-koh
_international	_internacional.	_een-tehr-nah-syoh-NAHL
_inexpensive	_no muy caro.	_noh muee KAH-roh
_very good	_muy bueno.	_muee BWEH-noh
Is that restaurant expensive?	¿Es caro ese restaurante?	ehs KAH-roh eh-seh rrehs-tow-RAHN-teh?
What's the name of the restaurant?	¿Cómo se llama el restaurante?	KOH-moh seh YAH-mah ehl rrehs-tow-RAHN-teh?
Where is it located?	¿Dónde está situado?	DOHN-deh ehs-TAH see-TWAH-doh?
Do I need reservations?	¿Se necesita una reservación?/	seh neh-seh-SEE-tah OO-nah rreh-sehr-bah-SYOHN?/
	. . . una reserva? (Spain)	. . . OO-nah rreh-SEHR-vah?
I'd like to reserve a table	Quisiera reservar una mesa	kee-SYEH-rah rreh-sehr-BAHR OO-nah MEH-sah
_for two people.	_para dos personas.	_PAH-rah dohs pehr-SOH-nahs
_for this evening.	_para esta noche.	_PAH-rah EHS-tah NOH-cheh
_for 8:00 P.M.	_para las ocho de la noche.	_PAH-rah lahs OH-choh deh lah NOH-cheh

_for tomorrow evening.	_para mañana en la noche.	_PAH-rah mah-NYAH-nah ehn lah NOH-cheh
_on the terrace.	_en la terraza.	_ehn lah teh-RRAH-sah
_by the window.	_cerca de la ventana.	_SEHR-kah deh lah behn-TAH-nah
_outside.	_afuera.	_ah-FWEH-rah
_inside.	_adentro.	_ah-DEHN-troh

DIALOGUE   At the Restaurant (En el restaurante)

Mesero*:	¿Puedo tomar su pedido?	PWEH-doh toh-MAHR soo peh-DEE-doh?
Cliente:	No sé. ¿Cuál es la especialidad?	noh SEH, kwal ehs lah ehs-peh-syah-lee-DAD?
Mesero:	Hoy le recomiendo la paella.	ohy leh rreh-koh-MYEHN-doh lah pah-EH-yah
Cliente:	Bien. Me trae eso, por favor.	byehn. meh TRAH-eh EH-soh, pohr fah-BOHR
Mesero:	¿Algo para tomar?	AHL-goh PAH-rah to-MAHR?
Cliente:	Sí, por favor. Quisiera una botella de agua mineral con gas.	see, pohr fah-BOHR kee-SYEH-rah OO-nah boh-TEH yah deh AH-gwah mee-neh-RAHL kohn GAHS

Waiter:	May I take your order?
Customer:	I don't know. What's the specialty?
Waiter:	I would recommend the *paella* today.
Customer:	Fine. I'll take that.
Waiter:	Something to drink?
Customer:	Yes, please. Bring me a bottle of fizzy mineral water.

Mesero is used in Mexico for "waiter," whereas *mozo* and *camarero* are used in Spain.

GOING TO A RESTAURANT

Waiter!	¡Mesero! (Mexico)/	meh-SEH-roh!/
	¡Mozo!	MOH-soh!/
	(Spain)/	
	¡Camarero!	cah-mah-REH-roh!
	(Spain)	
Waitress!	¡Mesera!/	meh-SEH-rah!/
	¡Camarera!	Kah-mah-REH-rah!
Miss!	¡Señorita!	seh-nyoh-REE-tah!
Can you bring	¿Puede traer	PWEH-deh trah-EHR
_the menu?	_la carta?	_lah KAHR-tah?
_the wine list?	_la lista de vinos?	_lah LEES-tah deh BEE-nohs
_an appetizer?	_un aperitivo?	_oon ah-peh-ree-TEE-voh?
Do you serve local dishes?	¿Tiene algún plato regional?	TYEH-neh ahl-GOON PLAH-toh rreh-hyoh-NAHL?
I'd like	Quisiera	kee-SYEH-rah
_something light.	_algo ligero.	_AHL-goh lee-HEH-roh
_a full meal.	_una comida completa.	_OO-nah koh-MEE-dah kohm-PLEH-tah
_the meal of the day.	_la comida corrida. (Mexico)/	_lah koh-MEE-dah ko-RREE-dah/
	el menú del día. (Spain)	ehl meh-NOO dehl DEE-ah
Do you have children's portions?	¿Tiene raciones para niños?	TYEH-neh rrah-SYOH-nehs PAH-rah NEE-nyohs?
I'm ready to order.	Estoy listo(-a) para pedir.	ehs-TOY LEES-toh(-tah) PAH-rah peh-DEER
Could I have . . .	Quisiera . . .	kee-SYEH-rah . . .
To begin . . .	Para comenzar . . .	PAH-rah koh-mehn-SAHR . . .
Next . . .	Después . . .	dehs-PWEHS . . .
Finally . . .	Para terminar . . .	PAH-rah tehr-mee-NAHR . . .

That's all.	Es todo.	ehs TOH-doh
Is the dish	¿Este plato es	EHS-teh PLAH-toh ehs
_baked?	_al horno?	_ahl OHR-noh?
_boiled?	_hervido?	_ehr-BEE-doh?
_braised?	_estofado?	_ehs-toh-FAH-doh?
_broiled?	_a la parrilla?	_ah lah pah-RREE-yah?
_fried?	_frito?	_FREE-toh?
I prefer the meat	Prefiero la carne	preh-FYEH-roh lah KAHR-neh
_well done.	_bien cocida.	_byehn koh-SEE-dah
_medium.	_en un término medio.	_ehn oon TEHR-mee-noh MEH-dyoh
_rare.	_poco cocida.	_POH-koh koh-SEE-dah
The soup is cold.	La sopa está fría.	lah SOH-pah ehs-TAH FREE-ah
I'd like another dish.	Quisiera otro plato.	kee-SYEH-rah OH-troh PLAH-toh
More water, please.	Más agua, por favor.	mahs AH-gwah, pohr fah-BOHR
I'm on a special diet.	Estoy en una dieta especial.	ehs-TOY ehn OO-nah DYEH-tah ehs-peh-SYAHL
Is it very spicy (hot)?	¿Es muy picante?/ . . . picoso? (Mexico)	ehs mwee pee-KAHN-teh?/ . . . pee-KOH-soh?
I'm diabetic.	Soy diabético(-a).	soy dee-ah-BEH-tee-koh(-kah)
I can't eat	No puedo comer	noh PWEH-doh koh-MEHR
_salt.	_sal.	_sahl
_fat.	_grasas.	_GRAH-sahs
_sugar.	_azúcar.	_ah-SOO-kahr
_flour.	_harina.	_ah-REE-nah
I don't eat pork.	No como puerco, carne de cerdo. (Spain)	noh KOH-moh PWEHR-koh, kahr-neh deh SEHR-doh

| I want to lose weight. | Quiero perder peso. | KYEH-roh pehr-DEHR PEH-soh |
| Where's the toilet? | ¿Dónde está el servicio? (Mexico)/ . . . el aseo? (Spain) | DOHN-deh es-TAH ehl ser-BEE-syoh?/ ehl ah-SAY-yoh? |

CONDIMENTS AND UTENSILS

silverware	cubiertos	koo-BYEHR-tohs
a fork	**un tenedor**	**oon teh-neh-DOHR**
a knife	**un cuchillo**	**oon koo-CHEE-yoh**
a spoon	**una cuchara**	**OO-nah koo-CHAH-rah**
a napkin	**una servilleta**	**OO-nah sehr-bee-YEH-tah**
a cup	**una taza**	**OO-nah TAH-sah**
a saucer	un platillo	oon plah-TEE-yoh
a plate	**un plato**	**oon PLAH-toh**
a glass	**un vaso**	**oon BAH-soh**
some bread	un poco de pan	oon POH-koh deh pahn
some butter	un poco de mantequilla	oon POH-koh deh mahn-teh-KEE-yah
water	agua natural	AH-gwah nah-too-RAHL
the salt	**la sal**	**lah sahl**
the pepper	**la pimienta**	**lah pee-MYEHN-tah**
the mustard	la mostaza	lah mohs-TAH-sah
the ketchup	la salsa de tomate el catsup	lah SAHL-sah deh toh-MAH-teh/ehl KAHT-sohp
the mayonnaise	la mayonesa	lah mah-yoh-NEH-sah
some coffee	**café**	**kah-FEH**
some tea	**té**	**teh**
some lemon	un poco de limón	oon POH-koh deh lee-MOHN
the sugar	**el azúcar**	**ehl ah-SOO-kahr**
some saccharine	un poco de sacarina	oon POH-koh deh sah-kah-REE-nah

an ashtray	un cenicero	oon seh-nee-SEH-roh
a toothpick	un palillo	oon pah-LEE-yoh
a beer	una cerveza	OO-nah sehr-BEH-sah

What the Waiter Says

¿Cuántas per- sonas son?	KWAHN-tahs pehr-SOH-nahs sohn?	How many people?
¿Está bien esta mesa?	ehs-TAH byehn EHS-tah MEH-sah?	Is this table all right?
¿Quiere una silla para niños?	KYEH-reh OO-nah SEE-yah PAH-rah NEE-nyohs?	Do you want a high chair?
¿Quieren pedir ahora?	KYEH-rehn peh-DEER ah-OH-rah?	Do you want to or- der now?
¿Quieren más agua?	KYEH-rehn mahs AH-gwah?	Do you want more water?
¿Desean algo más?	deh-SEH-ahn AHL-goh mahs?	Do you want any- thing else?
¿Todo va bien?	TOH-doh bah byehn?	Is everything all right?
¿Todo en la misma cuenta?	TOH-doh ehn lah MEES-mah KWEN-tah?	All on one bill?

THE BILL

May I have the check, please?	¿Me da la cuenta, por favor?	meh dah lah KWEHN-tah, pohr fah-BOHR?
Only one check, please.	Sólo una cuenta, por favor.	SOH-loh OO-nah KWEHN-tah, pohr fah-BOHR
Please give us separate checks.	Nos da cuentas separadas, por favor.	nohs dah KWEN-tahs seh-pah-RAH-dahs, pohr fah-BOHR
Is service included?	¿Está incluida la propina?	ehs-TAH een-KLUEE-dah lah proh-PEE-nah?
I think there's a mistake.	Creo que hay un error.	KREH-oh keh ahy oon eh-RROHR
Do you accept	¿Aceptan	ah-SEHP-tahn

_credit cards?	_tarjetas de crédito?	_tahr-HEH-tahs deh CREH-dee-toh?
_traveler's checks?	_cheques de viajero?	_CHEH-kehs deh byah-HEH-roh?
_dollars?	_dólares?	_DOH-lah-rehs?
This is for you.	Esto es para usted.	EHS-toh ehs PAH-rah oos-TEHD
Keep the change.*	Guarde el cambio.	GWAHR-deh ehl KAHM-byoh
The meal was excellent.	La comida estuvo deliciosa.	lah koh-MEE-dah ehs-TOO-boh deh-lee-SYOH-sah
And the service was very good.	Y el servicio estuvo muy bien.	ee ehl sehr-BEE-syoh ehs-TOO-boh MUEE byehn

*For information on tipping, see page 33.

ABOUT SPANISH FOOD

Spanish cuisine varies greatly from region to region. It reflects the influence of both the Arabs, who were in the south of Spain for nearly 700 years, and of Latin America.

Spanish meals normally consist of several courses. Foods commonly served are beef, pork, rabbit, and many different kinds of fish (especially in the coastal regions) as well as beans, vegetables, rice, and fruit. Sweet desserts are not common at the end of the meal, but wonderful pastries are always obtainable in pastry shops.

Some typical Spanish dishes are: *callos a la madrileña* and *gazpacho* (Andalucía), *cordero asado* (Castilla), *cocido madrileño* (Madrid), *migas de pastor* (Extremadura), *paella valenciana* (Levante), *lentejas a la babia* (León), *cabrito asado* (Aragón), *fabada asturiana* (Asturias), *caldo gallego* (Galicia), *merluza a la riojana* (Rioja and Navarra), and *bacalao a la vizcaína* (Vascongadas).

Depending on the town, you will find either a great variety of restaurants or perhaps just one or two local places. Local restaurants or *bares* (bars) in small towns tend to be family operated. Food is prepared for local tastes. Prices vary according to the type of restaurant. For breakfast you might try a *café* (kah-FEH) or *churrería* (choo-rreh-REE-ah). *Combinados* (kohm-bee-NAH-dohs), or combination dishes, are popular and inexpensive. A great variety of prepared dishes may be ordered à la carte by *raciones* (rrah-SYOH-nehs) or *medias raciones* (MEH-dyahs rrah-SYOH-nehs)—i.e., full or half portions—so you can try different kinds of food.

A very popular custom throughout Spain is that of *tapas* (TAH-pahs), small delicacies or hors d'oeuvres. Going out for a glass of wine accompanied by *tapas* is also an occasion to meet friends and to socialize. Bars are usually lined with an amazing variety of dishes—shrimp, olives, diced omelettes, artichokes, cheese, and sausage, to name a few. When you're ready to leave, count up the items you've eaten and pay. In Granada, Madrid and part of Andalucía, small *tapas* are often served free, courtesy of the house.

Spanish restaurants, like hotels, often display a rating scale outside—from one to five "forks" indicating the cost of eating at the restaurant.

Eating hours, except in the case of breakfast (*desayuno*[deh-sah-YOO-noh]), are usually quite late. Restaurants and bars usually serve lunch between 1:30 P.M. and 3:00 P.M. Dinner (*cena*/SE-nah/) is served from 8:30 to midnight. Menus are posted outside most restaurants, so you can make your choices before you enter.

SPANISH RESTAURANTS

café (kah-FEH)	A small locale for alcoholic and non-alcoholic drinks, plus simple snacks.
cafetería (kah-fe-teh-REE-ah)	A café-type place, specializing in foods such as sandwiches, snacks, and sweets (not self-service).
bar (bahr)	Typical bars which serve wine, *tapas*, and other light snacks.
fonda/posada/ hostería (FOHN-dah/poh-SAH- dah/ohs-teh-REE-ah)	Small restaurants, sometimes part of an inn, which specialize in regional dishes.

merendero (meh-rehn-DEH-roh)	Outdoor cafés, usually found near parks or on the coast, which serve seafood, soft drinks, ice cream, and so forth.
restaurante (rrehs-tow-RAHN-teh)	Restaurant, offering varied menus and prices. Most restaurants post menus outside showing the range of dishes and prices; many offer both local and international fare.

TYPICAL SPANISH DISHES

Tapas	TAH-pahs	Appetizers
alcachofas	ahl-kah-CHOH-fahs	artichokes
almejas	ahl-MEH-hahs	clams
anguilas	ahn-GHEE-lahs	eel
calamares	kah-lah-MAH-rehs	squid
caracoles	kah-rah-KOH-lehs	snails
chorizo	choh-REE-soh	sausage
gambas	GAHM-bahs	shrimp
huevos	WEH-bohs	eggs
jamón	hah-MOHN	ham
ostras	OHS-trahs	oysters
sardinas	sahr-DEE-nahs	sardines

Sopas (SOH-pahs)	Soups
caldo gallego (KAHL-doh gah-YEH-goh)	white bean, turnip green, and potato soup
fabada asturiana (fah-BAH-dah ahs-too-RYAN-nah)	bean soup with sausage
sopa de ajo (SOH-pah deh AH-hoh)	spicy garlic soup
gazpacho (gahs-PAH-choh)	cold fresh vegetable soup

Mariscos (mah-REES-kohs)	Seafood
almejas a la marinera (ahl-MEH-hahs ah lah mah-ree-NEH-rah)	clams in white wine sauce with garlic, onion, and tomatoes

bacalao al ajo arriero (bah-kah-LAH-oh ahl AH-hoh ah-RRY-eh-roh)	salt cod with tomatoes, onion, and garlic
besugo al horno (beh-SOO-goh ahl OHR-noh)	red snapper baked with potatoes
calamares en su tinta (kah-lah-MAH-rehs ehn soo TEEN-tah)	squid in its ink
merluza a la gallega (mehr-LOO-sah ah lah gah-YEH-gah)	poached hake with potatoes and tomato sauce
paella (pah-EH-yah)	saffron rice with seafood and chicken
zarzuela de mariscos (sahr-SWEH-lah deh mah-REES-kohs)	Catalonian shellfish stew

Carnes (KAHR-nehs)	**Meats**
callos a la madrileña (KAH-yohs ah lah mah-dree-LEH-nyah)	tripe stew with calves' feet, ham, and sausages
cocido madrileño (koh-SEE-doh mah-dree-LEH-nyoh)	boiled chicken, meats, and vegetables
riñones al jerez (rree-NYOH-nehs ahl heh-REHS)	sautéed kidneys with sherry sauce
ternera a la sevillana (tehr-NEH-rah ah lah seh-bee-YAH-nah)	sautéed veal with sherry and green olives

Aves (AH-behs)	**Poultry**
arroz con pollo (ah-RROHS kohn POH-yoh)	chicken with saffron rice and peas
empanada gallega (ehm-pah-NAH-dah gah-YEH-gah)	chicken-filled bread pie
pollo al chilindrón (POH-yoh ahl chee-leen-DROHN)	sautéed chicken with peppers, tomatoes, and olives

Huevos (WEH-bohs)	**Eggs**
tortilla de patata (tohr-TEE-yah deh pah-TAH-tah)	potato and onion omelet
huevos a la flamenca (WEH-bohs ah lah flah-MEHN-kah)	baked eggs with vegetables and meat
huevos fritos (WEH-bohs FREE-tohs)	fried eggs
huevos duros (WEH-bohs DOO-rohs)	hard-boiled eggs

huevos revueltos (WEH-bohs rreh-VWEHL-tohs)	scrambled eggs
huevos pasados por agua (WEH-bohs pah-SAH-dohs pohr AH-gwah)	poached eggs

Vegetales, arroz, ensaladas y salsas (beh-heh-TAH-lehs, ah-RROHS, ehn-sah-LAH-dahs ee SAHL-sahs)

Vegetables, rice, salads, and sauces

ali-oli (AH-lee-OH lee)	garlic mayonnaise
arroz con azafrán (ah-RROHS kohn ah-sah-FRAN)	saffron rice
espinacas con piñones y almendras (ehs-pee-NAH-kahs kohn pee-NYOH-nehs ee ahl-MEHN-drahs)	spinach with pine nuts and almonds
habas a la catalana (AH-bahs ah lah kah-tah-LAH-nah)	fava beans with sausages and mint
judías verdes con salsa de tomate (hoo-DEE-ahs BEHR-dehs kohn SAHL-sah deh toh-MAH-teh)	green beans in tomato sauce
patatas en salsa verde (pah-TAH-tahs ehn SAHL-sah BEHR-deh)	potatoes in parsley sauce

Panes y dulces (PAH-nehs ee DOOL-sehs)

Breads and Sweets

churros (CHOO-rrohs)	crisp-fried crullers
tortas de aceite (TOHR-tahs deh ah-SAY-teh)	anise and sesame-seed cookies

Postres y bebidas (POHS-trehs ee be-BEE-dahs)

Desserts and Drinks

Brazo gitano (BRAH-soh hee-TAH-noh)	sponge-cake roll with rum cream filling
flan de naranja (flahn deh nah-RAHN-hah)	orange caramel custard
leche frita (LEH-cheh FREE-tah)	fried custard squares
natillas (nah-TEE-yahs)	soft custard
torta moca (TOHR-tah MOH-kah)	mocha layer cake with rum
sangría (sahn-GREE-ah)	red wine and fruit punch

ABOUT MEXICAN FOOD

Mexico's restaurants come in all styles and sizes, from elegant dining rooms serving *nueva cocina Mexicana* (new Mexican cuisine) and imaginative international cuisine to simple stands selling snacks and family-operated restaurants in smaller towns, where food is prepared for local tastes. Although you will find Spanish dishes in Mexico, the roots of the nation's cuisine can be traced to the Aztecs, the Maya, and other indigenous cultures. The blend of flavors, spices, and styles of preparation is among the most unusual in the world.

Generally, the staples are corn, rice, and beans, often served with beef, pork, lamb, fish, or goat, depending on the region. A standard feature of typical meals is the *tortilla* (tohr-TEE-yah), made of specially prepared cornmeal, which is used to create *enchiladas* (ehn-chee-LAH-dahs), *tostadas* (tohs-TAH-dahs), *chilaquiles* (chee-lah-KEE-lehs), *garnachas* (gahr-NAH-chahs), *flautas* (FLOW-tahs), *sopes* (SOH-pehs), and *tacos* (TAH-kohs; eaten at any time of day). Cornmeal is also used in *tamales* (tah-MAH-lehs), which consist of a stewlike mixture stuffed inside dough that is wrapped in corn husks or banana leaves.

Mexican food uses many special ingredients and sauces. The popular *mole* (MOH-leh) sauce is based on peanuts, squash seeds, sunflower seeds, sesame seeds, or other ingredients; *mole poblano* (MOH-leh poh-BLAH-noh), from the state of Puebla, contains almonds, peanuts, and pine nuts as well as tomato, chocolate, and hot pepper. Because its preparation is complicated and laborious, *mole* is often served on special occasions, such as christenings, weddings, and birthdays.

Frijoles (free-HOH-lehs), beans, are part of the Mexican diet every day, beginning with breakfast. Sometimes, a small dish of *frijoles* signals the end of a meal. Many types of *frijoles* are used; especially common are pinto beans and black beans. There is an even greater variety of *chiles* (CHEE-lehs), hot peppers—some fifty different kinds.

Meat is usually served as a simple *barbacoa* (barhr-bah-KOH-ah), which means roasted in an underground pit, or *carnitas* (kahr-NEE-tahs), shredded meat; pork, beef and chicken, show up in *adobo* [ah-DOH-boh], a mixture of *achiote* and *chile*. *Carnes y quesos al carbón* (grilled meats over coals and melted cheese), usually accompanied by wheat flour tortillas, is a favorite. Also try *parrillada* (pah-rree-YAH-dah), an assortment of grilled meats. Some dishes combine several kinds of meat. *Pozole* (poh-SOH-leh), a soup that is made mainly in the states of Guerrero and Jalisco, is made from hulled corn (hominy), chicken, pork, and beef, and topped with oregano, radishes, lettuce, and hot pepper.

Vegetables are used mainly as garnish or in cooked soups. Peppers are probably the most widely consumed vegetable. *Chiles rellenos* (CHEE-lehs rreh-YEH-nohs), stuffed hot peppers, is made with the *chile poblano,* a large, dark-green chile that is not too hot once the seeds have been removed; the chiles are filled with cheese or ground meat, covered with an egg batter, fried, and sometimes served with a red sauce and rice. In August, you may well find *chiles en nogada* (CHEE-lehs ehn noh-GAH-dah), another Puebla specialty—*chile* stuffed with dried fruits, meat, and nuts, covered with a white sauce made of walnuts, and sprinkled with pomegranate seeds.

Every region has its specialties. In the state of Veracruz, for example, fish and seafood dishes stand out, including *huachinango a la veracruzana* (wah-chee-NAHN-goh ah lah beh-rah-kroo-SAH-nah), red snapper Veracruz-style, and *ceviche* (seh-BEE-cheh), raw fish or seafood marinated in lemon and lime juice. Other special dishes require a more adventurous palate. You might try the famous *maguey* (mah-GAY) worms, often one of the most expensive dishes on the menu; these are taken from the *maguey* plant, put into a sauce, and eaten in a *taco.* Another expensive delicacy is *escamoles* (ehs-kah-MOH-lehs), protein-rich ants' roe. Or sample the purple corn fungus, *huitlacoche* (ueet-lah-KOH-cheh), or squash blossoms, which come either fried or in soups.

Mexicans are also fond of Spanish cuisine, and dishes such as *paella* (pah-EH-yah), *gazpacho* (gahs-PAH-choh), and *sopa de mariscos* (SOH-pah deh mah-REES-kohs) are commonly served in restaurants and homes. Note that some of the "Mexican" dishes so well known in the United States—such as *chile con carne, burritos,* and *nachos*—are actually more typical of Texas and New Mexico and not often found in Mexico proper.

Mexico offers a great variety of regional drinks, both alcoholic and non-alcoholic. *Cerveza* (sehr-BEH-sah), beer, comes in many styles. And there are always the indigenous liquors—including *tequila* (teh-KEE-lah), *pulque* (POOL-keh), and *mezcal* (mehs-KAHL), all unique to Mexico.

Delicious and quite common are fruit-based drinks, *licuados* (lee-KWAH-dohs), made from practically every fruit: *papaya* (pah-PAH-yah), pineapple, melon, watermelon, banana, *guanábana* (gwah-NAH-bah-nah), *zapote* (sah-POH-teh), tamarind, guava, and strawberries, though it is not recommended that you eat strawberries, which have been known to cause stomach infections.

Water—*agua* (AH-gwah)—is used for another popular drink, a watered-down version of fruit juice mixed with sugar. Try the *agua de limón* (AH-gwah-deh lee-MOHN), "lemon water" or lemonade; *de papaya* (pah-PAH-yah); *de melón* (meh-LOHN); *de sandía* (sahn-DEE-ah), made of rice; and *atole* (ah-TOH-leh), made of cornstarch, water, cinnamon, sugar, and various flavorings.

When ordering plain water, you need to specify the kind you want; for mineral water, ask for *agua mineral* (AH-gwah mee-neh-RAHL) *con gas* (kahn gahz), carbonated, or *sin gas* (seen gahz), flat. And speaking of water, a word of caution: Avoid unboiled tap water wherever you go; in restaurants and homes, always request bottled mineral water. In addition, make sure that any drinks you order are made from boiled, purified, or bottled water, and that the ice they contain is, too. Similarly, avoid fresh vegetables or any uncooked food. Watch out for fresh cilantro leaves in sauces and unsterilized lettuce shreds.

When visiting restaurants, look for the *comida corrida* (koh-MEE-dah koh-RREE-dah), the fixed menú of the day, offered at a set price. Usually it costs less than the same meal ordered à la carte. Expect to see a 15 percent I.V.A. (*Impuesto al Valor Adquirido*) added to restaurant checks at the bottom of the bill. Plan to tip 10% to 15% of the pretax cost of the meal—in other words, roughly the same amount as the tax.

MEXICAN RESTAURANTS

bar (bahr)	For drinks and *botana* (boh-TAH-nah), or snacks.
cantina (kahn-TEE-nah)	Bars. They also serve *botana* and sometimes prepare special soups for that after-the-party hangover.

hacienda (ah-SYEHN-dah)	An old ranch turned restaurant that preserves some of the patios, gardens, and atmosphere; they serve indoors or outdoors, usually offering regional specialties.
hostería/posada/ fonda (ohs-teh-REE-ah/poh-SAH-dah/FOHN-dah)	Restaurants serving regional specialties or general Mexican food.
restaurante (rrehs-tow-RAHN-teh)	Restaurants, varying in size, price, style and type of menu, some catering especially to tourists.

TYPICAL MEXICAN DISHES

Botana	boh-TAH-nah	Appetizers
guacamole	gwah-kah-MOH-leh	mashed avocado, seasoned with condiments
camarones	kah-mah-ROH-nehs	shrimp
taquitos	tah-KEE-tohs	miniature *tacos*
cacahuates	kah-kah-WAH-tehs	peanuts

Sopas* (SOH-pahs)	Soups
consomé (kon-soh-MEH)	consommé/broth
caldo mexicano (KAHL-doh meh-hee-KAH-noh)	Mexican meat stock
sopa de frijol (SOH-pah deh free-HOHL)	black bean soup
sopa de aguacate (SOH-pah deh ah-gwah-KAH-teh)	avocado soup
sopa de elote (SOH-pah deh eh-LOH-teh)	corn soup
sopa de flor de calabaza (SOH-pah deh flohr deh kah-lah-BAH-sah)	squash blossom soup
sopa de tortilla (SOH-pah deh tohr-TEE-yah)	crisp tortilla soup

*Note: In Mexico, the starters *sopa de arroz* and *sopa de espaghetti* are not soups—they're seasoned rice or pasta fillers.

puchero a la mexicana (poo CHEH-roh ah lah meh-hee-KAH-nah)	Mexican boiled dinner, usually chicken or pork and vegetables in a soup
pozole (poh-SOH-leh)	hulled corn, chicken, beef, and pork soup

Arroz (ah-RROHS) — Rice

arroz a la mexicana (ah-RROHS ah lah meh-hee-KAH-nah)	rice with tomatoes
arroz verde (ah-RROHS BEHR-deh)	rice with green *chile* and green tomato

Huevos (WEH-bohs) — Eggs

huevos rancheros (WEH-bohs rrahn-CHEH-rohs)	fried eggs on tortilla topped with hot tomato sauce
huevos a la Mexicana (WEH-bohs ah lah meh-hee-KAH-nah)	scrambled eggs with onion, diced hot green chile, and tomato sauce

Carnes (KAHR-nehs) — Meats

carne asada (KAHR-neh ah-SAH-dah)	roast meat
carne de puerco en adobo (KAHR-neh deh PWEHR-koh ehn ah-DOH-boh)	pork loin in achiote and *chile* sauce
pipián (pee-PYAHN)	pork meat in pumpkin-seed sauce
albóndigas (ahl-BOHN-dee-gahs)	meatballs
cecina a la mexicana (seh-SEE-nah ah lah meh-hee-KAH-nah)	Mexican hung beef
picadillo (pee-kah-DEE-yoh)	Mexican hash
cochinita pibil (koh-chee-NEE-tah pee-BEEL)	suckling pig stuffed with fruit, *chile,* and spices, baked in a pit

Aves (AH-vehs) — Poultry

mancha manteles (MAHN-chah mahn-TEH-lehs)	turkey, sausage, and *chile* stew seasoned with almonds, pineapple, apples, banana, and cinnamon

mole de guajolote (MOH-leh deh gwah-hoh-LOH-teh)	turkey in chocolate, tomato, and nut sauce
arroz con pollo (ah-RROHS kohn POH-yah)	rice with chicken and tomato sauce

Antojitos mexicanos (ahn-toh-HEE-tohs meh-hee-KAH-nohs)	**Mexican Specialties**
enchiladas rojas (ehn-chee-LAH-dahs RROH-has)	rolled tortillas stuffed with chicken or meat and topped with tomato sauce
enchiladas verdes (ehn-chee-LAH-dahs BEHR-dehs)	rolled tortillas stuffed with chicken or cheese and topped with green tomato sauce
ceviche (seh-BEE-cheh)	raw fish or shellfish marinated in lime and orange juice and seasoned with tomato, onion, and hot pepper
guacamole (gwah-kah-MOH-leh)	mashed avocado with chopped tomato, onion, and chile
quesadillas (keh-sah-DEE-yahs)	tortillas folded in half and stuffed with squash flower, mushrooms, corn fungus, beans, cheese, etc.
sopes (SOH-pehs)	thick miniature tortillas topped with tomato sauce, cheese, meat, and/or beans or other garnish.
chilaquiles (chee-lah-KEE-lehs)	a stir-fry made with broken tortillas, mixed with tomato sauce and topped with cream and raw onion

Vegetales (beh-heh-TAH-lehs)	**Vegetables**
budín de elote (boo-DEEN deh eh-LOH-teh)	corn pudding
flores de calabaza rellenas (FLOH-rehs deh kah-lah-BAH-sah rreh-YEH-nahs)	stuffed squash blossoms
nopalitos rellenos (noh-pah-LEE-tohs rreh-YEH-nohs)	stuffed prickly-pear leaves
chiles rellenos (CHEE-lehs rreh-YEH-nohs)	stuffed *chiles*

Frijoles (free-HOH-lehs)	Beans
frijoles mexicanos (free-HOH-lehs meh-hee-KAH-nohs	boiled beans seasoned with salt, garlic, and—usually—lard
frijoles charros (free-HOH-lehs CHAH-rrohs)	beans cooked with beer
frijoles refritos (free-HOH-lehs rreh-FREE-tohs)	refried beans

Postres (POHS-trehs)	Desserts
arroz con leche (ah-RROHS kohn LEH-cheh)	rice with milk and cinnamon
chongos zamoranos (CHOHN-gohs sah-moh-RAH-nohs)	egg yolks with milk and sugar, cooked with cinnamon and syrup
flan (flahn)	caramel custard
capirotada (kah-pee-roh-TAH-dah)	bread, cheese, brown sugar, and pine nuts in a cakelike form
ate (AH-teh)	jellied paste made of different fruit, such as guava, apple, and quince

GENERAL FOOD CATEGORIES

Carne	KAHR-neh	Meat
cabrito	kah-BREE-toh	goat
carnero	kahr-NEH-roh	mutton
conejo	koh-NEH-hoh	rabbit
cordero	**kohr-DEH-roh**	**lamb**
puerco (Mexico)	**PWEHR-koh**	**pork**
cerdo (Spain)	**SEHR-doh**	**pork**
res	**rrehs**	**beef**
ternera	tehr-NEH-rah	veal
venado	beh-NAH-doh	venison

Cortes de carne	KOHR-tehs deh KAHR-neh	Cuts of Meat
bistec	bees-TEHK	steak
carne picada	KAHR-neh pee-KAH-dah	chopped beef

carne molida	KAHR-neh moh-LEE-dah	ground beef
chuletas	choo-LEH-tahs	chops
churrasco	choo-RRAHS-koh	T-bone steak
costilla	kohs-TEE-yah	ribs
corazón	koh-rah-SOHN	heart
hígado	EE-gah-doh	liver
lengua	LEHN-gwah	tongue
riñones	rree-NYOH-nehs	kidneys
sesos	SEH-sohs	brains
tripas	TREE-pahs	tripe
Aves	**AH-behs**	**Poultry**
capón	kah-POHN	capon
codorniz	koh-dohr-NEES	quail
ganso	GAHN-soh	goose
pato	**PAH-toh**	**duck**
pavo/ guajolote (*Mexico*)	**PAH-boh/** gwa-hoh-LOH-teh	**turkey**
perdiz	pehr-DEES	partridge
pollo	**POH-yoh**	**chicken**
Pescado y mariscos	pehs-KAH-doh ee mah-REES-kohs	**Fish and Seafood**

Names of fish and seafood vary greatly between Spain and Latin America, and even from country to country. Fish from tropical waters probably are the most varied in their names. Here are some of the more common.

almejas	**ahl-MEH-hahs**	**clams**
anchoas	ahn-CHOH-ahs	anchovies
arenque	ah-REHN-keh	herring
atún	**ah-TOON**	**tuna**
bacalao	bah-kah-LAH-oh	codfish
calamares	**kah-lah-MAH-rehs**	**squid**
cangrejos	kahn-GREH-hohs	crabs

gambas	GAHM-bahs	large shrimp
langostinos	lahn-gohs-TEE-nohs	crayfish
langosta	**lahn-GOHS-tah**	**lobster**
pulpo	POOL-poh	octopus
salmón	sahl-MOHN	salmon
sardinas	sahr-DEE-nahs	sardines
trucha	TROO-chah	trout

Vegetales	**veh-HEH-tah-lehs**	**Vegetables**
aceitunas	ah-say-TOO-nahs	olives
alcachofas	**ahl-kah-CHOH-fahs**	**artichokes**
apio	AH-pyoh	celery
berenjena	beh-rehn-HEH-nah	eggplant
calabaza	kah-lah-BAH-sah	squash
calabacín	kah-lah-bah-SEEN	zucchini
cebolla	seh-BOH-yah	onion
coliflor	koh-lee-FLOHR	cauliflower
champiñón	**chahm-pee-NYOHN**	**mushroom**
espárrago	ehs-PAH-rrah-goh	asparagus
espinaca	ehs-pee-NAH-kah	spinach
garbanzos	gahr-BAHN-sohs	chickpeas
guisantes/ chícharos (Mexico)	gee-SAHN-tehs, CHEE-chah-rohs	peas
habas/ frijoles (Mexico)	**AH-bahs, free-HOH-lehs**	**beans**
judías/ ejote (Mexico)	hoo-DEE-ahs, eh-HOH-teh	green beans
lechuga	**leh-CHOO-gah**	**lettuce**
maíz/elote (Mexico)	mah-EES, eh-LOH-teh	corn
papa/patata (Spain)	PAH-pah, pah-TAH-tah	potato
pepino	peh-PEE-noh	cucumber

pimiento	pee-MYEHN-toh	green/red pepper
puerro	PWEH-rroh	leek
repollo	rreh-POH-yoh	cabbage
tomate/ jitomate (*Mexico*)	**toh-MAH-teh,** hee-toh-MAH-teh	**tomato**
zanahoria	sah-nah-OH-ryah	carrot

Condimentos	**kohn-dee-MEHN-tohs**	**Herbs and Spices**
achiote	ah-CHYOH-teh	annatto, achiote (provides a red coloring for rice, etc.)
albahaca	ahl-bah-AH-kah	basil
azafrán	ah-sah-FRAHN	saffron
cilantro	see-LAHN-troh	coriander
comino	kohh-MEE-noh	cumin
orégano	oh-REH-gah-noh	oregano
pimienta (blanca/ negra)	pee-MYEHN-tah (BLAHN-kah/NEH-grah)	(white/black) pepper
romero	rroh-MEH-roh	rosemary

Frutas	**FROO-tahs**	**Fruits**
albaricoque	ahl-bah-REE-koh-keh	apricots
ciruela	see-RWEH-lah	plum
durazno/ melocotón (*Spain*)	doo-RAHS-noh, me-loh-koh-TOHN	peach
frambuesa	frahm-BWEH-sah	raspberry
fresa	FREH-sah	strawberry
higo	EE-goh	fig
lima	LEE-mah	lime
limón	lee-MOHN	lemon
mandarina	mahn-dah-REE-nah	tangerine
manzana	**mahn-SAH-nah**	**apple**
melón	**meh-LOHN**	**melon**
naranja	**nah-RAHN-hah**	**orange**

7 DINING OUT

pera	PEH-rah	pear
piña	PEE-nyah	pineapple
sandía	sahn-DEE-ah	watermelon
uvas	OO-bahs	grapes

Frutas tropicales	**FROO-tahs troh-pee-kahlehs**	**Tropical Fruits**
plátano	**PLAH-tah-noh**	**banana**
guayaba	gwah-YAH-bah	guava
mango	MAHN-goh	mango
tuna	TOO-nah	prickly pear
zapote	sah-POH-teh	sapodilla

Digestivos y licores	**dee-hehs-TEE-bohs ee lee-KOH-rehs**	**After-dinner Drinks (Liqueurs)**
crema de menta	KREH-mah deh MEHN-tah	creme de menthe
Kahlúa (*Mexico*)	kah-LOO-ah	coffee liqueur
coñac	koh-NYAHK	brandy

SOCIALIZING

Meeting people and making friends gives you the opportunity to learn about another culture and to discover important cultural differences regarding how Spanish speakers interact. While Spaniards tend to be a bit more formal than Latin Americans, you will see quickly that they are open and friendly.

In Spain and Mexico—and elsewhere in Latin America—people generally shake hands upon meeting or leave-taking. Close friends often embrace, and women usually kiss each other. You may notice that Latin Americans and Spaniards stand closer to people they're talking to than do North Americans and Northern Europeans. This subtle difference in sense of personal space can be disconcerting at first, until you get used to it. But observing such norms can show your hosts that you respect their way of doing things.

Note that in Spanish, it is customary to use the title *señor, señora,* and *señorita* to show respect, especially when speaking to people who are not close friends. These titles may be used with the last name, or alone.

DIALOGUE
Meeting Someone New (Conocer a alguien)

Turista:	**Buenos días, señor. Permítame presentarme. Soy Julie Adams.**	BWEH-nohs DEE-ahs, seh-NYOHR. pehr-MEE-tah-meh preh-sehn-TAHR-meh. soy Julie Adams.
Sr. Vargas:	**Encantado, señorita. Yo soy Juan Vargas.**	ehn-kahn-TAH-do, seh-nyoh-REE-tah. yoh soy HWAN BAHR-gahs.
Turista:	**Encantada.**	ehn-kahn-TAH-dah
Sr. Vargas:	**¿Está de vacaciones aquí?**	ehs-TAH deh bah-kah-SYOH-nehs ah-KEE?
Turista:	**Sí, estaré aquí por tres semanas.**	see, ehs-tah-REH ah-KEE pohr trehs seh-MAH-nahs
Sr. Vargas:	**¡Qué bueno! ¡Que tenga una buena estadía!**	keh BWEH-noh! keh TEHN-gah OO-nah BWEH-nah ehs-tah-DEE-ah!

Turista:	¡Gracias! Adiós, señor.	GRAH-syahs. ah-DYOHS, seh-NYOR.
Tourist:	Hello! May I introduce myself? My name is Julie Adams.	
Mr. Vargas:	Pleased to meet you, miss. I'm Juan Vargas.	
Tourist:	Pleased to meet you.	
Mr. Vargas:	Are you here on vacation?	
Tourist:	Yes, I'll be here for three weeks.	
Mr. Vargas:	How nice! Have a good stay.	
Tourist:	Thank you. Good-bye, sir.	

INTRODUCTIONS

I'd like to introduce you to	Quisiera presentarle	kee-SYEH-rah preh-sehn-TAHR-leh
_Mr. Vargas.	_al señor Vargas.	_ahl seh-NYOHR BAHR-gahs
_Mrs. Vargas.	_a la señora Vargas.	_ah lah seh-NYOH-rah BAHR-gahs
_Miss/Ms. . . .	_a la señorita . . .	_ah lah seh-nyoh-REE-tah . . .
Pleased to meet you.	**Encantado(-a).**	**ehn-kahn-TAH-doh (-dah)**
A pleasure.	**Mucho gusto.**	**MOO-choh GOOS-toh**
What is your name?	¿Cómo se llama?	KOH-moh seh YAH-mah?
My name is . . .	Me llamo . . .	meh YAH-moh . . .
_John.	_Juan.	_HWAHN
_Mary.	_María.	_mah-REE-ah
_Mr. Vargas	_Sr. Vargas.	_seh-NYOHR VAHR-gahs
I am Ramón Díaz	**Soy Ramón Díaz**	**soy Rah-MOHN DEE-ahs**
This is my	**Es mi**	**ehs mee**
_husband.	_esposo.	_ehs-POH-soh
_wife.	_esposa.	_ehs-POH-sah

_colleague.	_colega.	_koh-LEH-gah
_friend (*male*).	_amigo.	_ah-MEE-goh
_friend (*female*).	_amiga.	_ah-MEE-gah
How are you?	**¿Cómo está usted?**	**KOH-moh ehs-TAH oos-TEHD?**
Fine, thanks. And you?	**Bien, gracias. ¿Y usted?**	**BYEHN, GRAH-syahs. ee oos-TEHD?**

WHERE ARE YOU FROM?

Where are you from?	¿De dónde es usted?	deh DOHN-deh ehs oos-TEHD?
Where do you live?	**¿Dónde vive?**	**Dohn-deh BEE-veh?**
I'm from/**I live in**	Soy de/**Vivo en**	Soy deh/**BEE-voh ehn**
_the United States.	_los Estados Unidos.	_lohs ehs-TAH-dohs oo-NEE-dohs
_England.	_Inglaterra.	_een-glah-TEH-rrah
_Canada.	_Canadá.	_ka-nah-DAH
_New York.	_Nueva York.	_NWEH-bah yohrk
_California.	_California.	_kah-lee-FOHR-nyah
That's in the	Está en el	ehs-TAH ehn ehl
_north.	_norte.	_NOHR-teh
_south.	_sur.	_soor
_east.	_este.	_EHS-teh
_west.	_oeste.	_oh-EHS-teh
That's near	Está cerca de	ehs-TAH SEHR-kah deh
_the coast.	_la costa.	_lah KOHS-tah
_Canada.	_Canadá.	_kah-nah-DAH
_the border.	_la frontera.	_lah frohn-TEH-rah
_the ocean.	_el mar.	_ehl mahr
_the mountains.	_las montañas.	_lahs mohn-TAH-nyahs
I live in New York.	**Vivo en Nueva York.**	**BEE-boh ehn NWEH-bah yohrk**

How long will you be here?	¿Cuánto tiempo estará aquí?	KWAHN-toh TYEHM-poh ehs-tah-RAH ah-KEE?
I'll be here for	Estaré aquí por	ehs-tah-REH ah-KEE pohr
_a week.	_una semana.	_OO-nah seh-MAH-nah
_another week.	_otra semana.	_OH-trah seh-MAH-nah
_three weeks.	_tres semanas.	_trehs seh-MAH-nahs
_a short while.	_poco tiempo.	_POH-koh TYEHM-poh
_a long while.	_mucho tiempo.	_MOO-choh TYEHM-poh
What hotel are you staying at?	¿En qué hotel está?	ehn keh oh-TEHL ehs-TAH?
I am at the . . . hotel.	Estoy en el hotel . . .	ehs-TOY ehn ehl oh-TEHL . . .
How do you like	**¿Le gusta***	**leh GOOS-tah**
_Spain?	**_España?**	**_ehs-PAH-nyah?**
_Mexico?	**_México?**	**_MEH-hee-koh?**
I like it very much.	**Me gusta mucho.***	**meh GOOS-tah MOO-choh**
I just arrived.	Acabo de llegar.	ah-KAH-boh deh yeh-GAHR
I'm not sure yet.	No estoy seguro(-a) todavía.	noh ehs-TOY seh-GOO-roh(-rah) toh-dah-BEE-ah
Everything is so interesting.	**Todo es muy interesante.**	**TOH-doh ehs mwee een-tel-reh-SAHN-teh**
I like the people very much.	La gente me gusta mucho.*	lah HEHN-teh meh GOOS-tah MOO-choh
I like the countryside.	Me gusta el campo.*	meh GOOS-tah ehl KAHM-poh

*In Spanish, the verb *gustar* agrees with the object. The literal translation of "*Me gusta España*" is "Spain pleases me." "I like the shops here" would be translated as "*Me gustan las tiendas aquí*"—literally, "The shops here please me."

COUNTRIES AND NATIONALITIES

Note: In common usage, the names of the countries specified always take the article.

Country	País (pah-EES)	Nationality/Nacionalidad (nah-syoh-nah-lee-DAHD)
Argentina	la Argentina (lah ahr-hen-TEE-nah)	argentino(-a) (ahr-hehn-TEE-noh[-nah])
Bolivia	Bolivia (boh-LEE-byah)	boliviano(-a) (boh-lee-BYAH-noh[-nah])
Brazil	el Brasil (ehl brah-SEEL)	brasileño(-a) (brah-see-LEH-nyoh[-nyah])
Canada	Canadá (kah-nah-DAH)	canadiense (kah-nah-DYEHN-seh)
Chile	Chile (CHEE-leh)	chileno(-a) (chee-LEH-noh[-nah])
China	la China (lah CHEE-nah)	chino(-a) (CHEE-noh[-nah])
Colombia	Colombia (koh-LOHM-byah)	colombiano(-a) (koh-lohm-BYAH-noh[-nah])
Costa Rica	Costa Rica (KOHS-tah RREE-kah)	costarricense (kohs-tah-rree-SEHN-seh)
Cuba	Cuba (KOO-bah)	cubano(-a) (koo-BAH-noh[-nah])
Denmark	Dinamarca (dee-nah-MAHR-kah)	danés(-nesa) (dah-NEHS[NEH-sah])
Dominican Republic	la República Dominicana (lah rreh-POO-blee- kah doh-mee-nee- KAH-nah)	dominicano(-a) (doh-mee-nee-KAH-noh [-nah])
Ecuador	Ecuador (eh-kwah-DOHR)	ecuatoriano(-a) (eh-kwah-toh-RYAH-noh [-nah])
Egypt	Egipto (eh-HEEP-toh)	egipcio(-a) (eh-HEEP-syoh[-syah])
El Salvador	El Salvador (ehl sahl-bah-DOHR)	salvadoreño(-a) (sahl-bah-doh-REH-nyoh [-nyah])
England	Inglaterra (een-glah-TEH-rrah)	inglés(-glesa) (een-GLEHS[-GLEH-sah])

Finland	Finlandia (feen-LAHN-dyah)	finlandés(-desa) (feen-lahn-DEHS [-DEH-sah])
France	Francia (FRAHN-syah)	francés(-cesa) (frahn-SEHS[-SEH-sah])
Germany	Alemania (ah-leh-MAH-nyah)	alemán(-mana) (ah-leh-MAHN[-MAH-nah])
Greece	Grecia (GRE-syah)	griego(-a) (GRYEH-goh[-gah])
Guatemala	Guatemala (gwah-teh-MAH-lah)	guatemalteco(-a) (gwah-teh-mahl-TEH-koh [-kah])
Holland	Holanda (oh-LAHN-dah)	holandés(-desa) (oh-lahn-DEHS[-DEH-sah])
Honduras	Honduras (ohn-DOO-rahs)	hondureño(-a) (ohn-doo-REH-nyoh[-nyah])
Iceland	Islandia (ees-LAHN-dyah)	islandés(-desa) (eès-lahn-DEHS[-DEH-sah])
Ireland	Irlanda (eer-LAHN-dah)	irlandés(-desa) (eer-lahn-DEHS[-DEH-sah])
Israel	Israel (ees-rah-EHL)	israelí (ees-rah-eh-LEE)
Italy	Italia (ee-TAH-lyah)	italiano(-a) (ee-tah-LYAH-noh[-nah])
Japan	el Japón (ehl hah-POHN)	japonés(-nesa) (hah-poh-NEHS[-NEH-sah])
Mexico	México (MEH-hee-koh)	mexicano(-a) (meh-hee-KAH-noh[-nah])
Nicaragua	Nicaragua (nee-kah-RAH-gwah)	nicaragüense (nee-kah-rah-GWEHN-seh)
Norway	Noruega (noh-RWEH-gah)	noruego(-a) (noh-RWEH-goh[-gah])
Panama	Panamá (pah-nah-MAH)	panameño(-a) (pah-nah-MEH-nyoh[-nyah])
Paraguay	Paraguay (pah-rah-GWY)	paraguayo(-a) (pah-rah-GWAH-yoh[-yah])
Peru	el Perú (ehl peh-ROO)	peruano(-a) (peh-RWAH-noh[-nah])
Poland	Polonia (poh-LOH-nyah)	polaco(-a) (poh-LAH-koh[-kah])

Portugal	Portugal (pohr-too-GAHL)	portugués(-guesa) (pohr-too-GEHS [-GEH-sah])
Puerto Rico	Puerto Rico (PWEHR-toh RREE-koh)	puertorriqueño(-a) (pwehr-toh-rreé-KEH- nyoh[-nyah])
Russia	Rusia (RROO-syah)	ruso(-a) (RROO-soh[-sah])
Spain	España (ehs-PAH-nyah)	español(-a) (ehs-pah- NYOHL[-NYOH-lah])
Sweden	Suecia (SWEH-syah)	sueco(-a) (SWEH-koh[-kah])
Switzerland	Suiza (SWEE-sah)	suizo(-a) (SUEE-soh[-sah])
Turkey	Turquía (toor-KEE-ah)	turco(-a) (TOOR-koh[-kah])
United States	Estados Unidos (ehs-TAH-dohs oo-NEE-dohs)	estadounidense (ehs-tah-doh-oo-nee- DEHN-seh)
Uruguay	el Uruguay (ehl oo-roo-GWY)	uruguayo(-a) (oo-roo-GWAH- yoh[-yah])
Venezuela	Venezuela (beh-neh-SWEH-lah)	venezolano(-a) (beh-neh-soh-LAH-noh [-nah])

WHAT DO YOU DO?

Where do you work?	¿Dónde trabaja?	DOHN-deh trah-BAH- hah?
What do you do?	**¿En qué trabaja?**	**ehn keh trah-BAH-hah?**
What is your profession?	¿Cuál es su profesión?	kwahl ehs soo proh- feh-SYOHN?
I'm a	Soy	soy
_businessman.	_un hombre de negocios.	_oon OHM-breh deh neh- GOH-syohs
I'm retired.	Estoy jubilado(-a).	ehs-TOY hoo-bee-LAH- doh(-dah)
I'm not working any longer.	Ya no trabajo.	yah noh trah-BAH-hoh

79

JOBS AND OCCUPATIONS

Professions/ Occupations	Profesiones/ Oficios	pro-feh-SYOH-nehs/ oh-FEE-syohs
accountant	contador(-a)	kohn-tah-DOHR (-DOH-rah)
architect	arquitecto(-a)	ahr-kee-TEHK-toh(-tah)
artist	artista	ahr-TEES-tah
baker	panadero(-a)	pah-nah-DEH-roh(-rah)
blacksmith	herrero	eh-RREH-roh
butcher	carnicero(-a)	kahr-nee-SEH-roh(-rah)
cardiologist	cardiólogo(-a)	kahr-DYOH-loh-goh(-gah)
carpenter	carpintero	kahr-peen-TEH-roh
clerk	oficinista	oh-fee-see-NEES-tah
cook	cocinero(-a)	koh-see-NEH-roh(-rah)
dentist	dentista	dehn-TEES-tah
doctor	médico(-a)	MEH-dee-koh(-kah)
electrician	electricista	eh-lehk-tree-SEES-tah
engineer	ingeniero(-a)	een-heh-NYEH-roh(-rah)
eye doctor	óptico	OHP-tee-koh
lawyer	abogado(-a)	ah-boh-GHAH-doh(-dah)
locksmith	cerrajero	seh-rrah-HEH-roh
maid	sirviente(-a)	seer-BYEHN-teh(-tah)
neurologist	neurólogo(-a)	nehw-ROH-log-goh(-gah)
nurse	enfermero(-a)	ehn-fehr-MEH-roh(-rah)
ophthalmologist	oftalmólogo(-a)	ohf-tahl-MOH-loh-goh(-gah)
painter	pintor(-a)	peen-TOHR(-TOH-rah)
plumber	plomero	ploh-MEH-roh
salesperson	vendedor(-a)	behn-deh-DOHR(-DOH-rah)
sculptor	escultor(-a)	ehs-kool-TOHR(-TOH-rah)
shoemaker	zapatero	sah-pah-TEH-roh
shopkeeper	negociante	neh-goh-SYAHN-teh

waiter	mesero(-a) (Mexico)/	meh-SEH-roh(-rah)/
	camarero(-a) (Spain)	kah-mah-REH- roh(-rah)
writer	escritor(-a)	ehs-kree-TOHR(-TOH-rah)

MAKING FRIENDS

It's so good to see you.	Un gusto verle.	oon GOOS-toh BEHR- leh
It's nice to be here.	Es un placer estar aquí.	ehs oon plah-SEHR ehs-TAHR ah-KEE
Would you like a drink?	¿Le gustaría una bebida?	leh goos-tah-REE-ah OO-nah beh-BEE-dah?
With pleasure.	Con gusto.	kohn GOOS-toh
Cheers!	¡Salud!	sah-LOOD!
No, thanks.	No, gracias.	noh, GRAH-syahs

Note: Gracias (Thank you) is sometimes used alone to accept or decline something. In doing so, it is usually accompanied by a slight nod or shake of the head.

Would you like to go with us	¿Le gustaría acompañarnos	leh goos-tah-REE-ah ah- kohm-pah-NYAHR-nohs
_to the theater?	_al teatro?	_ahl teh-AH-troh?
_to the movies?	_al cine?	_ahl SEE-neh?
_to a restaurant?	_a un restaurante?	_ah oon rrehs-tow- RAHN-teh?
Gladly.	Con mucho gusto.	kohn MOO-choh GOOS-toh
Can I bring a friend?	¿Puedo llevar a un amigo?	PWEH-doh yeh-BAHR ah oon ah-MEE-goh?
Do you mind if I smoke?	¿Le importa si fumo?	leh eem-POHR-tah see FOO-moh?
Not at all.	Claro que no.	KLAH-roh keh noh
May I telephone you?	¿Puedo llamarle por teléfono?	PWEH-doh yah-MAHR- leh pohr teh-LEH-foh-noh?
What is your phone number?	¿Cuál es su número de teléfono?	KWAHL ehs soo NOO- meh-roh deh teh-LEH- foh-noh?

What is your address?	¿Cuál es su dirección?	KWAHL ehs soo dee-rehk-SYOHN?
Are you married?	**¿Es usted casado(-a)?**	**ehs oos-TEHD kah-SAH-doh(-dah)?**
No, I'm	**No, soy**	**noh, soy**
_single.	_soltero(-a).	_sohl-TEH-roh(-rah)
_divorced.	_divorciado(-a).	_dee-bohr-SYAH-doh(-dah)
_a widower (widow)	_viudo(-a).	_byoo-doh(-dah)
I'm traveling with a friend.	**Estoy viajando con un amigo(-a).**	**ehs-TOY byah-HAHN-doh kohn oon ah-MEE-goh (-gah).**
My family is with me.	Mi familia está conmigo.	mee fah-MEE-lyah es-TAH kohn-MEE-goh
Do you have any children?	¿Tiene usted hijos?	TYEH-neh oos-TEHD EE-hohs?
Yes, I have	Sí, tengo	see, TEHN-goh
_a child.	_un hijo.	_oon EE-hoh
_two children.	_dos hijos.	_dohs EE-hohs
_three children.	_tres hijos.	_trehs EE-hohs
_four children.	_cuatro hijos.	_KWAH-troh EE-hohs
_a son.	_un hijo.	_oon EE-hoh
_a daughter.	_una hija.	_OO-nah EE-hah
Here are pictures of my family.	Aquí tengo fotografías de mi familia.	ah-KEE TEHN-goh foh-toh-grah-FEE-ahs deh mee fah-MEE-lyah
It's getting late.	Se hace tarde.	seh AH-seh TAHR-deh
It's time to get back.	**Es hora de regresar.**	**ehs OH-rah deh rreh-greh-SAHR**
We're leaving tomorrow.	Nos vamos mañana.	nohs BAH-mohs mah-NYAH-nah
Thanks for everything.	Gracias por todo.	GRAH-syahs pohr TOH-doh
I had a very good time.	**Lo pasé muy bien.**	**loh pah-SEH mwee byehn**
We're going to miss you.	Vamos a extrañarle.	BAH-mohs ah eks-trah-NYAHR-leh

82

It was nice to have met you.	Gusto en conocerle.	GOOS-toh ehn koh-noh-SEHR-leh
Give my best to	Mis saludos a	mees sah-LOO-dohs ah
_your fiancé(e).	_su novio(-a).	_soo NOH-byoh(-vyah)
_your boyfriend (girlfriend).	_su amigo(-a).	_soo ah-MEE-goh (-gah)
_your family.	_su familia.	_soo fah-MEE-lyah
_your husband.	_su esposo.	_soo ehs-POH-soh
_your wife.	_su esposa.	_soo ehs-POH-sah
Can I give you a ride?	¿Puedo llevarlo?	PWEH-doh yeh-BAHR-loh?
Don't bother, thank you.	No se moleste, gracias.	noh seh moh-LES-teh, GRAH-syahs
I can take a taxi.	Puedo tomar un taxi.	PWEH-doh toh-MAHR oon TAHK-see
Bye.	Hasta luego.	AHS-tah LWEH-goh

THE FAMILY

I'm traveling	Viajo	BYA-hoh
_with my family.	_con mi familia.	_kohn mee fah-MEE-lyah
_without my family.	_sin mi familia.	_seen mee fah-MEE-lyah
My family lives in New York.	Mi familia vive en Nueva York.	mee fah-MEE-lyah BEE veh ehn NWEH-bah yohrk
My family is spread out.	Mi familia vive en diferentes lugares.	mee fah-MEE-lya BEE-veh ehn dee-feh-REHN-tehs loo-GAH-rehs
I have a . . . family.	Tengo una familia	TEHN-goh OO-nah fah-MEE-lyah
_big.	_grande.	_GRAHN-deh
_small.	_pequeña.	_peh-KEH-nyah
I have . . . _many relatives.	Tengo . . . _muchos parientes.	TEHN-goh . . . _MOO-chohs pah-RYEHN-tehs
_a baby.	_un bebé.	_oon beh-BEH

_a father.	_un padre.	_oon PAH-dreh
_a mother.	_una madre.	_OO-nah MAH-dreh
_a grandmother.	_una abuela.	_OO-nah ah-BWEH-lah
_a grandfather.	_un abuelo.	_oon ah-BWEH-loh
_a grandson.	_un nieto.	_oon NYEH-toh
_a granddaughter.	_una nieta.	_OO-nah NYEH-tah
_a cousin (*female*).	_una prima.	_OO-nah PREE-mah
_a cousin (*male*).	_un primo.	_oon PREE-moh
_an aunt.	_una tía.	_OO-nah TEE-ah
_an uncle.	_un tío.	_oon TEE-oh
_a sister.	_una hermana.	_OO-nah ehr-MAH-nah
_a brother.	_un hermano.	_oon ehr-MAH-noh
_in-laws.	_suegros.	_SWEH-grohs
_a father-in-law.	_un suegro.	_oon SWEH-groh
_a mother-in-law.	_una suegra.	_OO-nah SWEH-grah
_a sister-in-law	_una cuñada.	_OO-nah koo-NYAH-dah
_a brother-in-law.	_un cuñado.	_oon koo-NYAH-doh
How old are your children?	¿Cuántos años tienen sus hijos?	KWAHN-tohs AH-nyohs TYEH-nehn soos EE-hohs?
My children are	Mis hijos son	mees EE-hohs sohn
_very young.	_muy jóvenes.	_mwee HOH-behn-ehs
_all grown up.	_grandes.	_GRAHN-dehs
Peter is three years old.	Pedro tiene tres años.	PEH-droh TYEH-neh trehs AH-nyohs
He is older than Paul.	Él es mayor que Pablo.	ehl ehs mah-YOHR keh PAH-bloh
He is	Él es	ehl ehs
_my eldest son.	_mi hijo mayor.	_mee EE-hoh mah-YOHR
_my youngest son.	_mi hijo menor.	_mee EE-hoh meh-NOHR
She is	Ella es	EHL-yah ehs

_my eldest daughter.	_mi hija mayor.	_mee EE-hah mah-YOHR
_my youngest daughter.	_mi hija menor.	_mee EE-hah meh-NOHR
I am a widow.	Soy viuda.	soy BYOO-dah
I am a widower.	Soy viudo.	soy BYOO-doh

IN THE HOME

Make yourself at home.	Está en su casa.	ehs-TAH ehn soo KAH-sah
You may sit here.	Puede sentarse aquí.	PWEH-deh sehn-TAHR-seh ah-KEE
What a pretty house!	¡Qué casa tan bonita!	keh KAH-sah tahn boh-NEE-tah!
I really like this neighborhood.	Me gusta mucho este barrio.	meh GOOS-tah MOO-choh EHS-teh BAH-rryoh
Here is	Aquí está	ah-KEE ehs-TAH
_the kitchen.	_la cocina.	_lah koh-SEE-nah
_the living room.	_la sala.	_lah SAH-lah
_the dining room.	_el comedor.	_ehl koh-meh-DOHR
_the bedroom.	_el dormitorio/cuarto.	_ehl dohr-mee-TOH-ryoh/KWAHR-toh
_the bathroom.	_el baño.	_ehl BAH-nyoh
_the study.	_el estudio.	_ehl ehs-TOO-dyoh
_the attic.	_el desván	_ehl dehs-BAHN
_the cellar.	_el sótano.	_ehl SOH-tah-noh
_the couch.	_el sofá.	_ehl soh-FAH
_the armchair.	_el sillón.	_ehl see-YOHN
_the table.	_la mesa.	_lah MEH-sah
_the chair.	_la silla.	_lah SEE-yah
_the lamp.	_la lámpara.	_lah LAHM-pah-rah
_the door.	_la puerta.	_lah PWEHR-tah
It's	Es	ehs
_a house.	_una casa.	_OO-nah KAH-sah

_an apartment.	_un apartamento	_oon ah-pahr-tah-MEHN-toh
_a mansion.	_una mansión.	_OO-nah mahn-SYOHN
_a ranch.	_una hacienda.	_OO-nah ah-SYEHN-dah
Thanks for having invited us to your home.	Gracias por habernos invitado a su casa.	GRAH-syahs pohr ah-BEHR-nohs een-bee-TAH-doh ah soo KAH-sah
Please come to visit us sometime.	Debe venir a visitarnos también.	DEH-beh beh-NEER ah bee-see-TAHR-nos tahm-BYEHN

TALKING ABOUT LANGUAGE

Names of languages—*lenguas* (LEHN-gwahs), or *idiomas* (ee-DYOH-mahs)—are usually the same as the masculine form of the nationality. For example, the words for the German and Italian languages are *alemán* (ah-leh-MAHN) and *italiano* (ee-tah-LYAH-noh). Likewise, to say, "I speak Spanish," you say, "Yo hablo español" (yoh AH-bloh ehs-pah-NYOHL), or for "I speak English," you say, "Yo hablo inglés" (yoh AH-bloh een-GLEHS).

Do you speak	¿Habla usted	AH-blah oos-TEHD
_English?	_inglés?	_een-GLEHS?
_French?	**_francés?**	**_frahn-SEHS?**
_German?	**_alemán?**	**_ah-leh-MAHN?**
I only speak English.	Hablo solamente inglés.	AH-bloh soh-lah-MEHN-teh een-GLEHS
I don't speak Spanish.	No hablo español.	noh AH-bloh ehs-pah-NYOHL
I speak very little.	Hablo muy poco.	AH-bloh mwee POH-koh
I speak a little Spanish.	**Hablo un poco de español.**	**AH-bloh oon POH-koh deh ehs-pah-NYOHL**
I want to learn Spanish.	Quiero aprender español.	KYEH-roh ah-prehn-DEHR ehs-pah-NYOHL
I understand.	Comprendo/ Entiendo	kohm-PREHN-doh/ ehn-TYEHN-doh

I don't understand.	No comprendo/ No entiendo	noh kohm-PREHN-doh/ noh ehn-TYEHN-doh
Can you understand me?	**¿Me comprende?**	**meh kohm-PREHN-deh?**
Please repeat that.	**¿Puede repetir eso?**	**PWE-deh rreh-peh-TEER EH-soh?**
Speak more slowly.	Hable más despacio.	AH-bleh mahs dehs-PAH-syoh
Could you write that?	**¿Me lo escribe?**	**meh loh ehs-KREE-beh?**
How do you say . . .	¿Cómo se dice . . .	KOH-moh seh DEE-seh . . .
_in Spanish?	_en español?	_ehn ehs-pah-NYOHL?
_in English?	_en inglés?	_ehn een-GLES?
Is there anyone who speaks English here?	¿Hay alguien que habla inglés aquí?	ahy AHL-gyehn keh HAH-blah een-GLEHS ah-KEE?
Could you translate this?	**¿Puede traducir esto?**	**PWEH-deh trah-doo-SEER EHS-toh?**
Spanish is a beautiful language.	El español es una lengua hermosa.	ehl ehs-pah-NYOHL ehs OO-nah LEHN-gwah ehr-MOH-sah
I like Spanish a lot.	Me gusta mucho el español.	meh GOOS-tah MOO-choh ehl ehs-pah-NYOHL

9 PERSONAL CARE

DIALOGUE
Getting a Haircut (Cortarse el pelo)

Peluquera:	¿A quién le toca?	ah kyehn leh TOH-kah?
Cliente:	A mí. Quisiera un corte de pelo, por favor.	ah mee. kee-SYEH-rah oon KOHR-teh deh PEH-loh, pohr fah-BOHR
Peluquera:	¿Cómo lo quiere?	KOH-moh loh KYEH-reh?
Cliente:	Largo de atrás y más corto de los lados.	LAHR-goh deh ah-TRAHS ee mahs KOHR-toh deh lohs LAH-dohs
Peluquera:	¡Cómo no! ¿Quiere un champú también?	KOH-moh noh! KYEH-reh oon chahm-POO tahm-BYEHN?
Cliente:	No. Solamente el corte. Gracias.	noh. soh-lah-MEHN-teh ehl KOHR-teh. GRAH-syahs
Peluquera:	Está bien.	ehs-TAH byehn

Hairdresser:	Whose turn is it?
Client:	Mine. I'd like a haircut, please.
Hairdresser:	How would you like it?
Client:	Long in the back, but shorter on the sides.
Hairdresser:	Fine. Do you want a shampoo as well?
Client:	No. Just the haircut. Thank you.
Hairdresser:	Fine.

AT THE BARBERSHOP

I'd like a	Quisiera	kee-SYEH-rah
_haircut	_un corte de pelo.	_oon KOHR-teh deh PEH-loh
_shampoo.	_un lavado./ un champú.	_oon lah-BAH-doh/ oon chahm-POO

Leave it a little longer	Déjelo un poco más largo	DEH-heh-loh oon POH-koh mahs LAR-goh
_in the front.	_adelante.	_ah-deh-LAHN-teh
_on the sides.	_a los lados.	_ah lohs LAH-dohs
_in the back.	_atrás.	_ah-TRAHS
_on the top.	_arriba.	_ah-RREE-bah
Cut it short.	Córtelo corto.	KOHR-teh-loh KOHR-toh
Cut it a little shorter.	Córtelo un poco más corto.	KOHR-teh-loh oon POH-koh mahs KOHR-toh
I'd like the part	Quiero la raya	KYEH-roh lah RRAH-yah
_on the right.	_a la derecha.	_ah lah deh-REH-chah
_on the left.	_a la izquierda.	_ah lah ees-KYEHR-dah
_down the middle.	_al medio.	_ahl MEH-dyoh
Also trim my	También córteme	tahm-BYEHN KOHR-teh-meh
_beard.	_la barba.	_lah BAHR-bah
_mustache.	_el bigote.	_el bee-GOH-teh
_sideburns.	_las patillas.	_lahs pah-TEE-yahs
Cut a bit more right here	Corte un poco más aquí	KOHR-teh oon POH-koh mahs ah-KEE
_with the razor.	_con la navaja.	_kohn lah nah-BAH-hah
_with the scissors.	_con las tijeras.	_kohn lahs tee-HEH-rahs
It's fine like that.	Está bien así.	ehs-TAH byehn ah-SEE

AT THE BEAUTY PARLOR

I need to go to a hairdresser.	Debo ir a una peluquería.	DEH-boh eer ah OO-nah peh-loo-keh-REE-ah
Is there a beauty salon in this hotel?	¿Hay un salón de belleza en este hotel?	ahy oon sah-LOHN deh beh-YEH-sah ehn EHS-teh oh-TEHL?
Is there a long wait?	¿Debo esperar mucho?	DEH-boh ehs-peh-RAHR MOO-choh?
Do I need an appointment?	¿Necesito hacer una cita?	neh-seh-SEE-toh ah-SEHR OO-nah SEE-tah?

Can I make an appointment for	¿Puedo hacer una cita para	PWEH-doh ah-SEHR OO-nah SEE-tah PAH-rah
_later?	_más tarde?	_mahs TAHR-deh?
_this afternoon?	_esta tarde?	_EHS-tah TAHR-deh?
_three o'clock?	_las tres?	_lahs trehs?
_tomorrow?	_mañana?	_mah-NYAH-nah?
I'd like	**Quisiera**	**kee-SYEH-rah**
_a shampoo.	_un lavado.	_oon lah-VAH-doh
_a blowdry.	_un modelado.	_oon moh-deh-LAH-doh
_a set.	_un peinado.	_oon pay-NAH-doh
_a permanent.	_una permanente.	_OO-nah pehr-mah-NEHN-teh
_a manicure.	**_hacerme la manicura.**	**_ah-SEHR-meh lah mah-nee-KOO-rah**
_a touch-up.	_un retoque.	_oon rreh-TOH-keh
_a color rinse.	_un enjuague con color.	_oon ehn-HWAH-geh kohn koh-LOHR
Could I see a color chart?	¿Puedo ver una muestra de colores?	PWEH-doh behr OO-nah MWEHS-trah deh koh-LOH-rehs?
I prefer	Prefiero	preh-FYEH-roh
_auburn.	_castaño.	_kahs-TAH-nyoh
_ash blond.	_rubio ceniza.	_RROO-byoh seh-NEE-sah
_light blond.	_rubio claro.	_RROO-byoh KLAH-roh
_a darker shade.	_un tono más oscuro.	_oon TOH-noh mahs ohs-KOO-roh
_a lighter shade.	_un tono más claro.	_oon TOH-noh mahs KLAH-roh
Please use hairspray.	Con laca, por favor.	kohn LAH-kah, pohr fah-BOHR
No hairspray, please.	Sin laca, por favor.	seen LAH-kah, pohr fah-BOHR
That's perfect!	¡Está perfecto!	ehs-TAH pehr-FEK-toh!

LAUNDRY AND DRY CLEANING

I'm looking for	Estoy buscando	ehs-TOY boos-KAHN-doh
_a laundry.	_una lavandería.	_OO-nah lah-bahn-deh-REE-ah
_a dry cleaner.	_una tintorería.	_OO-nah teen-toh-reh-REE-ah
_a laundromat.	_una lavandería automática.	_OO-nah lah-bahn-deh-REE-ah ow-toh-MAH-tee-kah
I have a dress to be	Tengo un vestido para	TEHN-goh oon behs-TEE-doh PAH-rah
_washed.	_lavar.	_lah-BAHR
_ironed.	_planchar.	_plahn-CHAHR
_dry-cleaned.	_limpiar en seco.	_leem-PYAHR ehn SEH-koh
_mended.	_zurcir.	_soor-SEER
These clothes are dirty.	Esta ropa está sucia.	EHS-tah RROH-pah es-TAH SOO-syah
Can they be cleaned today?	¿La puede lavar hoy?	lah PWEH-deh loh-BAR ohy?
When will they be ready?	¿Cuando va a estar lista?	KWAHN-doh bah ah ehs-TAHR LEES-tah?
I need them	La necesito	lahs neh-seh-SEE-toh
_tomorrow.	_mañana.	_mah-NYAH-nah
_the day after tomorrow.	_pasado mañana.	_pah-SAH-doh mah-NYAH-nah
_in a week.	_en una semana.	_ehn OO-nah seh-MAH-nah
_as soon as possible.	_lo más pronto posible.	_loh mahs PROHN-toh poh-SEE-bleh
I'm leaving tomorrow.	Me voy mañana.	meh boy mah-NYAH-nah
Can you get this stain out?	**¿Puede sacar esta mancha?**	**PWEH-deh sah-KAHR EHS-tah MAHN-chah?**
Can you sew on this button?	¿Puede coser este botón?	PWEH-deh KOH-sehr EHS-teh boh-TOHN?
This isn't mine.	Esto no es mío.	EHS-toh noh ehs MEE-oh

There's an item missing.	Falta algo aquí.	FAHL-tah AHL-goh ah-KEE
Here is my list.	Aquí está mi lista.	ah-KEE ehs-TAH mee LEES-tah
_2 shirts	_dos camisas	_dohs kah-MEE-sahs
_5 pairs of men's undershorts	_cinco calzones/ calzoncillos (Spain)	_SEEN-koh kahl-SOH-nehs/ kahl-sohn-SEE-yohs
_a suit	_un traje	_oon TRAH-heh
_8 pairs of socks	_ocho pares de calcetines	_OH-choh PAH-rehs deh kahl-seh-TEE-nehs
_several handkerchiefs	_varios pañuelos	_BAH-ryohs pah-NYWEH-lohs
_2 ties	_dos corbatas	_dohs kohr-BAH-tahs
_a sweater	_un suéter	_oon SWEH-tehr
_2 pairs of pants	_dos pantalones	_dohs pahn-tah-LOH-nehs
_a jacket	_un saco/ una chaqueta	_oon SAH-koh/oo-nah chah-KEH-tah
_a bathing suit	_un traje de baño	_oon TRAH-heh deh BAH-nyoh
_3 blouses	_tres blusas	_trehs BLOO-sahs
_a skirt	_una falda	_OO-nah FAHL-dah
_a bra	_un sostén	_oon sohs-TEHN
_4 panties	_cuatro pantaletas/ bragas (Spain)	_KWAH-troh pahn-tah-LEH-tahs/ BRAH-gahs
_a dress	_un vestido	_oon behs-TEE-doh

You can usually locate English-speaking doctors in Spain and Mexico, especially in the big cities. Your embassy or consulate can help.

You should carry basic medicine, such as aspirin, and any prescription drugs you are currently using. Be sure to keep the prescription or label handy on your return trip, so that you can show it to the customs authorities, thus avoiding any problems.

The major health risk in Mexico is posed by consuming contaminated drinking water, fresh fruit, vegetables, herbs, and shellfish. So watch what you eat and drink. Avoid unpasteurized milk, milk products, and uncooked food, such as salads and even uncooked garnishes on cooked food. Stay away from fruits that you don't peel yourself. Drink only bottled water or water that has been boiled for at least 20 minutes. At establishments not frequented by tourists, ask for drinks without ice, *sin hielo* (sin hee-EH-lo). You can usually identify ice made commercially from purified water by its uniform shape and the hole in the center. *Refrescos* are sodas and are safe to drink. Hotels with water purification systems post signs to that effect in the rooms.

If your precautions fail, take liquid Pepto-Bismol, Imodium, or Lomotil—all available throughout Mexico. Rest as much as possible and drink plenty of purified water. In severe cases, rehydrate yourself with a salt-sugar solution (½ tsp. salt and 4 tbsp. sugar per quart of water) which is sold in pharmacies as *suero* (soo-eh-roh).

Air pollution in Mexico City can cause health problems, too. Avoid being outdoors on days of high smog alerts.

DIALOGUE
Finding a Doctor (Encontrar un doctor)

Turista:	**No me siento bien.**	noh meh SYEHN-toh byehn
Recepcionista:	**¿Necesita un doctor?**	neh-seh-SEE-tah oon dohk-TORH?
Turista:	**Creo que sí. ¿Puede recomendar uno?**	KREH-oh keh see. PWEH-deh reh-koh-mehn-DAHR OO-noh?
Recepcionista:	**Sí. Hay un Centro Médico en la esquina.**	see. ahy oon SEHN-troh MEH-dee-koh ehn lah ehs-KEE-nah
Turista:	**¿Hay algún doctor que hable inglés?**	ahy ahl-GOON dohk-TOHR keh AH-bleh een-GLEHS?
Recepcionista:	**No, pero la enfermera sí lo habla.**	noh, PEH-roh lah ehn-fehr-MEH-rah SEE loh AH-blah

Tourist:	I don't feel well.
Hotel clerk:	Do you need a doctor?
Tourist:	I think so. Can you recommend one?
Hotel clerk:	Yes. There's a Medical Center on the corner.
Tourist:	Is there a doctor who speaks English?
Hotel clerk:	No, but the nurse does.

FINDING A DOCTOR

Is there a doctor here?	¿Hay un doctor aquí?	ahy oon dohk-TOHR ah-KEE?
Could you call me a doctor?	**¿Puede llamarme a un doctor?**	**PWEH-deh yah-MAHR-meh ah oon dohk-TOHR?**
Where is the doctor's office?	¿Dónde está el consultorio del doctor?	DOHN-deh ehs-TAH ehl kohn-sool-TOH-ryoh dehl dohk-TOHR?
I need a doctor who speaks English.	Necesito un doctor que hable inglés.	neh-seh-SEE-toh oon dohk-TOHR keh AH-bleh een-GLEHS
When can I see the doctor?	¿Cuándo puedo ver al doctor?	KWAHN-doh PWEH-doh behr ahl dohk-TOHR?

Can the doctor see me now?	¿Puede verme el doctor ahora?	PWEH-deh BEHR-meh ehl dohk-TOHR ah-OH-rah?
It's an emergency.	Es una emergencia.	ehs OO-nah eh-mehr-HEHN-syah
Do I need an appointment?	¿Necesito hacer una cita?	neh-seh-SEE-toh ah-SEHR OO-nah SEE-tah?
Can I have an appointment	¿Puedo hacer una cita	PWEH-doh ah-SEHR OO-nah SEE-tah
_as soon as possible?	_lo más pronto posible?	_loh mahs PROHN-toh poh-SEE-bleh?
_for 2 o'clock?	_para las dos?	_PAH-rah lahs dohs?
What are the doctor's office hours?	¿Cuáles son las horas de consulta?	KWAH-lehs sohn lahs OH-rahs deh kohn-SOOL-tah?
I need	Necesito	neh-seh-SEE-toh
_a general practitioner.	_un médico general.	_oon MEH-dee-koh heh-neh-RAHL
_a pediatrician.	_un pediatra.	_oon peh-DYAH-trah
_a gynecologist.	_un ginecólogo.	_oon hee-neh-KOH-loh-goh
_an eye doctor.	_un oftalmólogo.	_oon ohf-tahl-MOH-loh-goh
_a dentist.	_un dentista.	_oon dehn-TEES-tah

TALKING TO THE DOCTOR

I don't feel well.	No me siento bien.	noh meh SYEHN-toh byehn
I'm sick.	Estoy enfermo(-a).	ehs-TOY ehn-FEHR-moh(-mah)
I don't know what I have.	No sé lo que tengo.	noh seh loh keh TEHN-goh
I feel	Me siento	meh SYEHN-toh
_weak.	_débil.	_DEH-beel
_dizzy.	_mareado(-a).	_mah-reh-AH-doh (-dah)

I have a fever.	Tengo fiebre.	TEHN-goh FYEH-breh
I don't have fever.	No tengo fiebre.	noh TEHN-goh FYEH-breh
I'm nauseated.	Tengo náuseas.	TEHN-goh NOW-seh-ahs
I can't sleep.	No puedo dormir.	noh PWEH-doh dohr-MEER
I threw up.	Vomité.	boh-mee-TEH
I have diarrhea.	Tengo diarrea.	TEHN-goh dyah-RREH-ah
I'm constipated.	Estoy estreñido(-a).	ehs-TOY ehs-treh-NYEE-doh(-dah)
I have	Tengo	TEHN-goh
_asthma.	_asma.	_AHS-mah
_a (animal) bite.	_una mordida.	_OO-nah mohr-DEE-dah
_bruises.	_hematomas.	_eh-mah-TOH-mahs
_a burn.	_una quemadura.	_OO-nah keh-mah-DOO-rah
_something in my eye.	_algo en el ojo.	_AHL-goh ehn ehl OH-hoh
_a cold.	_un resfriado.	_oon rehs-free-AH-doh
_a cough.	_tos.	_tohs
_cramps.	_calambres.	_kah-LAHM-brehs
_a cut.	_una cortadura	_oon KOHR-tah-DOO-rah
_the flu.	_gripe.	_GREE-peh
_a headache.	_dolor de cabeza.	_doh-LOHR deh kah-BEH-sah
_a lump.	_un bulto.	_oon BOOL-toh
_a rash.	_urticaria.	_oor-tee-KAH-ryah
_rheumatism.	_reumatismo.	_rreu-mah-TEES-moh
_a sore throat.	_dolor de garganta.	_doh-LOHR deh gahr-GAHN-tah
_a sting.	_una picadura.	_OO-nah pee-kah-DOO-rah

_a stomach ache.	_dolor de estómago.	_doh-LOHR deh ehs-TOH-mah-goh
_sunstroke.	_insolación.	_een-soh-lah-SYOHN
_a swelling.	_una hinchazón.	_OO-nah een-chah-SOHN
_an upset stomach.	**_malestar en el estómago.**	**_mah-lehs-TAHR ehn ehl ehs-TOH-mah-goh**
My . . . hurts (hurt).	**Me duele (-n)***	**meh DWEH-leh (-lehn)**
_stomach	_el estómago.	_ehl ehs-TOH-mah-goh
_feet	_los pies.	_lohs pyehs
_head	_la cabeza.	_lah kah-BEH-sah
_nose	_la nariz.	_lah nah-REES
_(inner) ear	_el oído.	_ehl oh-EE-doh
_mouth	_la boca.	_lah BOH-kah
_eye	_el ojo.	_ehl OH-hoh
_throat	**_la garganta.**	**_lah gahr-GAHN-tah**
_tongue	_la lengua.	_lah LEHN-gwah
_tooth	_el diente.	_ehl DYEHN-teh
_torso	_el torso.	_ehl TOHR-soh
_neck	_el cuello.	_ehl KWEH-yoh
_shoulder	_el hombro.	_ehl OHM-broh
_arm	_el brazo.	_ehl BRAH-soh
_elbow	_el codo.	_ehl KOH-doh
_chest	_el pecho.	_ehl PEH-choh
_breast	_el seno.	_ehl SEH-noh
_back	**_la espalda.**	**_lah ehs-PAHL-dah**
_hand	_la mano.	_lah MAH-noh
_wrist	_la muñeca.	_lah moo-NYEH-kah
_waist	_la cintura.	_lah seen-TOO-rah
_hip	_la cadera.	_lah kah-DEH-rah
_leg	_la pierna.	_lah PYEHR-nah
_knee	**_la rodilla.**	**_lah rroh-DEE-yah**

*In Spanish, the verb adds an -n when its subject is plural.

10 HEALTH CARE

97

_ankle	_el tobillo.	_ehl toh-BEE-yoh
_foot	_el pie.	_ehl pyeh
_heart	_el corazón.	_ehl koh-rah-SOHN
_liver	_el hígado.	_ehl EE-gah-doh
_appendix	_el apéndice.	_ehl ah-PEHN-dee-seh
_lungs	_los pulmones.	_lohs pool-MOH-nehs
_bladder	_la vejiga.	_lah beh-HEE-gah
_glands	_las glándulas.	_lahs GLAHN-doo-lahs
I'm allergic to	Soy alérgico(-a) a	soy ah-LEHR-hee-koh (-kah) ah
_penicillin.	_la penicilina.	_lah peh-nee-see-LEE-nah
_sulfa.	_la sulfa.	_lah SOOL-fah
_certain medicines.	_ciertas medicinas.	_SYEHR-tahs meh-dee-SEE-nahs
Here is the medicine I take.	Aquí está la medicina que tomo.	ah-KEE ehs-TAH lah meh-dee-SEE-nah keh TOH-moh
I've had this pain for two days.	He tenido este dolor por dos días.	eh teh-NEE-doh EHS-teh doh-LOHR pohr dohs DEE-ahs
I had a heart attack four years ago.	Tuve un infarto hace cuatro años.	TOO-beh oon een-FAHR-toh AH-seh KWAH-troh AH-nyohs
I'm four months pregnant.	Estoy embarazada de cuatro meses.	ehs-TOY ehm-bah-rah-SAH-dah deh KWAH-troh MEH-sehs
I have menstrual pains.	Tengo dolores menstruales.	TEHN-goh doh-LOH-rehs mehns-TRWAH-lehs

What the Doctor Says

¿Dónde le duele?	DOHN-deh leh DWEH-leh?	Where does it hurt?
¿Qué síntomas tiene?	keh SEEN-toh-mahs TYEH-neh?	What symptoms do you have?
Desvístase.	dehs-BEES-tah-seh	Get undressed.

Desvístase hasta la cintura.	dehs-BEES-tah-seh AHS-tah lah seen-TOO-rah	Undress to the waist.
Acúestese aquí.	ah-KWEHS-teh-seh ah-KEE	Lie down here.
Abra la boca.	AH-brah la BOH-kah	Open your mouth.
Tosa.	TOH-sah	Cough!
Respire a fondo.	rrehs-PEE-reh ah FOHN-doh	Breathe deeply.
Indíqueme donde le duele.	een-DEE-keh-meh DOHN-deh leh DWEH-leh	Show me where it hurts.
Saque la lengua.	SAH-keh lah LEHN-gwah	Stick out your tongue.
Vístase.	BEES-tah-seh	Get dressed.
Voy a tomarle la	boy ah toh-MAHR-leh lah	I'm going to take your
_temperatura.	_tehm-peh-rah-TOO-rah	_temperature.
_presión.	_preh-SYOHN	_blood pressure.
Necesito una muestra de	neh-seh-SEE-toh OO-nah MWEHS-trah deh	I need a sample of your
_sangre.	_SAHN-greh	_blood.
_materia fecal.	_mah-TEH-ryah feh-CAHL	_stool.
_orina.	_oh-REE-nah	_urine.
Le voy a dar un calmante.	leh boy ah dahr oon kahl-MAHN-teh	I'm going to give you a painkiller.
Usted necesita	oos-TEHD neh-seh-SEE-tah	You need
_una radiografía.	_OO-nah rrah-dyoh-grah-FEE-ah	_an X ray.
_una inyección.	_OO-nah een-yehk-SYOHN	_an injection.
_ir al hospital.	_eer ahl ohs-pee-TAHL	_to go to the hospital.
_ver a un especialista.	_behr ah oon ehs-peh-syah-LEES-tah	_to see a specialist.

No es serio.	noh ehs SEH-ryoh	It's not serious.
No es grave.	noh ehs GRAH-beh	It's not serious.
Es	ehs	It's
_serio.	_SEH-ryoh	_serious.
_un poco serio.	_oon POH-koh SEH-ryoh	_somewhat serious.
Está	ehs-TAH	It's
_dislocado.	_dees-loh-KAH-doh	_dislocated.
_roto.	_RROH-toh	_broken.
_luxado.	_loo-KSAH-doh	_sprained.
_infectado.	_een-fehk-TAH-doh	_infected.
Usted tiene	oos-TEHD TYEH-neh	You have
_apendicitis.	_ah-pehn-dee-SEE-tees	_appendicitis.
_una fractura.	_OO-nah frahk-TOO-rah	_a fracture.
_un hueso roto.	_oon WEH-soh RROH-toh	_a broken bone.
_gastritis.	_gahs-TREE-tees	_gastritis.
_gripe.	_GREE-peh	_the flu.
_una intoxi-cación.	_OO-nah een-tohk-see-kah-SYOHN	_food poisoning.
_pulmonía.	_pool-moh-NEE-ah	_pneumonia.
_viruela.	_bee-RWEH-lah	_smallpox.
_malaria.	_mah-LAH-ryah	_malaria.

Patient's Questions

Is it serious?	¿Es serio?	ehs SEH-ryoh?
Is it contagious?	¿Es contagioso?	ehs kohn-tah-HYOH-soh?
How long should I stay in bed?	¿Cuánto tiempo debo estar en cama?	KWAHN-toh TYEHM-poh DEH-boh ehs-TAHR ehn KAH-mah?
What exactly is wrong with me?	¿Qué es lo que tengo exactamente?	keh ehs loh keh TEHN-goh ehk-SAHK-tah-MEHN-teh?

How frequently should I take the medication?	¿Cada cuánto tiempo debo tomar la medicina?	KAH-dah KWAHN-toh TYEHM-poh DEH-boh toh-MAHR lah meh-dee-SEE-nah?
Do I need to see you again?	¿Debo verlo otra vez?/ . . . verle . . . (Spain)	DEH-boh BEHR-loh OH-trah vehs?/ . . . BEHR-leh . . .
Do I need a prescription?	¿Necesito una receta?	neh-seh-SEE-toh OO-nah rreh-SEH-tah?
When can I start traveling again?	¿Cuándo puedo empezar a viajar otra vez?	KWAHN-doh PWEH-doh ehm-peh-SAHR ah byah-HAHR OH-trah behs?
Can you give me a prescription for	¿Puede darme una receta para	PWEH-deh DAHR-meh OO-nah rreh-SEH-tah PAH-rah
_a painkiller?	_un calmante?	_oon kahl-MAHN-teh?
_a tranquilizer?	_un tranquilizante?	_oon trahn-kee-lee-SAHN-teh?
_a sleeping pill?	_una pastilla para dormir?	_OO-nah pahs-TEE-yah PAH-rah dohr-MEER?
Can I have a bill for my insurance?	¿Me puede dar un recibo para mi seguro?	meh PWEH-deh dahr oon rreh-SEE-boh PAH-rah mee seh-GOO-roh?
Could you fill out this medical form?	¿Puede llenar este formulario médico?	PWEH-deh yeh-NAHR EHS-teh fohr-moo-LAH-ryoh meh-DEE-koh?

AT THE HOSPITAL

Is there a hospital close by?	¿Hay un hospital por aquí?	ahy oon ohs-pee-TAHL pohr ah-KEE?
Call an ambulance!	¡Llame una ambulancia!	YAH-meh OO-nah ahm-boo-LAHN-syah!
Help me!	¡Ayúdeme!	ah-YOO-deh-meh!
Get me to the hospital!	**¡Lléveme al hospital!**	**YEH-beh-meh ahl ohs-pee-TAHL!**

I need first aid fast!	¡Necesito primeros auxilios rápido!	neh-seh-SEE-toh pree-MEH-rohs owk-SEE-lyohs RRAH-pee-doh!
I was in an accident!	**¡Tuve un accidente!**	**TOO-beh oon ahk-see-DEHN-teh!**
I cut my	**Me corté**	**meh kohr-TEH**
_hand.	_la mano.	_lah MAH-noh
_face.	_la cara.	_lah KAH-rah
_finger.	_el dedo.	_ehl DEH-doh
_leg.	**_la pierna.**	**_lah PYEHR-nah**
_neck.	_el cuello.	_ehl KWEH-yoh
I can't move.	No puedo moverme.	noh PWEH-doh moh-BEHR-meh
He hurt his head.	Se lastimó la cabeza.	seh lahs-tee-MOH lah kah-BEH-sah
His ankle is	**Tiene el tobillo**	**TYEH-neh ehl toh-BEE-yoh**
_broken.	_roto.	_RROH-toh
_twisted.	_torcido.	_tohr-SEE-doh
_swollen.	_hinchado.	_een-CHAH-doh
She (he) is bleeding heavily.	**Está sangrando mucho.**	**ehs-TAH sahn-GRAHN-doh MOO-choh**
He's (she's) unconscious.	**Está inconsciente.**	**ehs-TAH een-kohn-SYEHN-teh**
I burned myself.	**Me quemé.**	**meh keh-MEH**
I ate something poisonous.	Comí algo venenoso.	koh-MEE AHL-goh beh-neh-NOH-soh
When can I leave?	¿Cuándo puedo salir?	KWAHN-doh PWEH-doh sah-LEER?
When will the doctor come?	**¿Cuándo va a venir el doctor?**	**KWAHN-doh bah ah beh-NEER ehl dohk-TOHR?**
Where is the nurse?	**¿Dónde está la enfermera?**	**DOHN-deh ehs-TAH lah ehn-fehr-MEH-rah?**
I can't	No puedo	noh PWEH-doh

_eat.	_comer.	_koh-MEHR
_drink.	_beber.	_beh-BEHR
_sleep.	_dormir.	_dohr-MEER
What are the visiting hours?	¿Cuáles son las horas de visita?	KWAH-lehs sohn lahs OH-rahs deh bee-SEE-tah?

THE DENTIST

I need to see a dentist.	**Debo ver un dentista.**	**DEH-boh behr oon dehn-TEES-tah**
It's an emergency.	Es una emergencia.	ehs OO-nah eh-mehr-HEHN-syah
I'm in a lot of pain.	Tengo mucho dolor.	TEHN-goh MOO-choh doh-LOHR
I've lost a filling.	**He perdido un arreglo/empaste (Spain)**	**eh pehr-DEE-doh oon ah-RREH-gloh / ehm-PAH-steh**
This tooth is broken.	Este diente está roto.	EHS-teh DYEHN-teh ehs-tah RROH-toh
This tooth hurts.	Me duele este diente.	meh DWEH-leh EHS-teh DYEHN-teh
I don't want to have it extracted.	No quiero que me lo saque.	noh KYEH-roh keh meh loh SAH-keh
Can you fill it	**¿Puede rellenármelo**	**PWEH-deh reh-yeh-NAHR-meh-loh**
_with gold?	_con oro?	_kohn OH-roh?
_with silver?	**_con plata?**	**_kohn PLAH-tah?**
_temporarily?	_temporalmente?	_tehm-poh-rahl-MEHN-teh?
I want a local anesthetic.	Quiero anestesia local.	KYEH-roh ah-nehs-TEH-syah loh-KAHL
My denture is broken.	Mi dentadura postiza está rota.	mee dehn-tah-DOO-rah pohs-TEE-sah ehs-TAH RROH-tah

What the Dentist Says

Usted tiene	oos-TEHD TYEH-neh	You have
_una infección.	_OO-nah een-fehk-SYOHN	_an infection.
_una caries.	_OO-nah KAH-ryehs	_a cavity.
_un absceso	_oon ahb-SEH-soh	_an abscess.
¿Le duele esto?	leh DWEH-leh EHS-toh?	Does this hurt?
Debo sacarle esta muela.	DEH-boh sah-KAHR-leh EHS-tah MWEH-lah	This tooth must come out.
Puedo arreglar	PWEH-doh ah-rreh-GLAHR	I can fix
_este puente.	_EHS-teh PWEHN-teh	_this bridge.
_esta corona.	_EHS-tah koh-ROH-nah	_this crown.
Usted debe regresar	oos-TEHD DEH-beh rreh-greh-SAHR	You'll need to come back
_mañana.	_mah-NYAH-nah	_tomorrow.
_en unos días.	_ehn OO-nohs DEE-ahs	_in a few days.
_la próxima semana.	_lah PROK-see-mah seh-MAH-nah	_next week.

THE OPTICIAN

If you wear prescription glasses or contact lenses, be sure to bring an extra pair and a copy of your prescription. Note that in Mexico City, the smog may irritate your eyes if you wear contact lenses; don't forget your glasses.

I broke	Rompí	rrohm-PEE
_a lens.	_un lente.	_oon LEHN-teh
_the frame.	_la montura.	_lah mohn-TOO-rah
I lost a lens.	Perdí un lente.	pehr-DEE oon LEHN-teh
I've lost my	**He perdido mis**	**eh pehr-DEE-doh mees**
_glasses.	**_lentes.**	**_LEHN-tehs**

_contact lenses.	_lentes de contacto.	_LEHN-tehs deh kohn-TAHK-toh
Can you replace them right away?	**¿Puede reemplazarlos ahora?**	**PWEH-deh rrehm-plah-SAHR-lohs ah-OH-rah?**
When can I pick them up?	¿Cuándo puedo recogerlos?	KWAHN-doh PWEH-doh rreh-koh-HEHR-lohs?
Do you have sunglasses?	¿Tiene gafas (in Spain) para el sol?	TYE-neh gah-fahs PAH-rah ehl sohl?

AT THE PHARMACY

Pharmacies abound in Spain and Latin America. Often they are identified by the prescription symbol outside the establishment. When a pharmacy in an area is closed, there is usually a sign indicating which one is "on duty" (*de turno* [deh TOOR-noh]). Or you can check a local newspaper to see which one is open after regular hours.

Except for some unusual prescription drugs, you can find most medicines in pharmacies. However, you may feel more comfortable bringing medicine from home, as drug names vary from one country to another. Pharmacies in Spain tend to sell only medicinal products; however, in Mexico the *farmacias* (fahr-MAH-syahs) usually sell other items, such as beauty products, baby food, and toilet paper.

Is there a pharmacy nearby?	**¿Hay una farmacia por aquí?**	**ahy OO-nah fahr-MAH-syah pohr ah-KEE?**
When does the pharmacy open?	¿Cuándo abre la farmacia?	KWAHN-doh AH-breh lah fahr-MAH-syah?
What pharmacy is open now?	¿Cuál es la farmacia de turno?	KWAHL ehs lah fahr-MAH-syah deh TOOR-noh?
I need something for	**Necesito algo para**	**neh-seh-SEE-toh AHL-goh PAH-rah**
_a cold.	_el resfriado.	_ehl rehs-free-AH-doh
_constipation.	_el estreñimiento.	_ehl ehs-treh-nyee-MYEHN-toh

_a cough.	_la tos.	_lah tohs
_diarrhea.	_la diarrea.	_lah dyah-RREH-ah
_fever.	_la fiebre.	_lah FYEH-breh
_hay fever.	_la alergia.	_lah ah-LEHR-hyah
_headache.	_el dolor de cabeza.	_ehl doh-LOHR deh kah-BEH-sah
_an insect bite.	_una picadura.	_OO-nah pee-kah-DOO-rah
_sunburn.	_la quemadura de sol.	_lah keh-mah-DOO-rah deh sohl
_motion sickness.	_el mareo.	_ehl mah-REH-oh
_an upset stomach.	_el malestar de estómago.	_ehl mah-lehs-TAHR deh ehs-TOH-mah-goh
Other items:	Otros productos:	OH-trohs proh-DOOK-tohs
_alcohol	_alcohol	_ahl-KOHL
_analgesic	_analgésico	_ah-nahl-HEH-see-koh
_antiseptic	_antiséptico	_ahn-tee-SEHP-tee-koh
_aspirin	_aspirina	_ahs-pee-REE-nah
_bandages	_vendas	_BEHN-dahs
_Band-Aids	_curitas	_koo-REE-tahs
_contact lens solution	_líquido para lentes de contacto	_LEE-kee-doh PAH-rah LEHN-tehs deh kohn-TAHK-toh
_contraceptives	_anticonceptivos	_ahn-tee-kohn-sehp-TEE-vohs
_cotton	_algodón	_ahl-goh-DOHN
_cough drops	_pastillas para la tos	_pahs-TEE-yahs-PAH-rah lah tohs
_disinfectant	_desinfectante	_deh-seen-fehk-TAHN-teh
_eardrops	_gotas para el oído	_GOH-tahs PAH-rah ehl oh-EE-doh
_gauze	_gasa	_GAH-sah
_insect spray	_repelente	_rreh-peh-LEHN-teh
_iodine	_yodo	_YOH-doh

_laxative	_laxante	_lahk-SAHN-teh
_nose drops	_gotas para la nariz	_GOH-tahs PAH-rah lah nah-REES
_sanitary napkins	_toallas sanitarias	_toh-AH-yahs sah-nee-TAH-ryahs
_sleeping pills	_pastillas para dormir	_pahs-TEE-yahs PAH-rah dohr-MEER
_suppositories	_supositorios	_soo-poh-see-TOH-ryohs
_tablets	_comprimidos	_kohm-pree-MEE-dohs
_tampons	_tampones sanitarios	_tahm-POH-nehs sah-nee-TAH-ryahs
_thermometer	_termómetro	_tehr-MOH-meh-troh
_vitamins	_vitaminas	_bee-tah-MEE-nahs
It's urgent!	¡Es urgente!	ehs oor-HEHN-teh!

11 ON THE ROAD

CAR RENTALS

You may use your currently valid American driver's license to rent a car in Spain or Mexico. A good idea is to order your International Driver's License, available at a nominal charge from the American and Canadian Automobile Associations, and in the U.K. from the Automobile Association or the Royal Automobile Club. Most major car rental agencies have offices in Spain and Mexico. To get the best deal, book through a travel agent and shop around.

When driving in Mexico, carry proof of Mexican auto liability insurance at all times. It is usually provided by car-rental agencies and included in the cost of the rental. If you don't have proof of insurance and happen to injure someone—whether it's your fault or not—you stand the risk of being jailed.

Obey speed limits, parking regulations, and all highway rules, even if others do not.

DIALOGUE
At the Car-rental Agency (En el alquiler de coches)

Turista:	**Necesito alquilar un automóvil.**	neh-seh-SEE-toh ahl-kee-LAHR oon ow-toh-MOH-beel
Empleado:	**¿Tiene usted una reservación*?**	TYEH-neh oos-TEHD OO-nah rreh-sehr-bah-SYOHN?
Turista:	**No, ¿pero tiene uno disponible?**	noh, PEH-roh TYEH-neh OO-noh dees-poh-NEE-ble?
Empleado:	**Sí, ¿por cuánto tiempo lo quiere?**	see, pohr KWAHN-to TYEHM-poh loh KYEH-reh?
Turista:	**¿Cuál es la tarifa por día?**	kwahl ehs lah tah-REE-fah pohr DEE-ah?

*In Spain, you would say, "*una reserva* (rreh-SEHR-vah)."

Empleado:	**Cuesta €60 al día, más el kilometraje.**	KWEHS-tah seh-SEN-tah ee-OO-rohs ahl DEE-ah, mahs ehl kee-loh-meh-TRAH-heh
Turista:	**¿Es más barato por semana?**	ehs mahs bah-RAH-toh pohr seh-MAH-nah?
Empleado:	**¡Por supuesto! ¿Lo quiere llevar hoy?**	pohr soo-PWEH-toh! loh KYEH-reh yeh-BAHR ohy?
Turista:	**Sí, por favor. Lo quiero por una semana.**	see, pohr fah-BOHR. loh KYEH-roh pohr OO-nah seh-MAH-nah

....

Tourist:	I need to rent a car.
Clerk:	Do you have a reservation?
Tourist:	No, but do you have one available?
Clerk:	Yes, for how long do you want it?
Tourist:	What's the rate per day?
Clerk:	It's 60 Euros per day, plus mileage.
Tourist:	Is it cheaper by the week?
Clerk:	Of course! Do you want it today?
Tourist:	Yes, please. I'd like it for a week.

I need to rent	Necesito alquilar	neh-seh-SEE-toh ahl-kee-LAHR
_a car.	_un automóvil.	_oon ow-toh-MOH-beel
_a compact car.	_un automóvil pequeño.	_oon ow-toh-MOH-beel peh-KEH-nyoh
_an automatic car.	_un automóvil automático.	_oon ow-toh-MOH-beel ow-toh-MAH-tee-koh
_a station wagon.	_una camioneta.	_OO-nah kah-myoh-NEH-tah
How much is it per	¿Cuánto es por	KWAHN-toh ehs pohr
_hour?	_hora?	_OH-rah?
_day?	_día?	_DEE-ah?

_week?	_semana?	_seh-MAH-nah?
_month?	_mes?	_mehs?
_kilometer?	_kilómetro?	_kee-LOH-meh-troh?
How much is the insurance?	¿Cuánto cuesta el seguro?	KWAHN-toh KWEHS-tah ehl seh-GOO-roh?
Do you need	¿Necesita	neh-seh-SEE-tah
_a deposit?	_un depósito?	_oon deh-POH-see-toh?
_my driver's license?	_mi licencia de conducir?	_mee lee-SEHN-syah deh kohn-doo-SEER?
Do you accept credit cards?	¿Aceptan tarjetas de crédito?	ah-SEHP-tahn tahr-HEH-tahs deh KREH-dee-toh?
Can I leave the car in another city?	¿Puedo dejar el automóvil en otra ciudad?	PWEH-doh deh-HAR ehl ow-toh-MOH-beel ehn OH-trah syoo-DAHD?

DISTANCES AND LIQUID MEASURES

Distances in Spain, Mexico, and the rest of Latin America are expressed in kilometers, or *kilómetros* (kee-LOH-meh-trohs), and liquid measures (for gas and oil), in liters, or *litros* (LEE-trohs).

DISTANCE CONVERSIONS		LIQUID MEASURE CONVERSIONS	
1 kilometer (km.) =.62 miles		1 liter (l) = .26 gallon	
1 mile = 1.61 km.		1 gallon = 3.78 liters	
Kilometers	Miles	Liters	Gallons
1	0.62	10	2.6
5	3.1	15	4.0
8	5.0	20	5.3
10	6.2	30	7.9
15	9.3	40	10.6
20	12.4	50	13.2
50	31.0	60	15.8
75	46.6	70	18.5
100	62.1		

THE SERVICE STATION

Unleaded gas is widely available in Mexico. Gasoline stations, called *Pemex*, are owned and operated by the government and are few and far between, so don't let your tank run too low.

Where is there a service station?	¿Dónde hay una gasolinera?	DOHN-deh ahy OO-nah gah-soh-lee-NEH-rah?
Fill it with	Llénelo con	YEH-neh-loh kohn
_regular.	_regular.	_rreh-goo-LAHR
_super.	_super.	_SOO-pehr
_diesel.	_diesel.	_DEE-sehl
Give me 40 liters of regular.	Deme cuarenta litros de regular.	DEH-meh kwa-REHN-tah LEE-trohs deh rreh-goo-LAHR
Please check the	Por favor, revise	pohr fah-BOHR, rreh-BEE-seh
_carburetor.	_el carburador.	_ehl kahr-boo-rah-DOHR
_break fluid.	_el líquido de frenos.	_ehl LEE-kee-doh deh FREH-nohs
_spark plugs.	_las bujías.	_lahs boo-HEE-ahs
_tire pressure.	_la presión de las llantas.	_lah preh-SYOHN deh lahs YAHN-tahs
_water.	_el agua.	_ehl AH-gwah
_oil.	_el aceite.	_ehl ah-SAY-teh
Change the oil.	Cambie el aceite.	KAHM-byeh ehl ah-SAY-teh

DRIVING

Before taking off on a car trip, ask for a map of the country at a tourist office. Tourist offices are usually found in airports as well as in central locations in major cities.

Main highways are called *carreteras* (kah-rreh-TEH-rahs) and *autopistas* (ow-toh-PEES-tahs). These should be clearly indicated on the country's road map, showing toll roads and freeways. In Spain, toll roads are called *autopistas de peaje* (ow-toh-PEES-tahs deh peh-AH-heh), and in Mexico, *carretera cuota* (kah-rreh-TEH-rah KWOH-tah). In general, the national highways—*carreteras nacionales* (kah-rreh-TEH-rahs nah-syo-NAH-lehs)—of Spain are good.

The *carreteras libres* (kah-rreh-TEH-rahs lee-brehs) in Mexico, however, despite being scenic, are full of potholes and will add many hours to your journey. Some are actually dangerous. In Mexico, your best bet is to shell out for the toll freeways.

Speed Limits

Highways	120 km/h	(75 mph)
Double-lane highway	100 km/h	(62 mph)
Most local roads	90 km/h	(55 mph)
Urban areas	50 km/h	(37 mph)

In Spain and Mexico, drivers tend not to pay much attention to speed limits, though radar control is common and if you are found exceeding the speed limit, you may get a ticket. Mexico's automobile association, affiliated with the AAA in the United States, is the Asociación Mexicana Automovilística.

Is this the road to . . .	**¿Es éste el camino a . . .**	ehs EHS-teh ehl kah-MEE-noh a . . .
_Madrid?	_Madrid?	_mah-DREED?
_Guadalajara?	_Guadalajara?	_gwah-dah-lah-HAH-rah?
Is there a better road?	¿Hay un camino mejor?	ahy oon kah-MEE-noh MEH-hohr?
Is there a less congested road?	¿Hay un camino menos transi-tado?	ahy oon kah-MEE-noh MEH-nohs trahn-see-TAH-doh?
Is there a shortcut?	¿Hay un atajo?	_ahy oon ah-TAH-hoh?
I think we are	Creo que estamos	KREH-oh keh ehs-TAH-mohs
_lost.	_perdidos.	_pehr-DEE-dohs
_in the outskirts.	_en las afueras.	_ehn lahs ah-FWEH-rahs
_in the wrong lane.	_en el carril equivocado.	_ehn ehl kah-RREEL eh-kee-boh-KAH-doh
_in the wrong exit.	_en la salida equivocada.	_ehn lah sah-LEE-dah eh-kee-boh-KAH-dah.

_in the center of town.	_en el centro de la ciudad.	_ehn ehl SEHN-troh deh lah syoo-DAHD
_arriving at the next town.	_llegando al próximo pueblo.	_yeh-GAHN-doh ahl PROK-see-moh PWEH-bloh
How do I get to	**¿Cómo voy**	**KOH-moh boy**
_the Rex hotel?	_al hotel Rex?	_ahl oh-TEHL rrehks?
_the next town?	_al próximo pueblo?	_ahl PROHK-see-moh PWEH-bloh?
_the main highway?	**_a la carretera principal?**	**_ah lah kah-rreh-TEH-rah preen-see-PAHL?**
_the center of town?	_al centro de la ciudad?	_ahl SEHN-troh deh lah syoo-DAD?
Do I go	¿Voy	bohy?
_straight ahead?	_derecho?	_deh-REH-choh?
_to the right?	_a la derecha?	_ah lah deh-REH-chah?
_to the left?	_a la izquierda?	_ah lah ees-KYEHR-dah?
_two (three, etc.) more blocks?	_dos (tres, etc.) cuadras más?	_dohs (trehs) KWAH-drahs mahs?
Is it	**¿Queda**	**KEH-dah**
_nearby?	**_cerca?**	**_SEHR-kah?**
_far from here?	**_lejos de aquí?**	**_LEH-hohs deh ah-KEE?**
_near the hotel?	_cerca del hotel?	_SEHR-kah dehl oh-TEHL?
_far from the center?	_lejos del centro?	_LEH-hohs dehl SEHN-troh?
_close to the center?	_cerca del centro?	_SEHR-kah dehl SEHN-troh?
Are there any tourist services?	¿Hay servicios turísticos?	ahy sehr-BEE-syohs too-REES-tee-kohs?
May I park the car here?	**¿Puedo estacionar el auto aquí?**	**PWEH-doh ehs-tah-syoh-NAHR ehl OW-toh ah-KEE?**

EMERGENCIES AND CAR PROBLEMS

Sponsored by the Mexico Ministry of Tourism, the *Angeles Verdes* (Green Angels) patrol the highways daily in green-and-white cars. They carry emergency gasoline and oil, and an assortment of spare parts; they do not charge for labor. They also have two-way radios and first-aid equipment, and are prepared to offer tourism information and advice on highway and weather conditions ahead.

My car won't start.	Mi auto no arranca.	mee OW-toh noh ah-RRAHN-kah
Something must be wrong.	Debe tener algún problema.*	DEH-beh teh-NEHR ahl-GOON proh-BLEH-mah
I don't know what's wrong.	No sé que tiene.	noh seh keh TYEH-neh
I have a flat tire.	Tengo una llanta ponchada. (Mexico)/ ... pinchada. (Spain)	TEHN-goh OO-nah YAHN-tah pohn-CHAH-dah/ ... peen-CHAH-dah
I'm out of gas.	Se me terminó la gasolina.	seh meh tehr-mee-NOH la gah-soh-LEE-nah
The battery's dead.	No funciona la batería.	noh foon-SYOH-nah lah bah-teh-REE-ah
It's overheating.	Se está calentando mucho.	seh es-TAH kah-lehn-TAHN-doh MOO-choh
I left the keys inside the car.	Olvidé las llaves adentro.	ohl-bee-DEH lahs YAH-behs ah-DEHN-troh
I don't have an extra key.	No tengo una llave extra.	noh TEHN-goh OO-nah YAH-beh EHKS-trah
I don't have any tools.	No tengo herramientas.	noh TEHN-goh eh-rrah-MYEHN-tahs
I need	Necesito	neh-seh-SEE-toh
_a flashlight.	_una linterna.	_OO-nah leen-TEHR-nah
_a hammer.	_un martillo.	_oon mahr-TEE-yoh
_a jack.	_un gato.	_oon GAH-toh
_pliers.	_unas pinzas. (Mexico)/ un alicate. (Spain)	_OO-nahs PEEN-sahs/ oon ah-lee KAH-teh

_a bolt.	_un perno.	_oon PEHR-noh
_a nut.	_una tuerca.	_OO-nah TWEHR-kah
_a screwdriver.	_un destornillador.	_oon dehs-tohr-nee-yah-DOHR
Can you open the	¿Puede abrir	PWEH-deh ah-BREER
_hood?	_el cofre? (Mexico)/	_ehl KOH-freh?/
	el capó? (Spain)	_ehl kah-POH?
_trunk?	_la cajuela? (Mexico)/	_lah kah-HWEH-lah?/
	el maletero? (Spain)	_ehl mah-leh-TEH-roh?
_gas tank?	_el tanque de gasolina?	_ehl TAHN-keh deh gah-soh-LEE-nah?
Can you	**¿Puede**	**PWEH-deh**
_charge my battery?	_cargar la batería?	_kahr-GAHR lah bah-teh-REE-ah?
_change the tire?	**_cambiar la llanta?**	**_kahm-BYAHR la YAHN-tah?**
_tow the car to a garage?	**_remolcar el auto a un garaje?**	**_rreh-mohl-KAHR ehl OW-toh ah oon gah-RAH-heh?**

Car Repairs

When renting a car, be sure to ask for a list of authorized agencies and repair shops.

There's something wrong with the	Algo anda mal con	AHL-goh AHN-dah mahl kohn
_car.	_el automóvil.	_ehl ow-toh-MOH-beel
_brakes.	_los frenos.	_lohs FREH-nohs
_tires.	_las llantas.	_lahs YAHN-tahs
_spark plugs.	_las bujías.	_lahs boo-HEE-ahs
_motor.	_el motor.	_ehl moh-TOHR
Please check the	Por favor revise	pohr fah-BOHR rreh-BEE-seh
_oil.	_el aceite.	_ehl ah-SAY-teh
_water.	_el agua.	_ehl AH-gwah

_carburetor.	_el carburador.	_ehl kahr-boo-rah-DOHR
_battery.	_la batería.	_lah bah-teh-REE-ah
_radiator.	_el agua del radiador.	_ehl AH-gwah dehl rrah-dyah-DOHR
_brake fluid.	_el líquido para los frenos.	_ehl LEE-kee-doh PAH-rah lohs FREH-nohs
_tire pressure.	_la presión de las llantas.	_lah preh-SYOHN deh lahs YAHN-tahs
I have a problem with the	Tengo un problema con	TEHN-goh oon proh-BLEH-mah kohn
_gears.	_los cambios.	_lohs KAHM-byohs
_headlights.	_las luces delanteras.	_lahs LOO-sehs deh-lahn-TEH-rahs
_high beams.	_las altas.	_lahs AHL-tahs
_directional signals.	_las luces direccionales.	_lahs LOO-sehs dee-rehk-syo-NAH-lehs
_ignition.	_el encendido.	_ehl ehn-sehn-DEE-doh
_radiator.	_el radiador.	_ehl rrah-DYAH-dohr
_transmission	_la transmisión.	_la trahns-mee-SYOHN
_the windshield wipers.	_los limpiaparabrisas.	_lohs leem-pyah-pah-rah-BREE-sahs
Can you repair the	¿Puede reparar	PWEH-deh reh-pah-RAHR
_brakes?	_los frenos?	_lohs FREH-nohs?
_horn?	_la bocina?	_lah boh-SEE-nah?
_radio?	_la radio?	_lah RRAH-dyoh?
_starter?	_el arranque?	_ehl ah-RRAHN-keh?
_steering wheel?	_el volante?	_ehl boh-LAHN-teh?
_electrical system?	_el sistema eléctrico?	_ehl sees-TEH-mah eh-LEHK-tree-koh?
_door handle?	_la manija de la puerta?	_lah mah-NEE-hah deh lah PWEHR-tah?
_speedometer?	_el velocímetro?	_ehl beh-loh-SEE-meh-troh?

How long will this take?	¿Cuánto tiempo va a demorar?	KWAHN-toh TYEHM-poh bah ah deh-moh-RAHR?
How much will it cost?	¿Cuánto va a costar?	KWAHN-toh bah ah kohs-TAHR?
Other parts of the car	**Otras partes del automóvil**	**OH-trahs PAHR-tehs dehl ow-toh-MOH-veel**
the transmission	la transmisión	lah trahns-mee-SYOHN
the water pump	la bomba de agua	lah BOHM-bah deh AH-gwah
the directional signals	las luces direccionales	lahs LOO-sehs dee-rehk-syoh-NAH-lehs
the fuel pump	la bomba de gasolina	lah BOHM-bah deh gah-soh-LEE-nah
the distributor	el distribuidor	ehl dees-tree-BUEE-dohr
the gearshift	el cambio de velocidad	ehl KAHM-byoh deh beh-loh-see-DAHD
the headlights	las luces delanteras	lahs LOO-sehs deh-lahn-TEH-rahs
the taillights	los faros traseros	lohs FAH-rohs trah-SEH-rohs
the fan belt	la correa del ventilador	lah koh-RREH-ah dehl behn-tee-lah-DOHR

ROAD SIGNS

CASETA DE COBRO	kah-SEH-tah deh KOH-broh	Toll Booth
CAMBIO EXACTO	KAHM-byoh ehk-SAHK-toh	Exact Change
CARRIL (Mexico) (or) CANAL	kah-RREEL, kah-NAHL	Lane
CARRIL DERECHO	kah-RREEL deh-REH-choh	Right Lane
CARRIL IZQUIERDO	kah-RREEL ees-KYEHR-doh	Left Lane
CUNETA (Mexico) (or) HOMBRILLO	koo-NEH-tah ohm-BREE-yoh	Shoulder

VELOCIDAD MÁXIMA	beh-loh-see-DAHD MAHK-see-mah	Maximum Speed
VELOCIDAD MÍNIMA	beh-loh-see-DAHD MEE-nee-mah	Minimum Speed
REDUCIR LA VELOCIDAD	rreh-doo-SEER lah beh-loh-see-DAHD	Reduce Speed
DESVIACIÓN (*Mexico*) (*or*) DESVÍO	dehs-byah-SYOHN dehs-BEE-oh	Detour
PASO DE PEATONES	PAH-soh deh peh-ah-TOH-nehs	Pedestrian Crossing
CARRETERA EN OBRAS	kah-rreh-TEH-rah ehn OH-brahs	Road Construction

NO ENTRY FOR
MOTOR VEHICLES

DANGEROUS
INTERSECTION
AHEAD

STOP

NO ENTRY

MINIMUM SPEED
(km/hr)

SPEED LIMIT
(km/hr)

DIRECTION TO BE
FOLLOWED (at the
next intersection)

OVERHEAD
CLEARANCE
(meters)

ROTARY

NO PASSING

END OF
NO PASSING ZONE

END OF
RESTRICTION

NO LEFT TURN

NO U-TURN

NO PARKING

ONE WAY

DEAD END

PARKING

SUPERHIGHWAY

YIELD

GAS

DANGER AHEAD

DANGEROUS
DESCENT

BUMPS

ROAD NARROWS

LEVEL (RAILROAD)
CROSSING

TWO-WAY
TRAFFIC

SLIPPERY ROAD

CAUTION—
SHARP CURVE

PEDESTRIAN
CROSSING

TELEPHONES

The best way to make a call in Spain is by using a *tarjeta telefónica,* or phone card, in a pay phone, or by going to the *locutorio,* or local phone office (every town has one). To make an international call from Spain, dial 00, then the country code, area code, and number. For general information in Spain, dial 1003. International operators, who generally speak English, are at 025.

In Mexico, most pay phones take phone cards called Ladatel cards. Dial 040 for national directory assistance, 00 for international directory assistance. For assistance in English dial 090. To make an international call, dial 00, then the country code, area code and local number. A telephone booth in Spain is called a *cabina telefónica* (kah-BEE-nah teh-leh-FOH-nee-kah), and in Mexico, *caseta de teléfono* (kah-SEH-tah deh teh-LEH-foh-noh).

Is there a	¿Hay	ahy
_public telephone?	_un teléfono público?	_oon teh-LEH-foh-noh POO-blee-koh?
_telephone booth?	_una cabina telefónica?	_OO-nah kah-BEE-nah teh-leh-FOH-nee-kah?
_telephone directory?	_una guía telefónica?	_OO-nah GEE-ah teh-leh FOH-nee-kah?
Operator.	**Operadora.**	**oh-peh-rah-DOH-rah**
I'd like to call	Quisiera llamar a	kee-SYEH-rah yah-MAHR ah
_this number.	_este número.	_EHS-teh NOO-meh-roh
_information.	_información.	_een-fohr-mah-SYON
_the international operator.	_la operadora internacional.	_lah oh-peh-rah-DOH-rah een-tehr-nah-syoh-NAHL
I'd like to use my credit card.	Quisiera usar mi tarjeta de crédito.	kee-SYEH-rah oo-SAHR mee tahr-HEH-tah deh KREH-dee-toh

I'd like to make a	Quisiera hacer una llamada	kee-SYEH-rah ah-SEHR OO-nah yah-MAH-dah
_long-distance call.	_de larga distancia.	_deh LAHR-gah dees-TAHN-syah
_person-to-person call.	_de persona a persona.	_deh pehr-SOH-nah ah pehr-SOH-nah
_local call.	_local.	_loh-KAHL
_collect call.	_a cobro revertido.	_ah KOH-broh reh-behr-TEE-doh
_conference call.	_por conferencia.	_pohr kohn-feh-REHN-syah
_a call with time and charges.	_con tiempo y costo.	_kohn TYEM-poh ee KOHS-toh

What the Caller Says

Hello!	¡Hola! ¡Bueno!	OH-lah! BWEH-noh!
This is	Habla	AH-blah
_Mr. . . .	_el señor . . .	ehl seh-NYOHR
_Mrs. . . .	_la señora . . .	lah seh-NYOH-rah
_Miss/Ms. . . .	_la señorita . . .	lah seh-NYOH-REE-tah
May I speak to . . . ?	¿Puedo hablar con . . . ?	PWEH-doh ah-BLAHR kohn . . . ?
Is Juan there?	¿Se encuentra Juan?	seh ehn-KWEHN-trah wahn?
Can you repeat, please?	¿Puede repetir, por favor?	PWEH-deh rreh-peh-TEER, pohr fah-BOHR?
I can't hear very well.	No oigo muy bien.	noh OY-goh muee byehn
It's a bad connection.	Es una conexión mala.	ehs OO-nah koh-nehk-SYOHN MAH-lah
Speak louder, please.	Hable más fuerte, por favor.	AH-bleh mahs FWEHR-teh, pohr fah-BOHR
I'd like to leave a message.	Quisiera dejar un mensaje.	kee-SYEH-rah deh-HAHR oon mehn-SAH-he

My number is . . .	Mi número es . . .	mee NOO-meh-roh ehs . . .

What the Operator Says

La línea está ocupada.	lah LEE-nyah ehs-TAH oh-koo-PAH-dah	The line is busy.
No contestan.	noh kohn-TEHS-tahn	They don't answer.
¿Quiere que siga probando?	KYEH-reh keh SEE-gah proh-BAHN-doh?	Do you want me to keep trying?
¿Puede llamar más tarde?	PWEH-deh yah-MAHR mahs TAHR-deh?	Can you call later?
No cuelgue.	noh KWEHL-geh	Don't hang up.
Espere, por favor.	es-PEH-reh, pohr fah-BOHR	Please wait a moment.
Se interrumpió su llamada.	seh een-teh-rroom-PYOH soo yah-MAH-dah	Your call was disconnected.
¿Con quién desea hablar?	kohn kyen de-SEH-ah ah-BLAR?	Who do you want to speak to?
¿Quiere dejar un mensaje?	KYEH-reh deh-HAHR oon men-SAH-heh?	Do you want to leave a message?
¿Tiene otro número?	TYEH-neh OH-troh NOO-meh-roh?	Do you have another number?
Repita eso, por favor.	rreh-PEE-tah EH-soh, pohr fah-BOHR	Please repeat that.

THE POST OFFICE

Letters from Spain to the United States usually take from about one week to ten days. Look for stamps at the *estancos* (es-TAHN-kohs) as well as in the post office. *Estancos* can be found on almost every block in major cities.

In Mexico, stamps can be purchased only at a post office. Occasionally some stores and hotels that sell postcards also have a limited supply of stamps. But do not expect to find stamps there for other types of mail.

In both countries post offices are generally open from 9:00 A.M. to noon, and reopen again from 4:00 to 7:00 P.M., Monday to Friday. Post offices are also open until noon on Saturday. In

123

Mexico, mail to the United States may take about five days to a week from major cities, up to three weeks from smaller towns, and service to Europe takes about three weeks. The postal system is generally unreliable and only recommended for postcards.

Is this the post office?	¿Es el correo?	ehs ehl koh-RREH-oh?
I would like to send	Quisiera mandar	kee-SYEH-rah mahn-DAHR
_a letter.	_una carta.	_OO-nah KAHR-tah
_a postcard.	_una tarjeta postal.	_OO-nah tahr-HEH-tah pohs-TAHL
_a registered letter.	_una carta registrada.	_OO-nah KAHR-tah rreh-hees-TRAH-dah
_a special-delivery letter	_una carta con entrega inmediata.	_OO-nah KAHR-tah kohn ehn-TREH-gah een-meh-DYAH-tah
_a certified letter.	_una carta certificada.	_OO-nah KAHR-tah sehr-tee-fee-KAH-dah
_a package.	_un paquete.	_oon pah-KEH-teh
_a money order.	_un giro postal.	_oon HEE-roh pohs-TAHL
How many stamps do I need for	¿Cuántas/-tos estampillas/ sellos (Spain) necesito para	KWAHN-tahs/-tos ehs-tahm-PEE-yahs/ (SEH-yohs) neh-seh-SEE-toh PAH-rah
_surface mail?	_vía normal?	_BEE-ah nohr-MAHL?
_airmail?	_vía aérea?	_BEE-ah ah-EH-reh-ah?
_a postcard?	_una tarjeta postal?	_OO-nah tahr-HEH-tah pohs-TAHL?
_a letter to the United States?	_una carta a los Estados Unidos?	_OO-nah KAHR-tah ah lohs ehs-TAH-dos oo-NEE-dohs?
I'd also like to buy	También quisiera	tahm-BYEHN kee-SYEH-rah
_airmail envelopes.	_sobres aéreos.	_SOH-brehs ah-EH-reh-ohs
_aerograms.	_aerogramas.	_ah-eh-roh-GRAH-mahs
_airmail paper.	_papel aéreo.	_pah-PEHL ah-EH-reh-oh

_a collection of stamps.	_una colección de estampillas.	_OO-nah koh-lehk-SYOHN deh ehs-tahm-PEE-yahs
Where is the	¿Dónde está	DOHN-deh ehs-TAH
_letterbox?	_el buzón?	_ehl boo-SOHN?
_stamp machine?	_la máquina de estampillas?	_lah MAH-kee-nah deh ehs-tahm-PEE-yahs?
_the window for certified mail?	_la ventanilla para correo certificado?	_lah behn-tah-NEE-yah PAH-rah koh-RREH-oh sehr-tee-fee-KAH-doh?

E-MAIL AND THE INTERNET

Internet cafés have sprung up in most major Mexican cities, and in Spain, virtually every town with more than two traffic lights has one. Newer hotels in both countries provide data ports for Internet access. Always check with your hotel about surge protection as extreme electrical fluctuations or surges can damage or destroy your computer.

Where is the computer?	¿Dónde está la computadora?	DOHN-deh eh-STAH lah kohm-poo-tah-DOH-rah
I need to send an e-mail.	Necesito enviar un correo electrónico.	neh-seh-SEE-toh ehn-BYAHR oon koh-REH-yoh eh-lehk-TROH-nee-koh
Can I get on the Internet?	¿Puedo conectarme con el internet?	PWEH-doh koh-nehk-TAHR-meh ahl EEN-tehr-net
Do you have a Web site	¿Tiene página web?	TYEH-neh PAH-hee-nah web?

FAXES AND TELEGRAMS

Telegrams are still used in Mexico for all kinds of short messages. Telegraph offices are usually located near a post office and sometimes in the same building. A few hotels provide telegram service as well. Faxes are a fixture in Spain and common in larger businesses in Mexican cities.

May I send . . . to New York?	Puedo mandar . . . a Nueva York?	PWEH-doh mahn-DAHR . . . ah NWEH-bah yohrk?
_a telegram	_un telegrama	_oon teh-leh-GRAH-mah
_a telex	_un télex	_oon TEH-lehks
_a cable	_un cable	_oon KAH-bleh
_a night letter	_una carta nocturna	_OO-nah KAHR-tah nohk-TOOR-nah
_a fax	_un fax	_oon-FAHKS
I would like to wire some money.	Quisiera mandar dinero por cable.	kee-SYEH-rah mahn-DAHR dee-NEH-roh pohr KAH-bleh
How much is it per word?	¿Cuánto cuesta por palabra?	KWAHN-toh KWEHS-tah pohr pah-LAH-brah?
Will it arrive tomorrow morning?	¿Llegará mañana por la mañana?	yeh-gah-RAH mah-NYAH-nah pohr lah mah-NYAH-nah?

THE MEDIA

In Madrid you can get newspapers and magazines from all over the world. Among the English-language newspapers, look for the *London Times* and the *New York Times* (international editions), the *International Herald Tribune,* and the *Wall Street Journal.* In Mexico City you can also find a variety of English-language publications, especially at the airport and in Sanborns (a department store). Several bookstores specialize in English-language magazines and books. The *News* is a special English-language newspaper sold all over the country.

In Madrid, you can listen to the BBC radio from London. In Mexico, CBS affiliates feature syndicated news programs on a regular basis and there is also an English-speaking radio station. Thanks to Cablevisión (kah-bleh-vee-SYOHN) you can now watch CNN and other TV programs directly from the United States in Mexico. Spain also carries various foreign programs from other parts of Europe via satellite.

Books and Newspapers	Libros y periódicos	LEE-brohs ee peh-RYOH-dee-kohs
Do you have	¿Tienen	TYEH-nehn
_newspapers in English?	_periódicos en inglés?	_peh-RYOH-dee-kohs ehn een-GLEHS?

_magazines in English?	_revistas en inglés?	_rreh-BEES-tahs ehn een-GLEHS?
_books in English?	_libros en inglés?	_LEE-brohs ehn een-GLEHS?
_any publications in English?	_alguna publicación en inglés?	_ahl-GOO-nah poo-blee-kah-SYOHN ehn een-GLEHS?
Radio and Television	**Radio y televisión**	**RRAH-dyoh ee teh-leh-bee-SYOHN**
Is there a(an)	¿Hay una	ahy OO-nah
_English-speaking station?	_estación en inglés?	_ehs-tah-SYOHN ehn een-GLEHS?
_music station?	_estación con música?	_ehs-tah-SYOHN kohn MOO-see-kah?
_news station?	_estación que da noticias?	_ehs-tah-SYOHN keh dah noh-TEE-syahs?
_weather station?	_estación que da el tiempo?	_ehs-tah-SYOHN keh dah ehl TYEHM-poh?
What number is it on the dial?	¿En qué número se sintoniza?	ehn keh NOO-meh-roh seh seen-toh-NEE-sah?
What time is the program?	¿A qué hora es el programa?	ah ke OH-rah ehs ehl proh-GRAH-mah?
Is there an English-speaking channel?	**¿Hay un canal en inglés?**	**ahy oon kah-NAHL ehn een-GLEHS?**
Do you have a television guide?	¿Tiene un horario de televisión?	TYEH-neh oon oh-RAH-ryoh deh teh-leh-bee-SYOHN?
Do they have international news in English?	¿Tienen las noticias internacionales en inglés?	TYEH-nehn lahs noh-TEE-syahs een-tehr-nah-syoh-NAH-lehs ehn een-GLEHS?
When is the weather forecast?	¿Cuándo es el pronóstico del tiempo?	KWAHN-doh ehs ehl proh-NOHS-tee-koh dehl TYEHM-poh?

13 SIGHTSEEING

You can obtain information about what to see and do from national and local tourist offices and from guidebooks. The Internet is also useful for research. You'll find a plethora of links to the Web sites of local tourist offices, publications, attractions, and booking services at www.fodors.com. At your destination, ask your hotel for a guide to the city and activities of the week. You may also be able to obtain information about bus tours and places of interest to visit.

DIALOGUE
Touring the City (Visitar la ciudad)

Turista:	¿Cuáles son algunos de los lugares para visitar?	KWAH-lehs sohn ahl-GOO-nohs deh lohs loo-GAH-rehs PAH-rah bee-see-TAHR?
Empleado del hotel:	Hay muchas cosas interesantes en esta ciudad.	ahy MOO-chas KOH-sahs een-teh-reh-SAHN-tehs en ES-tah syoo-DAHD.
Turista:	¿Es fácil ir al distrito histórico?	ehs FAH-seel eer ahl dees-TREE-toh ees-TOH-ree-koh?
Empleado:	Sí, puede tomar un autobús en la esquina. Llega hasta la parte vieja de la ciudad.	see, PWEH-deh toh-MAHR oon ow-toh-BOOS ehn lah ehs-KEE-nah. YEH-gah AHS-tah lah PAHR-teh BYEH-hah deh lah syoo-DAHD
Turista:	¿Hay muchas iglesias allí?	ahy MOO-chahs ee-GLEH-syahs ah-YEE?
Empleado:	Sí, y también varios museos.	see, ee tahm-BYEHN BAH-ryohs moo-SEH-ohs
Turista:	Gracias por la información.	GRAH-syahs pohr lah een-fohr-mah-SYOHN

Tourist:	What are some places to visit?
Hotel clerk:	There are many interesting things to see in this city.
Tourist:	Is it easy to get to the historic district?
Hotel clerk:	Yes, you can take a bus at the corner. It goes right to the old part of town.
Tourist:	Are there many churches there?
Hotel clerk:	Yes, and also several museums.
Tourist:	Thanks for the information.

FINDING THE SIGHTS

I want to go to the	Quiero ir a	KYEH-roh eer ah
_cathedral.	_la catedral.	_lah kah-teh-DRAHL
_main market.	_al mercado central.	_ahl mehr-KAH-doh sehn-TRAHL
_art museum.	_al museo de arte.	_ahl moo-SEH-oh deh AHR-teh
_natural science museum.	_al museo de ciencias naturales.	_ahl moo-SEH-oh deh SYEHN-syahs nah-too-RAH-lehs
_folk-art museum.	_al museo de arte folklórico.	_ahl moo-SEH-oh deh AHR-teh fohl-KLOH-ree-koh
_national theater.	_al teatro nacional.	_ahl teh-AH-troh nah-syoh-NAHL
_business district.	_al sector comercial.	_ahl sehk-TOHR koh-mehr-SYAHL
_library.	_la biblioteca.	_lah bee-blyoh-TEH-kah
_government palace.	_al palacio de gobierno.	_ahl pah-LAH-syoh deh goh-BYEHR-noh
_botanical gardens.	_al jardín botánico.	_ahl hahr-DEEN boh-TAH-nee-koh
_zoo.	_al zoológico.	_ahl soh-LOH-hee-koh

Note: When "a" is followed by the indefinite masculine article "el," it becomes "al." For example, you say *Quiero ir al mercado* rather than *Quiero ir a el* mercado.

At what time do they open (close)?	¿A qué hora abren (cierran)?	ah keh OH-rah AH-brehn (SYEH-rrahn)?
Is it open today?	**¿Está abierto hoy?**	**ehs-TAH ah-BYEHR-toh ohy?**
How much is the admission?	**¿Cuánto es la entrada?**	**KWAHN-toh ehs lah ehn-TRAH-dah?**
How much is it for	¿Cuánto pagan	KWAHN-toh PAH-gahn
_children?	_los niños?	_lohs NEE-nyohs?
_students?	_los estudiantes?	_lohs ehs-too-DYAHN-tehs?
How much is it for a group?	¿Cuánto es para un grupo?	KWAHN-toh ehs PAH-rah oon GROO-poh?

AT THE MUSEUM

Where can I get an English-speaking guide?	¿Dónde hay un guía que habla inglés?	DOHN-deh ahy oon GEEH-ah keh AH-blah een-GLEHS?
How long does a tour take?	¿Cuánto tarda una visita con guía?	KWAHN-toh TAHR-dah oo-nah bee-SEE-tah kohn GEE-ah?
Where is the gift shop?	¿Dónde está la tienda del museo?	DOHN-deh ehs-TAH lah TYEHN-dah dehl moo-SEH-oh?
Do they sell prints?	¿Venden reproducciones?	BEHN-dehn rreh-proh-dook-SYOH-nehs?
Do they sell postcards?	¿Venden tarjetas postales?	BEHN-dehn tahr-HEH-tahs pohs-TAH-lehs?
Is there a restaurant here?	¿Hay un restaurante aquí?	ahy oon rrehs-tow-RAHN-teh ah-KEE?

IN THE OLD PART OF TOWN

Which are the historic sites?	**¿Cuáles son los sitios históricos?**	**KWAH-leh sohn lohs SEE-tyohs ees-TOH-ree-kohs?**
How many churches are there here?	¿Cuántas iglesias hay aquí?	KWAHN-tahs ee-GLEH-syahs ahy ah-KEE?

Is that church old?	¿Es vieja esa iglesia?	ehs BYEH-hah EH-sah ee-GLEH-syah?
What religion is it?	¿De qué religión es?	deh keh rreh-lee-HYOHN ehs?
Are there any monuments nearby?	¿Hay algún monumento por aquí?	ahy ahl-GOON moh-noo-MEHN-toh pohr ah-KEE?
What does that one commemorate?	¿Qué conmemora ése?	keh kohn-meh-MOH-rah EH-seh?
When was that built?	¿Cuándo fue construido eso?	KWAHN-doh fweh kohns-TRUEE-doh EH-soh?
How old is that building?	¿Es viejo ese edificio?	ehs BYEH-hoh EH-seh eh-dee-FEE-syoh?
Are there many statues here?	¿Hay muchas estatuas aquí?	ahy MOO-chahs ehs-TAH-twahs ah-KEE?
Whose statue is that?	¿De quién es esa estatua?	deh kyehn ehs EH-sah ehs-TAH-twah?
Who was he (she)?	¿Quién fue esa persona?	KYEHN fweh EH-sah pehr-SOH-nah?

IN THE BUSINESS DISTRICT

At what time are businesses open?	¿A qué hora abren los negocios?	ah keh OH-rah AH-brehn lohs neh-GOH-syohs?
Which are the department stores?	¿Cuáles son las tiendas grandes?	KWAH-lehs sohn lahs TYEHN-dahs GRAHN-dehs?
Are they open on weekends?	¿Abren los fines de semana?	AH-brehn lohs FEE-nes deh seh-MAH-nah?
Where is a souvenir shop?	¿Dónde hay una tienda de recuerdos?	DOHN-deh ahy OO-nah TYEHN-dah deh rreh-KWEHR-dohs?
Which is the main bank?	¿Cuál es el banco principal?	KWAHL ehs ehl BAHN-koh preen-see-PAHL?
Where is the money exchange?	¿Dónde hay una casa de cambio? (Mexico)	DOHN-deh ahy OO-nah KAH-sah deh KAHM-byoh?

131

IN THE COUNTRY

SIGHTSEEING 13

What is the best way to get to the country?	¿Cuál es la mejor manera de ir al campo?	kwahl ehs lah meh-HOHR mah-NEH-rah deh eer ahl KAHM-poh?
Is there a bus from here?	¿Hay un autobús desde aquí?	ahy oon ow-toh-BOOS DEHS-deh ah-KEE?
How long does it take?	¿Cuánto tarda?	KWAHN-toh TAHR-dah?
Is there any place to eat there?	¿Hay algún lugar para comer allí?	ahy ahl-GOON loo-GAHR PAH-rah koh-MEHR ah-YEE?
Should we take some food?	¿Debemos llevar comida?	deh-BEH-mohs yeh-BAHR koh-MEE-dah?
Are there restrooms?	¿Hay baños públicos?	ahy BAH-nyohs POO-blee-kohs?
I like (the)	**Me gustan**	**meh GOOS-tahn**
_mountains.	_las montañas.	_lahs mohn-TAH-nyahs
_plants.	_las plantas.	_lahs PLAHN-tahs
_flowers.	_las flores.	_lahs FLOH-rehs
_fields.	_los campos.	_lohs KAHM-pohs
_hills.	_las colinas.	_lahs koh-LEE-nahs
_woods.	_los bosques.	_lohs BOHS-kehs
_birds.	_los pájaros.	_lohs PAH-ha-rohs
_wild animals.	_los animales silvestres.	_lohs ah-nee-MAH-lehs seel-BEHS-trehs
_farms.	_las granjas.	_lahs GRAHN-hahs
_houses.	_las casas.	_lahs KAH-sahs
_cottages.	_las cabañas.	_lahs kah-BAH-nyahs
_villages.	_los pueblitos.	_lohs pweh-BLEE-tohs
Look! There's a	¡Mire! Ahí hay	MEE-reh! ah-EE ahy
_barn.	_un granero.	_oon grah-NEH-roh
_bridge.	_un puente.	_oon PWEHN-teh
_castle.	_un castillo.	_oon kahs-TEE-yoh

132

_waterfall.	_una catarata.	_OO-nah kah-tah-RAH-tah
_stream.	_un arroyo.	_oon ah-RROH-yoh
_lake.	_un lago.	_oon LAH-goh
_beach.	_una playa.	_OO-nah PLAH-yah
_pond.	_un estanque.	_oon ehs-TAHN-keh
_village.	_un pueblo.	_oon PWEH-bloh
The view is	**La vista es**	**lah BEES-tah ehs**
_breathtaking.	_impresionante.	_eem-preh-syoh-NAHN-teh
_magnificent.	**_magnífica.**	**_mahg-NEE-fee-kah**
This place is	Este lugar es	EHS-teh loo-GAHR ehs
_beautiful.	_hermoso.	_ehr-MOH-soh
_very pretty.	_muy bonito.	_muee boh-NEE-toh
_very touristy.	_muy turístico.	_muee too-REES-tee-koh
What is a typical souvenir from here?	¿Cuál es el recuerdo típico de aquí?	kwahl ehs ehl rreh-KWEHR-doh TEE-pee-koh deh ah-KEE?
Do you tip the guide?	¿Se da propina al guía?	seh dah proh-PEE-nah ahl GEE-ah?

PLACES TO SEE IN SPAIN

Some of the principal tourist attractions of the capital, Madrid, are listed below.

Plaza Mayor
(PLAH-sah mah-YOHR)

You can get to this main square through the famous Arco de Cuchilleros, which also takes you into old Madrid, a fascinating part of the city. The Plaza Mayor has many shops and outdoor cafés, and is one of the most visited places in the city.

Puerta del Sol
(PWEHR-tah dehl sohl)

This area is considered the center of the city. Most bus and metro lines start and end here. It is a good place to do your shopping since you will find both tourist shops and department stores here.

Calle Serrano
(KAH-ye seh-rrah-noh)

This street is famous for its fashionable stores and its many excellent restaurants.

Parque del Retiro
(PAHR-keh dehl rreh-TEE-roh)

Located in the middle of Madrid, the grounds of this park once belonged to a royal palace. Here you will find rose gardens, fountains, two nightclubs, many outdoor cafés, and a lake for boating.

Rastro
(RRAHS-troh)

This flea market on Ribera de Curtidores Street is open Sunday only. Here you will find trinkets, antiques, toys, and artwork. As in other flea markets in Spain, it's a good place to use your bargaining skills.

Palacio Real
(pah-LAH-syoh rreh-AHL)

This palace is used only for important official events. It makes for an interesting visit and you will enjoy its treasure of fine arts—including porcelain, tapestries, crystal, and paintings.

Calle de Alcalá y la Gran Vía
(KAH-yeh deh ahl-kah-LAH ee lah grahn BEE-ah)

Two of Madrid's main thoroughfares are where you will find innumerable shops.

Museo del Prado
(moo-SEH-oh dehl PRAH-doh)

This museum has some of the most famous works of art in the world. It is particularly rich in works of Spanish, Flemish, and Italian artists.

Museo Thyssen-Bornemisza
(moo-SEH-oh TEE-sehn bohr-neh-MEE-zah)

A collection of 800 paintings includes examples from every important movement in the history of Western art.

Centro de Arte Reina Sofía
(SEHN-troh deh AHR-teh RAY-nah soh-FEE-yah)

The focus of this museum is modern art, most notably paintings by Picasso, Dalí, and Miró.

Museo de las Américas
(moo-SEH-oh deh lahs ah-MEH-ree-kahs)

This museum has collections of items brought from pre-Columbian America.

Museo Arqueológico
(moo-SEH-oh ahr-keh-oh-LOH-hee-kah)

Here, the focal point is the collection of reproductions of the Altamira caves, paintings of Altamira, and some 2,000 archaeological objects.

Museo del Pueblo Español (moo-SEH-oh dehl PWEH-bloh ehs-pah-NYOHL)	Regional dress and household items in this museum come from all over Spain.
Teatro de la Zarzuela (teh-AH-troh deh lah sahr-SWEH-lah)	This theater behind Las Cortes (the Spanish Parliament) offers not only zarzuela—light opera—but also ballet and opera.
Plaza de España (PLAH-sah ehs-PAH-nyah)	Here you will see the statue of Cervantes accompanied by his two most famous literary characters, Don Quixote and Sancho Panza.
Teatro Real (teh-AH-troh reh-AHL)	Madrid's royal opera house, built in 1850, is a state-of-the-art theater in a beautiful, neoclassical building.

Another city worth visiting is Toledo, near Madrid, to the south. In this medieval city, you will be able to visit an impressive palace as well as the home of the famous painter El Greco. A museum there contains many of his works. Not far from Madrid you can also visit El Escorial (ehl ehs-koh-RYAHL), the enormous monastery, mausoleum, and palace that was built by King Felipe II, and Segovia, another medieval town, famous for its Roman aqueduct.

Other cities of interest, if you have time, are Granada, Seville, Córdoba, and Barcelona. The first three, in the south of Spain, offer prime examples of the Moorish influence in art and architecture.

PLACES TO SEE AROUND MEXICO CITY

Mexico City, with over 20 million inhabitants in the greater metropolitan area, is a vibrant and lively place to visit.

Getting around the capital is not too difficult—there is an abundance of taxis, whose fares are quite reasonable, and a metro system that rivals any in the world.

Following are some of the city's principal attractions.

Plaza de la Constitución (PLAH-sah deh lah kohns-tee-too-SYOHN)	The main public square of Mexico City, it is second only to the Red Square in size. It is known by most people as the Zócalo (SOH-kah-loh). Virtually every Mexican

135

town has a *zócalo*, or main square, around which you will normally also find a church and a government building.

Catedral Metropolitana
(kah-teh-DRAHL me-troh-poh-lee-TAH-nah)

Also at the Zócalo, it is said to be the largest cathedral in Latin America. The magnificent structure was started in 1573 and completed in 1813, 240 years later. It houses many works of art from the colonial era.

Palacio Nacional
(pah-LAH-syoh nah-syoh-NAHL)

The oldest building on the square, it covers about two city blocks, and was built on the site of Moctezuma's opulent palace and constructed from its rubble. A series of Diego Rivera murals, painted over a period of 25 years, can be seen here. These extensive murals impressively depict many episodes in the history of Mexico, from pre-Columbian myth, all the way up to the Revolution of 1910.

Monte de Piedad
(MOHN-teh deh pyeh-DAHD)

This is the national pawn shop and a popular tourist attraction. The massive structure stands on the site of Moctezuma's brother's palace.

Museo de las Culturas
(moo-SEH-oh deh lahs kool-TOO-rahs)

This museum houses a rich collection of artifacts from all over the world.

Iglesia de Santo Domingo
(ee-GLEH-syah deh SAHN-toh doh-MEEN-goh)

A beautiful church that played an important role in the days of the Inquisition, it is set on a plaza a few blocks north of the Zócalo. Today, scribes often work under the arches of this charming place, typing out business memos and love letters for the illiterate.

Bazar del Sábado
(bah-SAHR dehl SAH-bah-doh)

This bazaar in San Ángel is held only on Saturdays, and offers samples of artifacts from all over the country. Prices range from reasonable—outside— to very expensive—inside.

Xochimilco
(soh-chee-MEEL-koh)

Floating gardens are reminiscent of the Aztec era, when canals laced the city. You can ride in one of the flower-covered boats, be serenaded, and eat, all at the same time. On Sunday you will find the most activity, but it's also harder to get an empty boat then.

Bosque de Chapultepec
(BOHS-keh deh chah-pool-teh-PEHK)

Chapultepec Park—with acres of woods and open spaces, picnic areas, restaurants, a zoo, pony rides, and boats for rent—is a popular place for recreation and leisure. In addition, Chapultepec is the site of several important museums, including the renowned Museo de Antropología.

Museo de Antropología
(moo-SEH-oh deh ahn-troh-poh-loh-HEE-ah)

Located in Chapultepec Park, this museum, with its massive architecture and spectacular display of archaeological artifacts—among them the 27-ton Aztec Calendar stone—is one of the great museums of the world.

Palacio de Bellas Artes
(pah-LAH-syoh deh BEH-yahs AHR-tehs)

It contains many of the most famous murals of Rivera, Orozco, Siqueiros, and Tamayo, and also houses the auditorium where the famous Ballet Folklórico de México performs.

Torre Latinoamericana
(TOH-reh lah-tee-noh-ah-meh-ree-KAH-nah)

Once the tallest building in Mexico, it offers an impressive bird's-eye view of the entire city.

La Ciudadela
(lah syoo-dah-DEH-lah)

This market has possibly the best display of artifacts from around the country. Be sure to shop around for the best buys and bargains, as many vendors carry the same items.

Ciudad Universitaria
(syoo-DAHD oo-nee-behr-see-TAH-ryah)

The grounds and buildings of the National University are worth a visit. The many mosaic-covered buildings are in themselves works of art, as is the impressive botanical garden.

Basílica de Guadalupe
(bah-SEE-lee-kah deh gwah-dah-LOO-peh)

A church built in honor of Our Lady of Guadalupe, the Patron Saint of Mexico and the Americas. The original basilica was closed to visitors, as it is slowly sinking into the ground. The modern church built next to it is visited by thousands of pilgrims each year.

137

Teotihuacán	Climb the pyramids dedicated to the
(teh-oh-tee-wah-	moon and the sun, and walk the streets of
KAHN)	this ancient Toltec city. Be sure not to miss
	the temple of Quetzalcóatl, the feathered
	serpent.

Polanco	The fashionable business district in Me-
(poh-LAHN-koh)	xico City. Many four- and five-star hotels
	are located here, as well as both interna-
	tional and Mexican designer boutiques.
	You will also find some of the city's best
	restaurants.

Zona Rosa	The somewhat seedy Zona Rosa is a lively
(SOH-nah RROH-sah)	night spot full of trendy bars and dance
	clubs, as well as restaurants and shops.

From Mexico City, it's a short bus trip to many other places. Cuernavaca, under two hours away, is known for its excellent climate (it is called the City of Eternal Spring). Two hours beyond Cuernavaca is the silver capital of Mexico, Taxco, a colonial gem well worth seeing. Taxco is also the midpoint between Mexico City and Acapulco. Just northwest of Mexico City, Morelia is known for its Monarch butterfly sanctuaries, and Pátzcuaro, which still resembles a bustling 16th century town, is home to the Purépecha Indians. Heading east from Mexico City, you'll approach two volcanoes on your way to Puebla, a splendid colonial town known for its numerous churches and the preparation of *mole* sauce. Continue down the coast of the Gulf of Mexico to the tropical and lively port of Veracruz, or head south over the mountains to the picturesque old city of Oaxaca, where you can see archaeological sites such as Monte Alban and Mitla. You can also fly to Mérida in Yucatán where you can visit the famous Maya ruins in Chichen Itzá or Uxmal.

SHOPPING IN SPAIN

Spain is a wonderful place to shop. Though there are a few bargains left, notably for saffron, prices in Spain have caught up with, and in many areas surpassed, those of northern Europe. There is a great variety of things to buy: small handicrafts, pottery, embroidery, and leather goods, to name just a few. Wooden sculptures of saints—both old and new—are typical. You can find antiques along major streets in Madrid like the Paseo del Prado and Carrera de San Jerónimo, as well as in the famous flea market, the Rastro.

Special stores called *artespaña* (ahr-tehs-PAH-nyah) carry wares from the various regions of Spain. Department stores are good sources for fine merchandise. The main department store in Madrid is El Corte Inglés, which has several locations throughout the city and the country. Note that bargaining is customary only at flea markets.

SHOPPING IN MEXICO

Each region of Mexico offers its own array of crafts. Look for embroidered dresses in Cuernavaca, Taxco, and Oaxaca; the fashionable *guayabera* shirts (gwah-yah-BEH-rahs) in Yucatán and Veracruz. *Sarapes, guaraches,* leather goods, and hand-knitted sweaters are found all over Mexico. But other items—like silver, onyx, amber, and opal jewelry and certain heavy wool sweaters—are found primarily in certain regions.

If you decide to buy silver in Mexico make sure you are buying the real thing. Look for the engraved seal indicating 900—i.e., pure silver and not an alloy (*alpaca*). Certain silver items may be marked "Taxco," indicating not only that it is silver but also that it comes from Taxco, the silver capital of Mexico.

Certain names in the world of merchandising carry special significance for the cognoscenti—for example, Tane silver shops, Aca Joe sportswear, Víctor (known for his handicrafts), and Sergio Bustamante (famous for his papier-mâché). There are also numerous copper and bronze artists, and their items are available in many places. Also look for Fonart, a government store with fixed prices, and Sanborns, a department store that carries quality handicrafts at high prices.

For a fine selection of Mexican artifacts, the Bazar del Sábado in San Ángel is a must. Prices are generally higher, but they have the largest selections of pottery, paper flowers, jewelry, bark paintings, *sarapes*, baskets, and leather goods. The smaller regional markets may have similar items at more economical prices. (See next page for a glossary of folk art.)

DIALOGUE
At the Gift Shop (En la tienda de regalos)

Turista:	¿Tiene cosas típicas del país?	TYEH-neh KOH-sahs TEE-pee-kahs dehl pah-EES?
Vendedor:	Sí, tenemos muchos objetos típicos.	see, teh-NEH-mohs MOO-chohs ohb-HEH-tohs TEE-pee-kohs
Turista:	¿Puedo ver algo en cuero?	PWEH-doh behr AHL-goh ehn KWEH-roh?
Vendedor:	Claro. Hay bolsas, carteras y muchas otras cosas.	KLAH-roh. ahy BOHL-sahs, kahr-TEH-rahs, ee MOO-chahs OH-trahs KOH-sahs
Turista:	Muy bien. ¿Me muestra una bolsa?	mwee byehn. meh MWEHS-trah OO-nah BOHL-sah?
Vendedor:	¿De qué color la quiere?	deh keh koh-LOHR lah KYEH-reh?
Turista:	Negra, creo.	NEH-grah, KREH-oh
Vendedor:	Un momento, por favor.	oon moh-MEHN-toh, pohr fah-VOHR
Turista:	Gracias.	GRAH-syahs

Tourist:	Do you have handicrafts from the country?
Vendor:	Yes, we have many typical items.
Tourist:	May I see something in leather?
Vendor:	Of course. We have bags, billfolds, and many other things.

Tourist:	Fine. Would you show me a bag?
Vendor:	What color would you like?
Tourist:	In black, I think.
Vendor:	One moment, please.
Tourist:	Thank you.

TYPES OF FOLK ART

basketwork	cestería	ses-teh-REE-ah
blanket	sarape	sah-RAH-peh
ceramics	cerámica	seh-RAH-mee-kah
clay	barro	BAH-rroh
copper	cobre	KOH-breh
embroidery	bordados	bohr-DAH-dohs
feather decorations	adornos de plumas	ah-DOHR-nohs de PLOO-mahs
glass	vidrio	BEE-dryoh
blown glass	vidrio soplado	BEE-dryoh soh-PLAH-doh
gold	oro	OH-roh
jade	jade	HAH-deh
lacquerware	lacas	LAH-kahs
leather	cuero	KWEH-roh
tooled leather embossed leather	cuero labrado cuero repujado	KWEH-roh lah-BRAH-doh KWEH-roh rreh-poo-HAH-doh
marble	mármol	MAHR-mohl
mask	máscara	MAHS-kah-rah
musical instrument	instrumento musical	eens-troo-MEHN-toh moo-see-KAHL
onyx	ónix	OH-neeks
paper cutouts	papel recortado	pah-PEHL rreh-kohr-TAH-doh

paper toys	juguetes de cartón	hoo-GEH-tehs deh kahr-TOHN
pottery	cerámica	seh-RAH-mee-kah
saddle	montura	mohn-TOO-rah
shawl	mantón	man-TOHN
silver	plata	PLAH-tah
thread	hilo	EE-loh
toy	juguete	hoo-GEH-teh
weaving	tejidos	teh-HEE-dohs
wood carvings	madera tallada	mah-DEH-rah tah-YAH-dah
wool	lana	LAH-nah
yarn	hilo	EE-loh

BARGAINING

In Spain, bargaining is acceptable in only a few places, such as the Rastro flea market in Madrid. In some places that sell regional souvenirs in cities like Granada and Seville, you might ask for a discount. In Latin America, bargaining is far more common. But even there, it is done primarily in markets and with street vendors.

Many people consider bargaining an art. To get the best price, you should first go from one vendor to another inquiring about prices for the same item in order to establish a range. Then return to the booth that asked for the lowest price and begin bargaining. Remember not to show too much interest: Act casual, mildly curious. If you seem uncommitted, you will have a better chance of obtaining a lower price. But remember that no matter how well you bargain, there is a limit below which the vendor cannot make a profit. The price may be lowered more significantly for costly items than for less expensive ones.

What the Shopper Says

Excuse me.	Perdón.	pehr-DOHN
I'm interested in this.	Me interesa esto.	meh een-teh-REH-sah EHS-toh

How much is it?	¿Cuánto cuesta?	KWAHN-toh KWEHS-tah?
It's very expensive!	¡Es muy caro!	ehs muee KAH-roh!
It's overpriced. (It's not worth so much.)	No vale tanto.	noh VAH-leh TAHN-toh
Do you have a cheaper one?	¿Tiene uno más barato?	TYEH-neh OO-noh mahs bah-RAH-toh?
This is damaged—do you have another one?	Está dañado, ¿hay otro?	ehs-TAH dah-NYAH-doh, ahy OH-troh?
What is the lowest price?	¿Cuál es el precio mínimo?	KWAHL ehs ehl PREH-syoh MEE-nee-moh?
Is that the final price?	¿Es el último precio?	ehs ehl OOL-tee-moh PREH-syoh?
Can't you give me a discount?	¿No me da una rebaja?	noh meh dah OO-nah rreh-BAH-hah?
I'll give you . . .	Le doy . . .	leh doy . . .
I won't pay more than . . .	No pago más de . . .	noh PAH-goh mahs deh . . .
I'll look somewhere else.	Voy a ver en otro sitio.	voy ah behr ehn OH-troh SEE-tyoh
No, thank you.	No, gracias.	noh, GRAH-syahs

What the Vendor Says

¡Cliente!	KLYEN-teh!	Customer!
¿Qué se le ofrece?	keh seh leh oh-FREH-seh?	What would you like? (What can I offer you?)
¿Qué se lleva?	keh seh YEH-vah?	What will you buy?
¡Lléveselo!	YEH-veh-seh-loh!	Buy it!
Se lo vendo en . . .	seh loh BEHN-doh ehn . . .	I'll sell it to you for . . .
Se lo dejo en . . .	seh loh DEH-hoh ehn . . .	I'll let you have it for . . .
Es lo mínimo.	ehs loh MEE-nee-moh.	That's the lowest price.
No se puede.	noh seh PWEH-deh	It's not possible.

143

| ¿Se lo lleva? | seh loh YEH-bah? | Will you take it? |
| Gracias. Que le vaya bien. | GRAH-syahs. keh leh BAH-yah, byehn | Thank you. Have a good day. |

GENERAL SHOPPING LIST

I need to buy	Necesito comprar	neh-seh-SEE-toh kohm-PRAHR
_books.	_libros.	_LEE-brohs
_a roll of film.	_un rollo de película.	_oon RROH-yoh deh peh-LEE-koo-lah
_some food.	_comida.	_koh-MEE-dah
_candy.	_dulces.	_DOOL-sehs
_shoes.	_zapatos.	_sah-PAH-tohs
_clothes.	_ropa.	_RROH-pah
_medicine.	_una medicina.	_OO-nah meh-dee-SEE-nah
_jewelry.	_joyas.	_HOH-yahs
_cigarettes.	_cigarillos.	_see-gah-REE-yohs
_gifts.	_regalos.	_rreh-GAH-lohs
_souvenirs.	_recuerdos.	_rreh-KWEHR-dohs
_postcards.	_tarjetas postales.	_tahr-HEH-tahs pohs-TAH-lehs

TYPES OF STORES

shop	tienda	TYEHN-dah
bookstore	librería	lee-breh-REE-ah
camera shop	tienda de artículos fotográficos	TYEHN-dah deh ahr-TEE-koo-lohs foh-toh-GRAH-fee-kohs
grocery store	tienda de comestibles	TYEHN-dah deh koh-mehs-TEE-blehs
bakery	panadería	pah-nah-deh-REE-ah
candy store	confitería	kohn-fee-teh-REE-ah
shoe store	zapatería	sah-pah-teh-REE-ah

clothing store	tienda de ropa	TYEHN-dah deh RROH-pah
jewelry store	joyería	hoh-yeh-REE-ah
local market	mercado	mehr-KAH-doh
butcher shop	carnicería	kahr-nee-seh-REE-ah
department store	tienda por departamentos	TYEHN-dah pohr deh-pahr-tah-MEHN-tohs
flower shop	florería	floh-reh-REE-ah
fruit stand	frutería	froo-teh-REE-ah
gift shop	tienda de regalos	TYEHN-dah deh rreh-GAH-lohs
liquor store	licorería	lee-koh-reh-REE-ah
hardware store	ferretería	feh-rreh-teh-REE-ah
record store	tienda de discos	TYEHN-dah deh DEES-kohs
tobacco shop	tabaquería	tah-bah-keh-REE-ah
newsstand	puesto de periódicos	PWEHS-toh deh peh-RYOH-dee-kohs
supermarket	supermercado	soo-pehr-mehr-KAH-doh

CLOTHING

I want to buy	Quiero comprar	KYEH-roh kohm-PRAHR
_a blouse.	_una blusa.	_oo-nah BLOO-sah
_a sweater.	_un suéter.	_oon SWEH-tehr
_a dress.	_un vestido.	_oon behs-TEE-doh
_a skirt.	_una falda.	_OO-nah FAHL-dah
_stockings.	_medias.	_MEH-dyahs
_an evening gown.	_un traje de noche.	_oon TRAH-heh deh NOH-cheh
_a tie.	_una corbata.	_OO-nah kohr-BAH-tah
_a shirt.	_una camisa.	_OO-nah kah-MEE-sah
_a belt.	_un cinturón.	_oon seen-too-RHON
_a hat.	_un sombrero.	_oon sohm-BREH-roh
_a robe.	_una bata.	_OO-nah BAH-tah

145

_an overcoat.	_un abrigo.	_oon ah-BREE-goh
_handkerchiefs.	_pañuelos.	_pah-NYWEH-lohs
My size is	**Mi talla es**	**mee TAH-yah ehs**
_small.	_pequeña.	_peh-KEH-nyah
_medium.	_mediana.	_meh-DYAH-nah
_large.	_grande.	_GRAHN-deh
_extra-large.	_extra-grande.	_EHKS-trah GRAHN-deh
_10.	_diez.	_dyehs
_12.	_doce.	_DOH-seh
_14.	_catorce.	_kah-TOHR-seh

Note: See pages 147–148 for a complete chart of size equivalents.

Do you have it in	**¿Lo tiene en**	**loh TYEH-neh ehn**
_black?	_negro?	_NEH-groh?
_blue?	_azul?	_ah-SOOL?
_brown?	_marrón?	_mah-RROHN?
_gray?	_gris?	_grees?
_white?	_blanco?	_BLAHN-koh?
_red?	_rojo?	_RROH-hoh?
_green?	_verde?	_BEHR-deh?
_yellow?	_amarillo?	_ah-mah-REE-yoh?
_orange?	_anaranjado?	_ah-nah-rahn-HAH-doh?
I prefer something in	**Prefiero algo en**	**preh-FYEH-roh AHL-goh ehn**
_cotton.	_algodón	_ahl-goh-DOHN
_silk.	_seda.	_SEH-dah
_corduroy.	_pana.	_PAH-nah
_denim.	_tela vaquera	_TEH-lah bah-KEH-rah
_gabardine.	_gabardina.	_gah-bahr-DEE-nah
_lace.	_encaje.	_ehn-KAH-heh
_linen.	_hilo.	_EE-loh
_leather.	_cuero.	_KWEH-roh
_nylon.	_nilón.	_nee-LOHN
_rayon.	_rayón.	_rrah-YOHN

146

_satin.	_satén.	_sah-TEHN
_suede.	_gamuza.	_gah-MOO-sah
_synthetic.	_sintético.	_seen-TEH-tee-koh
_taffeta.	_tafetán.	_tah-feh-TAHN
_terrycloth.	_tela de toalla.	_TE-lah deh TWAH-yah
_velvet.	_terciopelo.	_tehr-syoh-PEH-loh
_wool.	**_lana.**	**_LAH-nah**
_worsted.	_estambre.	_ehs-TAHM-breh
I'd like to try it on.	**Quiero probármelo.**	**KYEH-roh proh-BAHR-meh-loh**
It does not fit me.	No me queda bien.	noh meh KEH-dah byehn
It fits well.	**Me queda bien.**	**meh KEH-dah byehn**
I'll take it.	**Me lo llevo.**	**meh loh YEH-boh**

WOMEN'S CLOTHING SIZES

We recommend trying on all clothing before buying because sizes vary and do not always correlate exactly with U.S. sizes. Also, returning clothing that you have purchased is unusual in Spain and Latin America, except at the large department stores in major cities.

In Mexico, many clothing companies use U.S. sizes.

Suits/Dresses

U.S.	6,8	8,10	10,12	12,14	14,16
Mexico	30,32	32,34	34,36	36,38	38,40
Spain	36,37,38	40	42	44	46

Blouses/Sweaters

U.S.	small		medium		large
Mexico	*chico(-a)*		*mediano(-a)*		*grande*
Spain	*pequeño(-a)*		*mediano(-a)*		*grande*

Shoes

U.S.	5	6	7	8	9
Mexico	2–3	3–4	4–5	5–6	6–7
Spain	38	39	41	42	43

MEN'S CLOTHING SIZES

Suits/Coats

U.S.	36	38	40	42	44
Mexico	36	38	40	42	44
Spain	46	48	50	52	54

Dress Shirts

U.S.	14	14¼	15	15½	16	16½	17	17½
Mexico may be same as U.S. or Europe
Spain		36	37	38	40	41	42	43

Sleeve Lengths

corto	(KOHR-toh)	=	short
mediano	(me-DYAH-noh)	=	medium
largo	(LAHR-goh)	=	long

Shoes

U.S.	7	8	9	10	11	12
Mexico	6	7	8	9	10	11
Spain	41	42	43	44	46	47

THE JEWELRY STORE

I'd like to see some	Quisiera ver	kee-SYEHR-ah behr
_rings.	_unos anillos.	_OO-nohs ah-NEE-yohs
_necklaces.	_unos collares.	_OO-nohs koh-YAH-res
_chains.	_unas cadenas.	_OO-nahs kah-DEH-nahs
_bracelets.	_unas pulseras.	_OO-nahs pool-SEH-rahs
_brooches.	_unos broches.	_OO-nohs BROH-chehs
_earrings.	_unos aretes.	_OO-nohs ah-REH-tehs
_pins.	_unos alfileres.	_OO-nohs ahl-fee-LEH-rehs
_wristwatches.	_unos relojes pulsera.	_OO-nohs rreh-LOH-hes pool-SEHR-ah

Do you have this in	¿Lo tiene en	loh TYEH-neh ehn
_gold?	_oro?	_OH-roh?
_white gold?	_oro blanco?	_OH-roh BLAHN-koh?
_silver?	_plata?	_PLAH-tah?
_stainless steel?	_acero inoxidable?	_ah-SEH-roh ee-noh-ksee-DAH-bleh?
_platinum?	_platino?	_plah-TEE-noh?
I would like it with	Lo quisiera con	loh kee-SYEH-rah kohn
_jade.	_jade.	_HAH-deh
_onyx.	_ónix.	_OH-neeks
_a pearl.	_una perla.	_OO-nah PEHR-lah
_ivory.	_marfil.	_marh-FEEL
_a diamond.	_un diamante.	_oon dyah-MAHN-teh
_an emerald.	_una esmeralda.	_OO-nah ehs-meh-RAHL-dah
_an aquamarine.	_un aguamarina	_oon ah-gwah-mah-REE-nah
_an amethyst.	_una amatista.	_OO-nah ah-mah-TEES-tah

THE PHOTO SHOP

Film is expensive in Spain and Mexico, so it's a good idea to bring it from home. Wait until you return home to have film developed, as this, too, is expensive.

I would like a roll of film	Quisiera un rollo de película.	kee-SYEHR-ah oon RROH-yoh deh pe-LEE-koo-lah
Do you have	¿Tiene película	TYEH-neh peh-LEE-koo-lah
_film for prints?	_para fotografías?	_PAH-rah foh-toh-grah-FEE-ahs?
_film for slides?	_para diapositivas?	_PAH-rah dy-ah-poh-see-TEE-bahs?
_movie film?	_de cine?	_deh SEE-neh?
_color film?	_en colores?	_ehn koh-LOH-rehs?
_black-and-white film?	_en blanco y negro?	_ehn BLAHN-koh ee NEH-groh?

149

_35 mm film, 36 exposures?	_de treinta y cinco milímetros con treinta y seis fotografías?	_deh TRAYN-tah ee SEEN-koh mee-LEE-mee-trohs kohn TRAYN-tah ee says foh-toh-grah-FEE-ahs?
Do you develop film here?	¿Revelan películas aquí?	rreh-BEH-lahn peh-LEE-koo-lahs ah-KEE?
How much does it cost?	¿Cuánto cuesta?	KWAHN-toh KWEHS-tah?
How long does it take?	¿Cuánto tiempo tarda?	KWAHN-toh TYEHM-poh TAHR-dah?
When can I pick up the pictures?	¿Cuándo puedo recoger las fotografías?	KWAHN-doh PWEH-doh rreh-koh-HEHR lahs foh-toh-grah-FEE-ahs?

MUSIC

Do you have	**¿Tiene**	**TYEH-neh**
_records?	_discos?	_DEES-kohs?
_tapes?	_cintas?	_SEEN-tahs?
_compact disks?	**_discos compactos?**	**_DEES-kohs kom-PAK-tohs**
Where is the . . . music?	¿Dónde está la música . . .	DOHN-deh ehs-TAH lah MOO-see-kah
_classical	_clásica?	_KLAH-see-kah?
_folk	_folklórica?	_fohl-KLOH-ree-kah?
_popular	_popular?	_poh-poo-LAHR?
_Spanish	_española?	_ehs-pah-NYOH-lah?
_Latin American	_latinoamericana?	_lah-tee-noh-ah-meh-ree-KAH-nah?
_rock 'n' roll	_rocanrol?	_roh-kahn-ROHL?
Do you sell	¿Vende	BEHN-deh
_maracas?	_maracas?	_mah-RAH-kahs?
_castanets?	_castañuelas?	_kahs-tah-NYWEH-lahs?
_other musical instruments?	_otros instrumentos musicales?	_OH-trohs eens-troo-MEHN-tohs MOO-see-kah-lehs?

BOOKS, MAGAZINES, AND PAPER GOODS

Where is there a bookstore?	¿Dónde hay una librería?	DOHN-deh ahy OO-nah lee-breh-REE-ah?
Is there a bookstore that carries English books?	**¿Hay una librería que vende libros en inglés?**	**ahy oo-nah lee-breh-REE-ah keh BEHN-deh LEE-brohs ehn een-GLEHS?**
Do you have the book . . . ?	¿Tiene el libro . . . ?	TYEH-neh ehl LEE-broh . . . ?
Do you have this guide book in English?	¿Tiene esta guía en inglés?	TYEH-neh EHS-tah GEE-ah ehn een-GLEHS?
Do you have a Spanish-English dictionary?	**¿Tiene un diccionario español-inglés?**	**TYEH-neh oon deek-syoh-NAH-ryoh ehs-pah-NYOHL-een-GLEHS?**
Do you have	¿Tiene	TYEH-neh
_novels?	_novelas?	_noh-BEH-lahs?
_books?	_libros?	_LEE-brohs?
_magazines?	_revistas?	_rreh-BEES-tahs?
_a guide book?	_una guía?	_OO-nah GEE-ah?
_a map of the city?	_un mapa de la ciudad?	_oon MAH-pah deh lah syoo-DAHD?
_a pocket dictionary?	_un diccionario de bolsillo?	_oon deek-syoh-NAH-ryoh deh bohl-SEE-yoh?
_a ball-point pen?	_un bolígrafo?	_oon boh-LEE-grah-foh?
_envelopes?	_sobres?	_SOH-brehs?
_a notebook?	_un cuaderno?	_oon kwah-DEHR-noh?
_posters?	_carteles?	_kahr-TEH-lehs?
_ribbon?	_cinta?	_SEEN-tah?
_Scotch tape?	_cinta adhesiva?	_SEEN-tah ah-deh-SEE-vah?
_stamps?	_timbres (*Mexico*)/ sellos (*Spain*)?	_TEEM-brehs/ SEH-yohs?
_stationery?	_papel de correspondencia?	_pah-PEHL deh koh-rrehs-pohn-DEHN-syah?
_string?	_hilo?	_EE-loh?

_wrapping paper?	_papel de envolver?	_pah-PEHL deh ehn-bohl-BEHRenvolver?
_a writing pad?	_un bloc de papel?	_oon blohk deh pah-PEHLenvolver?

TOILETRIES

toiletries	objetos de baño	ohb-JEH-tohs deh BAH-nyoh
a brush	un cepillo	oon seh-PEE-yoh
cologne	colonia	koh-LOH-nyah
a comb	un peine	oon PAY-neh
deodorant	desodorante	deh-soh-doh-RAHN-teh
disposable diapers	pañales desechables	pah-NYAH-lehs deh-seh-CHAH-blehs
hairspray	laca	LAH-kah
a mirror	un espejo	oon ehs-PEH-hoh
moisturizing lotion	loción humectante	loh-SYOHN oo-mehk-TAHN-teh
mouthwash	enjuague bucal	ehn-HWAH-geh boo-KAHL
nail clippers	cortauñas	kohr-ta-OO-nyahs
nail polish	esmalte de uñas	ehs-MAHL-teh deh OO-nyahs
nail polish remover	quitaesmalte	kee-tah-ehs-MAHL-teh
perfume	perfume	pehr-FOO-meh
sanitary napkins	toallas sanitarias	toh-AH-yahs sah-nee-TAH-ryahs
shampoo	champú	chahm-POO
shaving cream	crema de afeitar	KREH-mah deh ah-fay-TAHR
soap	jabón	hah-BOHN
a sponge	una esponja	OO-nah ehs-POHN-hah
tampons	tampones	tahm-POH-nehs
tissues	pañuelos de papel	pah-NYWEH-lohs deh pah-PEHL
toilet paper	papel higiénico	pah-PEHL ee-HYEH-ee-koh
a toothbrush	un cepillo de dientes	oon seh-PEE-yoh deh DYEHN-tehs

| toothpaste | pasta de dientes | PAHS-tah deh DYEHN-tehs |
| tweezers | pinzas | PEEN-sahs |

FOOD SHOPPING

I would like a	Me gustaría	meh goos-tah-REE-ah
_bottle of juice.	_una botella de jugo/zumo. (Spain)	_oo-nah boh-TEH-yah deh HOO-goh/ THOO-moh
_bottle of milk.	_una botella de leche.	_OO-nah boh-TEH-yah deh LEH-cheh
_box of cereal.	_una caja de cereales.	_OO-nah KAH-hah deh seh-reh-AH-lehs
_box of cookies.	_una caja de galletas.	_OO-nah KAH-hah deh gah-YEH-tahs
_can of tomato sauce.	_una lata de salsa de to-mate.	_OO-nah LAH-tah deh SAHL-sah deh toh-MAH-teh
_dozen eggs.	_una docena de huevos.	_OO-nah doh-SEH-nah deh WEH-bohs
_package of candies.	_un paquete de caramelos.	_oon pah-KEH-teh deh kah-rah-MEH-lohs
Do you have	¿Tiene	TYEH-neh
_cold cuts?	_embutidos?	_ehm-boo-TEE-dohs?
_cheese?	_queso?	_KEH-soh?
_soft drinks?	_refrescos?	rreh-FREHS-kohs?
_cigarettes?	_cigarrillos?	_see gah-RREE-yohs?
_matches?	_fósforos?	_FOHS-foh-rohs?

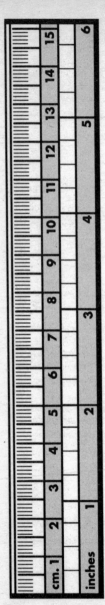

WEIGHTS AND MEASURES

METRIC WEIGHT	U.S.
1 gram (g)	0.035 ounce
28.35 grams	1 ounce
100 grams	3.5 ounce
454 grams	1 pound
1 kilogram (kilo)	2.2 pounds

LIQUIDS	U.S.
1 liter (l)	4.226 cups
1 liter	2.113 pints
1 liter	1.056 quarts
3.785 liters	1 gallon

DRY MEASURE	U.S.
1 litre	0.908 quart
1 decalitre	1.135 pecs
1 hectolitre	2.837 bushels

One inch = 2.54 centimeters
One centimeter = .39 inch

inches	feet	yards	
1 mm.	0.039	0.003	0.001
1 cm.	0.39	0.03	0.01
1 dm.	3.94	0.32	0.10
1 m.	39.40	3.28	1.09

.39 (# of centimeters) = (# of inches)
2.54 (# of inches) = (# of centimeters)

	mm.	cm.	m.
1 in.	25.4	2.54	0.025
1 ft.	304.8	30.48	0.304
1 yd.	914.4	91.44	0.914

154

ENTERTAINMENT

In Spain and Mexico, you will see people sitting in parks and cafés reading a magazine or newspaper, talking, or just relaxing. Movies, plays, operas, concerts, sports events (primarily soccer), bullfights, and going to the beach are also popular to see or do.

DIALOGUE   Swimming (Natación)

Juan:	¡Hace tanto calor!	ah-seh TAHN-toh kah-LOHR!
María:	Sí, ¿qué tal si nos vamos a nadar?	see, keh tahl see nohs BAH-mohs ah nah-DAHR?
Juan:	Buena idea. ¿Vamos a la playa o a la piscina?	BWEH-nah ee-DEH-ah. BAH-mohs ah lah PLAH-yah oh ah lah pee-SEE-nah?
María:	¡Me encanta el mar! ¿Pero no es peligroso por aquí?	meh ehn-KAHN-tah ehl mahr! PEH-roh noh ehs peh-lee-GROH-soh pohr ah-KEE?
Juan:	No. El mar aquí es muy tranquilo.	noh. ehl mahr ah-KEE ehs muee trahn-KEY-loh
María:	¡Qué bien! Entonces nos vemos en la playa en cinco minutos.	key byehn! ehn-TOHN-sehs nohs BEH-mohs ehn lah PLAH-yah ehn SEEN-koh mee-NOO-tohs
Juan:	¡Perfecto! No te olvides de la loción bronceadora. El sol está muy fuerte.	pehr-FEHK-toh! noh teh ohl-BEE-dehs deh lah loh-SYOHN brohn-sehy-ah-DOH-rah. ehl sohl ehs-TAH muee FWEHR-teh

John:	It's so hot out!
Mary:	Yes. Why don't we go swimming?
John:	Good idea! Shall we go to the beach or the pool?
Mary:	I love the sea. But isn't it dangerous around here?
John:	No! The sea here is very calm.

Mary:	Good. Then I'll see you on the beach in five minutes.
John:	Right. And don't forget the suntan lotion! The sun is very strong.

Where are the best beaches?	¿Dónde están las mejores playas?	DOHN-deh ehs-TAHN lahs meh-HOH-rehs PLAH-yahs?
How do we get there?	¿Cómo se puede ir allí?	KOH-moh seh PWEH-deh eer ah-YEE?
Is it a private or a public beach?	¿Es una playa privada o pública?	ehs OO-nah PLAH-yah pree-BAH-dah o POO-blee-kah?
Is there a lifeguard?	**¿Hay un salvavidas?**	**ahy oon sahl-bah-BEE-dahs?**
Is it dangerous for children?	¿Es peligroso para niños?	ehs peh-lee-GROH-soh PAH-rah NEE-nyohs?
Are there dangerous currents?	¿Hay corrientes peligrosas?	ahy koh-RRYEHN-tehs peh-lee-GROH-sahs?
When is	¿Cuándo hay	KWAHN-doh ahy
_high tide?	_marea alta?	_mah-REH-ah AHL-tah?
_low tide?	_marea baja?	_mah-REH-ah BAH-hah?
We need	**Necesitamos**	**neh-seh-see-TAH-mohs**
_some beach chairs.	_unas sillas de playa.	_OO-nahs SEE-yahs deh PLAH-yah
_some beach towels.	_unas toallas de playa.	_OO-nahs TWAH-yahs deh PLAH-yah
_suntan lotion	_loción bronceadora.	_loh-SYOHN brohn-seh-yah-DOH-rah
Is the pool . . .	**¿Está la piscina . . .**	**eh-STAH lah pee-SEE-nah . . .**
_outdoors?	_afuera?	_ah-FWEH-rah
_indoors?	_adentro?	_ah-DEHN-troh
_heated?	_climatizada?	_klee-mah-tee-ZAH-dah

156

CAMPING

Can we camp here?	¿Podemos acampar aquí?	poh-DEH-mohs ah-kahm-PAHR ah-KEE?
Is there room for a trailer?	¿Hay lugar para un trailer?	ahy loo-GAHR PAH-rah oon TRY-lehr?
What does it cost	¿Cuánto cuesta	KWAHN-toh KWEHS-tah
for one night?	por una noche?	pohr OO-nah NOH-cheh?
Is/Are there	**¿Hay**	**ahy**
_drinking water?	_agua potable?	_AH-gwah poh-TAH-bleh?
_electricity?	_electricidad?	_eh-lehk-tree-see-DAHD?
_showers?	_duchas?	_DOO-chahs?
_a grocery store?	_una tienda de comestibles?	_OO-nah TYEHN-dah deh koh-mehs-TEE-blehs?
_butane gas?	_gas?	_gahs?

MOVIES

Check the entertainment page of local newspapers to find out what's playing at the movies. Some English-speaking films are dubbed into Spanish, but nearly all recent releases are available in the original language version. Look for VO (*versión original*) or VOSE (*versión original con subtítulos españoles*) listings. Watching locally produced movies can help improve your language skills, even if you don't understand everything you hear. Note that theaters can be crowded on weekends; some sell numbered tickets in advance.

Let's go to the movies.	Vamos al cine.	BAH-mohs ahl SEE-neh
What's playing?	¿Qué presentan?	keh preh-SEHN-tahn?
Is it in Spanish or English?	¿Es en español o en inglés?	ehs ehn ehs-pah-NYOHL oh ehn een-GLEHS?
What kind of film is it?	**¿Qué tipo de película es?**	**keh TEE-poh deh peh-LEE-koo-lah ehs?**

157

It's	Es	ehs
_a comedy.	_una comedia.	_OO-nah koh-MEH-dyah
_a drama.	_un drama.	_oon DRAH-mah
_With subtitles?	_¿Con subtítulos?	kohn soob-TEE-too-lohs?
Is it dubbed?	¿Está doblada?	ehs-TAH doh-BLAH-dah?
When does the show start?	¿Cuándo empieza la función?	KWAHN-doh ehm-PYEH-sah lah foon-SYOHN?
How much are the tickets?	¿Cuánto cuestan las entradas?	KWAHN-toh KWEHS-tahn lahs ehn-TRAH-dahs?
What theater is showing the new film	¿En qué teatro pasan la película nueva	ehn keh teh-AH-troh PAH-sahn lah peh-LEE-koo-lah NWEH-vah
_by . . . ?	_de . . . ?	_deh . . . ?
_with . . . ?	_con . . . ?	_kohn . . . ?

THEATER, CONCERTS, OPERA, AND BALLET

In Spain, you can get a *Guía del ocio* (GEE-ah dehl OH-syoh), a "leisure guide," from any newsstand. The guide provides information about schedules and admission fees for daily, weekly, and monthly events.

Madrid has many theaters. While most of them present some form of comedy or drama, the Teatro de la Zarzuela (teh-AH-troh deh lah sahr-SWEH-lah) is perhaps the most typical of all. *Zarzuela* is light opera, combining drama, comedy, singing, and dance, all in one choreographed piece. In the summer, *zarzuelas* are performed open-air at the Plaza de Colón, free of charge. Many musical groups, including some major conductors, perform at the Teatro Real. Whereas most Spanish cities offer some form of theatrical activities, be prepared for other options in smaller towns.

In Mexico, the major theater companies are in the capital city. In the provinces, local universities and other cultural centers often mount productions. In Mexico City some theaters have translated Broadway musicals into Spanish.

There are several dance companies, specializing in different forms of dance. There are two major companies that specialize in folk repertoires. The best-known is the Ballet Folklórico de México (bah-LEHT fohl-KLOH-ree-koh deh MEH-hee-koh), or the Mexican Folkloric Ballet Company, which performs at the famous Palacio de Bellas Artes (pah-LAH-syoh deh BEH-yahs AHR-tehs), or Fine Arts Palace. The other is the Ballet de la Ciudad de México (bah-LEHT deh lah syoo-DAHD deh MEH-hee-koh), or the Mexico City Ballet Company, which offers another interpretation of Mexican folk dances. You will also find classical ballet companies. Many local universities have their own ballet company, performing primarily Mexican pieces. Note that it is not unusual to give a small tip to ushers in theaters.

What's playing at the theater?	¿Qué dan en el teatro?	keh dahn ehn ehl teh-AH-troh?
I'd like to go to	Me gustaría ir a	meh goos-tah-REE-ah eer ah
_a play.	_una obra.	_OO-nah OH-brah
_an opera.	_una ópera.	_OO-nah OH-peh-rah
_an operetta.	_una zarzuela.	_OO-nah sahr-SWEH-lah
_a ballet.	_un ballet.	_oon bah-LEHT
_a musical.	_una obra musical.	_OO-nah OH-brah moo-see-KAHL
_a concert.	_un concierto.	_oon kohn-SYEHR-toh
What kind of play is it?	¿Qué tipo de obra es?	keh TEE-poh deh OH-brah ehs?
Who wrote it?	¿Quién la escribió?	KYEHN lah ehs-kree-BYOH?
Are there tickets for today?	¿Hay entradas para hoy?	ahy ehn-TRAH-dahs PAH-ray oy?
How much are the tickets?	¿Cuánto cuestan las entradas?	KWAHN-toh KWEHS-tahn lahs ehn-TRAH-dahs?
Do we need a reservation?	¿Necesitamos una reservación?/	neh-seh-see-TAH-mohs OO-nah rreh-sehr-bah-SYOHN?/
	. . . una reserva? (Spain)	. . . OO-nah rreh-SEHR-bah?

159

Please give me . . . tickets.	Me da . . . entradas, por favor.	meh dah . . . ehn-TRAH-dahs, pohr fah-BOHR
I'd like	**Quisiera**	**kee-SYEH-rah**
_an orchestra seat.	_asientos en la galería.	_ah-SYEHN-tohs ehn lah gah-leh-REE-ah
_seats in the balcony.	_asientos en el balcón.	_ah-SYEHN-tohs ehn ehl bahl-KOHN
_a mezzanine seat.	_un asiento en anfiteatro.	_oon ah-SYEHN-toh ehn ahn-fee-teh-AH-troh
_seats up front.	**_asientos adelante.**	**_ah-SYEHN-tos ah-deh-LAHN-teh**
_seats in back.	_asientos atrás.	_ah-SYEHN-tos ah-TRAHS
_seats on the side.	_asientos a los lados.	_ah-SYEHN-tos ah los LAH-dohs
_good seats.	_buenos asientos.	_BWEH-nohs ah-SYEHN-tohs
_inexpensive tickets.	_entradas no muy caras.	_ehn-TRAH-dahs noh muee KAH-rahs
_tickets for the matinee.	_entradas para la matinée.	_ehn-TRAH-dahs PAH-rah lah mah-tee-NEH
_tickets for the evening.	_entradas para la tanda de la tarde (or) de la noche.	_ehn-TRAH-dahs PAH-rah lah TAHN-dah deh lah TAR-deh (de lah NOH-cheh)
A program, please.	Un programa, por favor.	oon proh-GRAH-mah, pohr fah-BOHR
Who's	**¿Quién**	**kyehn**
_playing?	**_actúa?**	**_ahk-TOO-ah?**
_singing?	**_canta?**	**_KAHN-tah?**
_dancing?	**_baila?**	**_BAH-ee-lah?**
_directing?	_dirige?	_dee-REE-heh?
_speaking?	_habla?	_AH-blah?
_announcing?	_anuncia?	_ah-NOON-syah?

CLUBS, DISCOS, AND CABARETS

In some restaurants in Spain you can see a show while you eat. In Madrid, which has many of these establishments, some feature *flamenco* (flah-MEHN-koh) dancing and singing. On weekends, it is customary to eat as late as midnight, enjoying regularly scheduled music performances. There are also innumerable discos, which play everything from American-style music to Europop. Cabarets and boîtes are concentrated in certain parts of town, and reservations are sometimes needed—as at Madrid's Café de Chinitas (kah-FEH deh chee-NEE-tahs), one of the best-known places for *flamenco*. Most nightclubs are open from 7:00 P.M. till 3:00 A.M.

In Mexico City and Acapulco, as in Spain, many clubs offer dinner and a show; cabarets usually serve only drinks and snacks with the show. For information about nightlife, consult a *Guía turística* (GEE-ah too-REES-tee-kah), distributed at no charge by the tourist office.

Why don't we go dancing tonight?	¿Por qué no vamos a bailar esta noche?	pohr keh noh BAH-mohs ah bah-ee-LAHR EHS-tah NOH-cheh?
Can you suggest a good nightclub?	¿Podría recomendar un buen club nocturno?	poh-DREE-ah rreh-koh-mehn-DAHR oon bwehn kloob nohk-TOOR-noh?
Do they serve dinner?	¿Sirven cena?	SEER-behn SEH-nah?
What kind of show do they have?	¿Qué clase de función tienen?	keh-KLAH-seh deh foon-SYOHN TYEH-nehn?
Is there an entrance fee?	¿Se cobra la entrada?	seh KOH-brah lah ehn-TRAH-dah?
There's a minimum charge.	Se cobra un consumo mínimo.	seh KOH-brah oon kohn-SOO-moh MEE-nee-moh
What kind of dress is required? (*lit.,* How should one dress?)	Cómo se debe vestir?	KOH-moh seh DEH-beh behs-TEER?

Is there a place to go after dinner?	¿Hay algún lugar adonde ir después de cenar?	ahy ahl-GOON loo-GAHR ah-DOHN-deh eer dehs-PWEHS deh seh-NAHR?
Good evening.	Buenas noches.	BWEH-nahs NOH-chehs
We would like a table	Quisiéramos una mesa	kee-SYEH-rah-mohs OO-nah MEH-sah
_near the stage.	_cerca del escenario.	_SEHR-kah dehl eh-se-NAH-ryoh
_near the dance floor.	_cerca de la pista de baile.	_SEHR-kah deh lah PEES-tah deh BAH-ee-leh
How much do you charge for drinks?	¿Cuánto cuestan las bebidas?	KWAHN-toh KWEHS-tahn lahs beh-BEE-dahs?
Do you have any special drinks? (drinks of the house)	¿Tienen alguna bebida de la casa?	TYEH-nehn ahl-GOO-nah beh-BEE-dah deh lah KAH-sah?
What kind of non-alcoholic beverages do you serve?	¿Qué tipo de bebidas sin alcohol tienen?	keh TEE-poh deh beh-BEE-dahs seen ahl-KOHL TYEH-nehn?
Could we see the menu?	¿Podemos ver el menú?	poh-DEH-mohs behr ehl meh-NOO?
At what time is the show?	¿A qué hora es el espectáculo?	ah keh OH-rah ehs ehl ehs-pehk-TAH-koo-loh?
How many shows are there?	¿Cuántas veces se da el espectáculo?	KWAHN-tahs BEH-sehs seh dah ehl ehs-pehk-TAH-koo-loh?

SPORTS

Soccer is the most popular sport in Spain and Latin America. In Mexico, soccer is played nearly year-round, while in Spain the season is primarily from September through June. There are many teams, and both Spanish and Mexican fans are passionate about their favorite.

I would like to see a soccer match.	Quisiera ver un partido de fútbol.	kee-SYEH-rah behr oon pahr-TEE-doh deh FOOT-bohl

Who is playing?	¿Quiénes juegan?	KYEH-nehs HWEH-gahn?
Which is the best team?	¿Cuál es el mejor equipo?	kwahl ehs ehl meh-HOHR eh-KEE-poh?
Is the stadium near here?	¿Está cerca de aquí el estadio?	ehs-TAH SEHR-kah deh ah-KEE ehl ehs-TAH-dyoh?
How much are the tickets?	¿Cuánto cuestan las entradas?	KWAHN-toh KWEHS-tahn lahs ehn-TRAH-dahs?
Are there better seats?	¿Hay asientos mejores?	ahy ah-SYEHN-tohs meh-HOH-rehs?
What is the score?	¿Cuál es la anotación?	KWAHL ehs lah ah-noh-tah-SYOHN?
Who is winning?	¿Quién gana?	KYEHN GAH-nah?

BULLFIGHTS

The popularity of this ritual dance-confrontation between man and beast, long a fixture of life in the Spanish-speaking world, has seen some decline with the protests of animal rights activists and the rise of soccer and other spectator sports. Bullfighting is considered an art, not a sport, and likened to a ballet in which the *matador* acts out a series of poses and gracious steps, cape in hand, as he confronts the bull. Part of the art revolves around a series of classical positions, each with a specific name, some more daring and dangerous than others.

The *matador* is the primary bullfighter or *torero*, and the names of *matadores* are well known throughout the Spanish-speaking world. They are the principal actors, masters in the art of capework, expert in a variety of positions, through which they demonstrate their courage as they confront their adversary. After an initial performance with the cape, the bull is then weakened, first by the *picador* on horseback who strikes at the bull's massive neck muscles with a long lance. He is followed by the *banderilleros*, who insert pairs of *banderillas* (bahn-deh-REE-yahs), or sharp darts, into the bull's neck and back muscles. This is usually an extremely dangerous maneuver, accomplished while the bull is charging, and without the cape to help distract and confuse the animal.

The last segment of a bullfight is called the *faena* (fah-EH-nah). Here, the *matador* holds in his left hand a red, heart-shaped cloth, the *muleta* (moo-LEH-tah), and in his right hand a sword, which he will eventually use to kill the bull. The accomplishment of a good *faena* requires an extremely skilled *torero*. Such *toreros* gain fame throughout Spain and Latin America and often travel from one country to another at different times of the year.

Most bullfights, or *corridas de toros* (koh-RREE-dahs deh TOH-rohs), feature six bulls and three principal bullfighters. Each bullfighter kills one bull in each of the two segments of the afternoon's event. Following are some of the principal figures in a bullfight.

In Mexico, the bullfight season begins when the rains end, in November, and continues until April or May. Bullfights normally begin after lunch at 4 PM. Mexico City has the world's largest bull ring, but bullfighting is in decline here as well. You will find finer performances in a more intimate, beautiful ring in Puebla through May.

el torero (ehl toh-REH-roh)	A bullfighter. The matador, the picador, and the banderillero are all toreros. However, common usage often refers only to the matador as the torero, and to the others by their specific titles.
el matador (ehl mah-tah-DOHR)	The principal bullfighter, the one who kills the bull.
el picador (ehl pee-kah-DOHR)	Assistant on horseback who helps to weaken the bull by using a pica (PEE-kah), or lance.
el banderillero (ehl bahn-deh-ree-YEH-roh)	Often the matador himself—or an assistant he may designate—who places pairs of banderillas (bahn-deh-REE-yahs) on the bull's back and neck.
la cuadrilla (lah kwah-DREE-yah)	The team of bullfighters under the orders of the matador.
el monosabio (ehl moh-noh-SAH-byoh)	An orderly who does various jobs in the ruedo (RWEH-doh) or bullfight ring.
Is there a bullfight today?	**¿Hay una corrida hoy?**	ahy OO-nah koh-RREE-dah oy?

164

Where is the bull-ring?	¿Dónde está la plaza de toros?	DOHN-deh ehs-TAH lah PLAH-sah deh TOH-rohs?
Who is the main bullfighter?	¿Quién es el torero principal?	KYEHN ehs ehl toh-REH-roh preen-SEE-pahl?
Do you have seats in the	¿Tiene asientos en	TYEH-neh ah-SYEHN-tohs ehn
_shade?	_la sombra?	_lah SOHM-brah?
_sun?	_el sol?	_ehl sohl?
Bravo!	¡Olé!	oh-LEH!

16 GRAMMAR IN BRIEF

The format of this book allows you to find and use essential phrases without formal study of the grammar. However, by learning some of the basic patterns of the language, you will also be able to construct your own sentences. No book can predict or contain every sentence a traveler may need to use or understand, so any time you invest in learning grammatical patterns will contribute to your ability to communicate.

DEFINITE AND INDEFINITE ARTICLES

Spanish articles have several different forms because Spanish nouns have gender—which means that they are viewed as either masculine or feminine—and an article must agree in gender with its noun. The article must also agree with its noun in number—singular or plural. For example, *pasaporte* (passport) is masculine; hence the article it takes might be either *un* or *el* (*un pasaporte* or *el pasaporte*). Likewise, *maleta* (suitcase) is feminine, and its article might be *una* or *la*. The plural form of the masculine or feminine articles would be used if the nouns were plural. Finally, Spanish definite articles contract with prepositions in two cases, which occur frequently. The chart below outlines the uses of the various articles.

	Indefinite Article	Definite Article	Contraction with Prepositions *de* (of)	*a* (to)
Masculine, singular	un (a)	el (the)	del (of the) [*de* + *el* = del]	al (to the) [*a* + *el* = al]
Feminine, singular	una (a)	la (the)	de la (of the)	a la (to the)
Masculine, plural	unos (some)	los (the)	de los (of the)	a los (to the)
Feminine, plural	unas (some)	las (the)	de las (of the)	a las (to the)

Definite articles are used in Spanish more than they are in English. They are used with:

1. abstract nouns   **la libertad**

2. certain countries and cities   **el Japón; la Habana; el Ecuador**

3. countries and cities when qualified	**el Brasil hermoso; la Lima señorial**
4. days of weeks, seasons	**llegó el lunes; voy en la primavera**
5. verbal nouns	**el viajar es muy costoso**
6. names of languages	**el español es fácil**
7. titles (when not in direct address)	**éste es el señor Fernández**
8. parts of the body and articles of clothing (instead of the possessive adjective used in English)	**me duele la cabeza** (my head hurts); **me puse la camisa** (I put my shirt)

Articles are omitted:

| 1. with simple predicate nouns [Except: when the predicate noun is modified by an adjective] | **mi tío es abogado** (my uncle is a lawyer) [**mi tío es un buen abogado** (my uncle is a good lawyer)] |
| 2. with otro(-a) | **quiero otro libro** (I want another book) |

Other aspects of articles in Spanish to take into account are:

1. Definite and indefinite articles are used to convert adjectives into nouns: *un joven* (a young man); *la vieja* (the old woman).

2. There is also a neutral (no gender), definite article, *lo*, which is used with adjectival nouns (which always appear with a masculine ending), as in *lo bello* (the beautiful).

3. The neutral, definite article, *lo* (in both singular and plural forms), is also used to convert possessive pronouns into nouns: *lo mío* (that which is mine); *lo tuyo* (that which is yours).

NOUNS

Nouns in Spanish are either masculine or feminine. As a general rule, words ending in -*o* are masculine, while words ending in -*a*, -*d*, or -*cion* are feminine. [Two exceptions worth noting: *el día* (the day) and *la mano* (the hand), which are masculine and feminine, respectively.] With other endings, you simply have to learn the gender when you learn the words.

To form the plural of nouns ending in -o or -a, just add -s. If a word ends in a consonant, then add -es.

el pasaporte (the passport)	los pasaportes (the passports)
la oficina (the office)	las oficinas (the offices)
un boleto (a ticket)	unos boletos (some tickets)
una maleta (a suitcase)	unas maletas (some suitcases)

ADJECTIVES

Descriptive Adjectives

Most adjectives agree in number and gender with the noun they accompany. Unlike English adjectives, adjectives in Spanish, with few exceptions (e.g., *gran* and *buen*), usually follow the noun.

el señor viejo (the old man)

la señora vieja (the old woman)

los señores viejos (the old men)

las señoras viejas (the old women)

When an adjective ends in -e it does not change to agree with the noun in gender. The plural is formed by adding -s to the singular.

el señor inteligente (the intelligent man)

la señora inteligente (the intelligent woman)

los señores inteligentes (the intelligent men)

las señoras inteligentes (the intelligent women)

If an adjective ends in a consonant, such as: *difícil* (difficult), *común* (common), *cruel* (cruel), there is no change for gender. Plurals of both masculine and feminine are formed by adding -es to the singular.

un ejercicio difícil (a difficult exercise)

una tarea difícil (a difficult task)

unos ejercicios difíciles (some difficult exercises)

unas tareas difíciles (some difficult tasks)

[Exception: Adjectives ending in -*ón*, -*án*, or -*or* add -*a* to form the feminine, as in *trabajador, trabajadora*.]

Demonstrative Adjectives

Singular		Plural	
este, esta	this (near me)	estos, estas	these (near me)
ese, esa	this (near you)	esos, esas	these (near you)
aquel, aquella	that (remote)	aquellos, aquellas	those (remote)

Possessive Adjectives

Singular	Plural	
mi	mis	my
tu	tus	your (sing., familiar)
nuestro(-a)	nuestros(-as)	our
vuestro(-a)	vuestros(-as)	your (pl., familiar/ Spain only)
su	sus	his, her, its, their, your (sing., formal; and pl.)

The possessive adjective must agree in gender and number with the noun it modifies:

Mi cuarto es bonito.	(My room is pretty.)	
Mis cuartos son bonitos.	(My rooms are pretty.)	
Su hija es bonita.	(Her/his daughter is pretty.) [or]	(your [sing., formal; or pl.] daughter is pretty.)
Sus hijas son bonitas.	(Her/his daughters are pretty.)	(your [sing., formal; or pl.] daughters are pretty.)

ADVERBS

Adverbs of Manner

In English, -ly is added to an adjective to form an adverb. Spanish forms adverbs by adding -mente to the feminine form of an adjective.

	Adjective	
(Masc.)	(Fem.)	Adverb
lento	lenta	lentamente (slowly)
rápido	rápida	rápidamente (rapidly)
fácil	fácil*	fácilmente (easily)

[Exceptions: *despacio* (slow or slowly), *demasiado* (too much).]

*Note: The feminine and masculine forms of this word are the same.

Affirmative and Interrogative Adverbs

donde (where)	dónde (where?)
como (how, as)	cómo (how?)
cuando (when)	cuándo (when?)
cuanto (as much as)	cuánto (how much?)

COMPARISONS WITH ADJECTIVES AND ADVERBS

In Spanish, you form the comparative by placing the word *más* (more) before the noun, adjective, or adverb compared, followed by the word *que*.

más caro que (more expensive than)

más antiguo que (older than)

más despacio que (more slowly than)

Most adjectives and adverbs are regular in the formation of their comparatives, as above.

The superlative is formed by adding the corresponding definite article before the comparative.

el (libro) más caro (the most expensive book)

la (casa) más antigua (the oldest house)

los libros más caros (the most expensive books)

las casas más antiguas (the oldest houses)

A common exception, however, is *bueno* (good), whose comparative form is *mejor* (better).

The superlative is formed by adding the definite article before *mejor*.

PRONOUNS

Personal Pronouns

The pronoun takes the place of the subject in a sentence, and assumes its gender and number.

Subject Pronoun		Indirect Object Pronouns		Direct Object Pronouns	
yo	I	me	to me	me	me
tú	you (familiar)	te	to you	te	you
vos	you (familiar/Arg., Uru., & Central America)	te	to you	te	you
usted	you (formal)	le	to you	lo (m.) la (f.)	you
él	he	le	to him	lo	him
ella	she	le	to her	la lo	her it
nosotros	we	nos	to us	nos	us
vosotros	you (familiar/Spain only)	os	to you	os	you
ustedes	you (formal or familiar in Latin America; formal in Spain)	les	to you	los (m.) las (f.)	you
ellos	they (m.)	les	to them	los (m.)	them
ellas	they (f.)	les	to them	las (f.)	them

Note: With plural pronouns, the masculine form is used when referring both to a group (more than one) of males and to a group composed of both males and females.

Reflexive Pronouns

Reflexive pronouns are used when the action of the verb reflects back on the subject. Prepositional reflexive pronouns are used following prepositions.

		Simple Reflexive	Prepositional
(yo)	me	mí	myself
(tú)	te	ti	yourself
(vos)	te	vos	yourself
(él/ella)	se	sí	himself herself itself
(usted)	se	usted	yourself
(nosotros)	nos	nosotros	ourselves
(vosotros) [Spain]	os	vosotros	yourselves
(ustedes) [Lat. Amer.]	se	ustedes	themselves
(ellos/ellas)	se	sí	themselves
(ustedes)	se	sí	yourselves

Some common verbs can become reflexive by adding -se to the infinitive, producing changes such as:

lavar (to wash)	lavarse (to wash [oneself])
despertar (to wake up)	despertarse (to wake [oneself] up)
vestir (to dress)	vestirse (to dress [oneself])

Here are some common reflexive verbs:

despertarse (to wake up)	arreglarse (to fix oneself up)
levantarse (to get up)	vestirse (to get dressed)
lavarse (to get washed)	desvestirse (to get undressed)
bañarse (to bathe oneself)	acostarse (to go to bed)
peinarse (to get combed)	irse (to go away)

Relative Pronouns

Relative pronouns must always be expressed in Spanish. They are:

que	who, whom, which, that (invariable; refers to persons or things)
quien, quienes	who, whom, that (inflected for number only, and refers to persons only)
(el/la) cual (que); (los/las) cuales (que)	whom, which (used for clarity)
cuyo, cuya, cuyos, cuyas	whose (possessive, and must precede and agree in gender and number with person or thing possessed)

Interrogative Pronouns

The interrogative pronouns are relative pronouns used to ask questions. They differ from relative pronouns in that they bear an accent mark:

Singular	Plural	
¿quién?	¿quiénes?	who?, whom?
¿cuál?	¿cuáles?	which?
¿qué?		what? qué es
¿cuánto(-a)?	¿cuántos(-as)?	how much?/ aquel? how many?

Demonstrative Pronouns

Demonstrative pronouns have written accents to distinguish them from the demonstrative adjectives:

Singular		Plural	
éste, ésta	this (near me)	éstos, éstas	these (near me)
ése, ésa	that (near you)	ésos, ésas	those (near you)
aquél, aquélla	that (yonder)	aquéllos, aquéllas	those (yonder)

PREPOSITIONS

Some of the most common prepositions in Spanish are:

a (at, to, with time)	hasta (until, up to)
con (with)	para (for, in order to, to)
contra (against)	por (for, by, through, because)

de (from, of, about)	según (according to)
en (in, on)	sin (without)
entre (between, among)	sobre (on, about)
hacia (towards)	

Some prepositions combine with other words to form compounds.

además de (besides, in addition to)	después de (after)
al lado de (beside, at the side of)	detrás de (behind)
antes de (before [references to time])	en vez de (instead of)
cerca de (near)	encima de (on top of)
debajo de (under, underneath)	enfrente de (in front of, facing, opposite)
delante de (in front of)	fuera de (outside of)
dentro de (inside of, within)	lejos de (far from)

NEGATIVE SENTENCES

To form the negative in Spanish, place the word *no* in front of the verb. For example:

Yo hablo español. (I speak Spanish.)

*Yo **no** hablo español.* (I don't speak Spanish.)

When the personal subject pronoun is omitted, then the phrase starts with *no*.

Viajo mañana. (I travel tomorrow.)

***No** viajo mañana.* (I don't travel tomorrow.)

Other negative words are:

nada (nothing)	ninguno(-a) (none)
nadie (no one/nobody)	tampoco (neither)
nunca (never)	

Unlike *no*, all of these words can go before or after the verb. They can also be used along with the negative *no*. Sometimes there may even be as many as three negatives in a single sentence:

| No dio nada a nadie. | (He did not give anything to anyone. [literally: He did not give nothing to no one.]) |

QUESTIONS

Questions are easy to form in Spanish, and can be done in several ways. The simplest form is to raise your voice at the end of a statement to indicate a question, similar to what is done in English. For example: "*Vas a México.*" (You are going to Mexico) becomes: "*¿Vas a México?*" (You are going to Mexico?). Notice, however, that Spanish includes an "upside-down" question mark in front of the written sentence as well as the "right-side-up" one at the end.

A second easy way to form a question is to invert the order of the subject and verb. This again is similar to what is done in English. "*Usted tiene un boleto.*" (You have a ticket) becomes: "*¿Tiene usted un boleto?*" (Do you have a ticket?).

VERBS

There are three verb conjugations in Spanish. In the infinitive, all verbs end in either *-ar, -er,* or *-ir.* Regular verbs are conjugated as follows:

-ar *hablar* (I) (to talk)	*-er* *comer* (II) (to eat)	*-ir* *vivir* (III) (to live)
Present Tense		
yo hablo	como	vivo
tú hablas	comes	vives
usted habla	come	vive
él/ella habla	come	vive
nosotros hablamos	comemos	vivimos
vosotros habláis	coméis	vivís
ustedes hablan	comen	viven
ellos/ellas hablan	comen	viven

-ar hablar (I) (to talk)	-er comer (II) (to eat)	-ir vivir (III) (to live)
Past Tense (Preterite)		
yo hablé	comí	viví
tú hablaste	comiste	viviste
usted habló	comió	vivió
él/ella habló	comió	vivió
nosotros hablamos	comimos	vivimos
vosotros hablasteis	comisteis	vivisteis
ustedes hablaron	comieron	vivieron
ellos/ellas hablaron	comieron	vivieron

Other regular verbs which follow these patterns are: **comprar** (to buy), **viajar** (to travel), **beber** (to drink), **perder** (to lose), **partir** (to leave), and **pedir** (to ask for).

Irregular Verbs

Some commonly used verbs which do not follow the patterns given above, and have slightly irregular forms, are:

dar (to give)	*hacer* (to do/make)	*decir* (to tell/say)
Present Tense		
yo doy	hago	digo
tú das	haces	dices
usted da	hace	dice
él/ella da	hace	dice
nosotros damos	hacemos	decimos
vosotros dais	hacéis	decís
ustedes dan	hacen	dicen
ellos/ellas dan	hacen	dicen
Past Tense (Preterite)		
yo di	hice	dije
tú diste	hiciste	dijiste

usted dio	hizo	dijo
él/ella dio	hizo	dijo
nosotros dimos	hicimos	dijimos
vosotros disteis	hicisteis	dijisteis
ustedes dieron	hicieron	dijeron
ellos/ellas dieron	hicieron	dijeron

tener (to have)	*poder* (to be able/can)	*ver* (to see)
Present Tense		
yo tengo	puedo	veo
tú tienes	puedes	ves
usted tiene	puede	ve
él/ella tiene	puede	ve
nosotros tenemos	podemos	vemos
vosotros tenéis	podéis	veis
ustedes tienen	pueden	ven
ellos/ellas tienen	pueden	ven
Past Tense (Preterite)		
yo tuve	pude	vi
tú tuviste	pudiste	viste
usted tuvo	pudo	vio
él/ella tuvo	pudo	vio
nosotros tuvimos	pudimos	vimos
vosotros tuvisteis	pudisteis	visteis
ustedes tuvieron	pudieron	vieron
ellos/ellas tuvieron	pudieron	vieron

ir (to go)
Present Tense

yo voy	nosotros vamos
tú vas	vosotros vais
usted va	ustedes van
él/ella va	ellos/ellas van

Future Tense

There are two ways of forming the future in Spanish. One is the simple future, which requires only a spelling change; the other is formed with the verb "to go to" plus an infinitive. Use depends on the region of the Spanish-speaking world you are in. Although both convey the idea of the future, the meanings are slightly different:

Hablaré con el gerente. (I will speak to the manager.)

Voy a hablar con el gerente. (I am going to speak to the manager.)

The endings for the simple future of regular verbs for all three conjugations are demonstrated below.

yo hablaré	comeré	viviré
tú hablarás	comerás	vivirás
usted hablará	comerá	vivirá
él/ella hablará	comerá	vivirá
nosotros hablaremos	comeremos	viviremos
vosotros hablaréis	comeréis	viviréis
ustedes hablarán	comerán	vivirán
ellos/ellas hablarán	comerán	vivirán

To form the future with "going to," just add the preposition *a* and leave the verb in the infinitive:

Voy a comer. (I am going to eat.)

Voy a viajar. (I am going to travel.)

Note that the personal subject pronoun is sometimes omitted. This is possible since the verb ending indicates the person referred to. An exception is made sometimes when there is need to clarify or stress the persons referred to. This is common, for example, when the third person singular or plural is involved (*él, ella, ellos, ellas*), in which case one might say:

Ella va a comer. (She is going to eat.)

Verbs *Ser* and *Estar*

The verb "to be" is expressed in Spanish by two different verbs: ser and estar.

Ser is conjugated as follows:		**Estar** is conjugated as follows:	
yo soy	I am	yo estoy	I am
tú eres	you are	tu estás	you are
usted es	you are	usted está	you are
él/ella es	he/she/it is	él/ella está	he/she/it is
nosotros somos	we are	nosotros estamos	we are
vosotros sois	you are	vosotros estáis	you are
ustedes son	you are	ustedes están	you are
ellos/ella son	they are	ellos/ellas están	they are

These examples show how the verbs are used:

ser

1. Used in impersonal expressions:

¿Qué hora es? (What time is it?)

Es hermoso. (It's beautiful.)

2. With prepositions, except those expressing temporary place at, or location in:

Es para mí. (It's for me.)

Él es de Colombia. (He's from Colombia.)

3. With a predicate noun or pronoun:

Son nuestros. (They're ours.)

4. With predicate adjectives to express an inherent quality:

Es bueno. (It's good.)

Somos mexicanos. (We're Mexicans.)

estar

1. To express temporary location:

Estoy aquí. (I'm here.)

Está en la casa. (He's in the house.)

2. With an adjective that does not express an inherent quality:

Está contento. (He's happy.)

Estoy cansado. [temporary condition] (I'm tired.)

3. To form progressive tenses:

Estoy comiendo.* (I'm eating.)

Estoy viajando.* (I'm traveling.)

Estoy viviendo.* (I'm living.)

Note: *The gerund (present participle) is formed as follows: -ar verbs drop the -ar ending from the infinitive and add -ando. -er verbs drop the -er ending from the infinitive and add -iendo. -ir verbs drop the -ir ending and add -iendo.

Special Uses of *Tener* and *Hacer*

Tener is used to express *to be* in cases such as: to be thirsty, to be hungry, to be cold, to be warm, to be . . . years old.

Tengo hambre. (I am hungry.)

¿Tienes sed? (Are you thirsty?)

Tenemos calor. (We are hot/warm.)

Tienen frío. (They are cold.)

Tiene veinte años. (He is twenty years old.)

Hacer is also used to express the idea of *to be*. It is always used in the third person singular.

Hace frío. (It is cold.)

Hace calor. (It is hot/warm.)

Finally, *hacer* is used in expressions of time, as when referring to the length of time since an event took place or to the continuation of an action through time.

Hace tres meses leí ese libro. (I read that book three months ago.)

Hace diez años que vivo en esta casa. (I have lived in this house for ten years.)

ENGLISH-SPANISH DICTIONARY

List of Abbreviations

abbr. *abbreviated as*
adj. *adjective*
conj. *conjunction*
f. *feminine noun*
m. *masculine noun*
Mex. *Mexico usage*

pl. *plural*
pron. *pronoun*
sing. *singular*
Sp. *Spain usage*
v. *verb*
w/ *with*

A

a, an un, una (f.) *(oon, OO-nah)*
able, to be poder *(poh-DEHR)*
about acerca de *(ah-SEHR-kah deh)*
above arriba, encima de *(ah-RREE-bah, ehn-SEE-mah deh)*
abscess absceso (m.) *(ahb-SEH-soh)*
accelerator acelerador (m.) *(ah-seh-leh-rah-DQHR)*
accept aceptar *(ah-sehp-TAHR)*
accident accidente (m.) *(ahk-see-DEHN-teh)*
ache, head dolor de cabeza (m.) *(doh-LOHR deh kah-BEH-sah)*
stomachache dolor de estómago *(doh-LOHR deh ehs-TOH-mah-goh)*
toothache dolor de muelas *(doh-LOHR deh MWEH-lahs)*
across a través de *(ah trah-BEHS deh)*
address dirección (f.) *(dee-rehk-SYOHN)*
adhesive tape esparadrapo (m.) *(ehs-pah-rah-DRAH-poh)*
adjust ajustar, arreglar *(ah-hoos-TAHR, ah-rreh-GLAHR)*
admittance, no se prohibe la entrada *(seh proh-EE-beh lah ehn-TRAH-dah)*

afraid, to be tener miedo *(teh-NEHR MYEH-doh)*
after después de *(dehs-PWEHS deh)*
afternoon tarde (f.) *(TAHR-deh)*
again otra vez, de nuevo *(OH-trah behs, deh NWEH-boh)*
against contra *(KOHN-trah)*
ago hace (with time expressions) *(AH-seh)*
agree estar de acuerdo *(ehs-TAHR deh ah-KWEHR-doh)*
ahead adelante *(ah-deh-LAHN-teh)*
aid ayuda (f.) *(ah-YOO-dah)*; **first aid** primeros auxilios (m.pl.) *(pree-MEH-rohs owk-SEE-lyohs)*
air aire (m.) *(AHY-reh)*; **airmail** correo aéreo (m.) *(koh-RREH-oh ah-EH-reh-oh)*
airline línea aérea (f.) *(LEE-neh-ah ah-EH-reh-ah)*
airplane avión (m.) *(ah-BYOHN)*
airport aeropuerto (m.) *(ah-eh-roh-PWEHR-toh)*
alarm clock despertador (m.) *(dehs-pehr-tah-DOHR)*
all todo *(TOH-doh)*
allow permitir *(pehr-mee-TEER)*
almond almendra (f.) *(ahl-MEHN-drah)*
almost casi *(KAH-see)*

181

alone solo *(SOH-loh)*
already ya *(yah)*
also también *(tahm-BYEHN)*
always siempre *(SYEHM-preh)*
a.m. de (por) la mañana *(deh [pohr] lah mah-NYAH-nah)*
am, I soy, estoy *(sohy, ehs-TOHY)*
American norteamericano (-a) *(nohr-teh-ah-meh-ree-KAH-noh)(-nah)*
among entre *(EHN-treh)*
and y *(ee)*
ankle tobillo (m.) *(toh-BEE-yoh)*
annoy molestar *(moh-lehs-TAHR)*
another otro *(OH-troh)*
answer (response) respuesta (f.) *(rrehs-PWEHS-tah)*
any algún *(ahl-GOON)*
anybody (anyone) alguien *(AHL-gyehn)*
anything algo *(AHL-goh)*;
  anything else? ¿algo más? *(AHL-goh mahs?)*
apartment piso (m./Sp.), apartamento (m.) *(PEE-soh, ah-pahr-tah-MEHN-toh)*
aperitif aperitivo (m.) *(ah-peh-ree-TEE-boh)*
appetizers entremeses (m.pl.), bocadillos (m.pl.) *(ehn-treh-MEH-sehs, boh-kah-DEE-yohs)*
apple manzana (f.) *(mahn-SAH-nah)*
apricot albaricoque (m.) *(ahl-bah-ree-KOH-keh)*
April abril (m.) *(ah-BREEL)*
Arab árabe *(AH-rah-beh)*
are, they son; están *(sohn; ehs-TAHN)*
Argentine argentino(-a) *(ahr-hehn-TEE-noh)(-nah)*
arm brazo (m.) *(BRAH-soh)*

armchair sillón (m.) *(see-YOHN)*
around alrededor de *(ahl-reh-deh-DOHR deh)*
arrival llegada (f.) *(yeh-GAH-dah)*
article artículo (m.) *(ahr-TEE-koo-loh)*
as como *(KOH-moh)*
ashtray cenicero (m.) *(seh-nee-SEH-roh)*
ask (a question) preguntar *(preh-goon-TAHR)*;
  ask for pedir *(peh-DEER)*
asparagus espárragos (m.pl.) *(ehs-PAH-rrah-gohs)*
aspirin aspirina (f.) *(ahs-pee-REE-nah)*
at en; a *(ehn; ah)*;
  at once en seguida *(ehn seh-GEE-dah)*
attention atención (f.); cuidado (m.) *(ah-tehn-SYOHN; kuee-DAH-doh)*
August agosto (m.) *(ah-GOHS-toh)*
aunt tía (f.) *(TEE-ah)*
Austrian austríaco(-a) *(ows-TREE-ah-koh) (-kah)*
automobile automóvil (m.), carro (m.), coche (m.) *(ow-toh-MOH-beel, KAH-rroh, KOH-cheh)*
autumn otoño (m.) *(oh-TOH-nyoh)*
avoid evitar *(eh-bee-TAHR)*
awful terrible *(teh-RREE-bleh)*

B

baby bebé (m./f.), nene (-a) (m.,f.) *(beh-BEH, NEH-neh [-nah])*
back (body part) espalda (f.) *(ehs-PAHL-dah)*;
  (behind) detrás de *(deh-TRAHS deh)*;

(direction, movement)
atrás *(ah-TRAHS)*

bacon tocino (m.) *(toh-SEE-noh)*

bad malo *(MAH-loh)*

badly mal *(mahl)*

bag bolsa (f.) *(BOHL-sah);*
handbag cartera (f.) *(kahr-TEH-rah);*
(valise) maleta (f.) *(mah-LEH-tah)*

baggage equipaje (m.) *(eh-kee-PAH-heh)*

baked al horno *(ahl OHR-noh)*

balcony (theater) galería (f.) *(gah-leh-REE-ah);*
(house) balcón (m.) *(bahl-KOHN)*

ball pelota (f.) *(peh-LOH-tah)*

banana plátano (m.) *(PLAH-tah-noh)*

bandage venda (f.) *(BEHN-dah)*

bank banco (m.) *(BAHN-koh)*

barber barbero *(bahr-BEH-roh)*

barbershop barbería *(bahr-beh-REE-yah)*

bargain ganga (f.) *(GAHN-gah)*

basket cesta (f.), canasta (f.) *(SEHS-tah, kah-NAHS-tah)*

bath baño *(BAH-nyoh)*

bathe bañarse *(bah-NYAR-seh)*

bathing suit traje de baño (m.) *(TRAH-heh deh BAH-nyoh)*

bathroom cuarto de baño (m.) *(KWAHR-toh deh BAH-nyoh)*

battery (automobile) acumulador (m.), batería (f.) *(ah-koo-moo-lah-DOHR, bah-teh-REE-ah)*

be ser; estar *(sehr; ehs-TAHR);*
to be back estar de vuelta *(ehs-TAHR deh BWEHL-tah)*

beach playa (f.) *(PLAH—yah)*

beautiful bello, hermoso *(BEH-yoh, ehr-MOH-soh)*

beauty salon salón de belleza (m.) *(sah-LOHN deh beh-YEH-sah)*

because porque *(POHR-keh)*

bed cama (f.) *(KAH-mah)*

bedroom alcoba (f.), dormitorio (m.) *(ahl-KOH-bah, dohr-mee-TOH-ryoh)*

beef carne de res (f.) *(KAHR-neh deh rehs);*
roast beef rosbif *(rrohs-BEEF)*

beer cerveza (f.) *(sehr-BEH-sah)*

beet remolacha (f.), betabel (f./Mex.) *(rreh-moh-LAH-chah, beh-tah-BEHL)*

before antes de *(AHN-tehs deh)*

begin comenzar *(koh-mehn-SAHR)*

behind detrás de *(deh-TRAHS deh)*

Belgian belga *(BEHL-gah)*

believe creer *(kreh-EHR)*

bell (door) timbre (m.) *(TEEM-breh)*

bellhop botones (m.) *(boh-TOH-nehs)*

belong pertenecer *(pehr-teh-neh-SEHR)*

belt cinturón (m.) *(seen-too-ROHN)*

best el/la mejor *(ehl/lah meh-HOHR)*

bet apuesta (f.) *(ah-PWEHS-tah);*
I'll bet apuesto a que *(ah-PWEHS-toh ah keh)*

better mejor *(meh-HOHR)*

between entre *(EHN-treh)*

bicarbonate of soda bicarbonato de soda (m.) *(bee-kahr-boh-NAH-toh deh SOH-dah)*

big grande *(GRAHN-deh)*
bill (restaurant check) cuenta (f.) *(KWEHN-tah)*
billion mil millones *(meel mee-YOH-nehs)*
bird pájaro (m.) *(PAH-hah-roh)*
bite mordida (f.) *(mohr-DEE-dah)*;
  to bite morder *(mohr-DEHR)*
bitter amargo *(ah-MAHR-goh)*
black negro *(NEH-groh)*
blade, razor hoja de afeitar (f.) *(OH-hah deh ah-fay-TAHR)*
blank form formulario (m.) *(fohr-moo-LAH-ryoh)*
block (city) cuadra (f.) *(KWAH-drah)*;
  square (city) block manzana (f.) *(mahn-SAH-nah)*
blood sangre (f.) *(SAHN-greh)*
blouse blusa (f.) *(BLOO-sah)*
blue azul *(ah-SOOL)*
boat bote (m.) *(BOH-teh)*
body cuerpo (m.) *(KWEHR-poh)*
boiled hervido *(ehr-BEE-doh)*
bolt perno (m.) *(PEHR-noh)*
bone hueso (m.) *(WEH-soh)*
book libro (m.) *(LEE-broh)*;
  guidebook guía (f.) *(GEE-ah)*
bookstore librería (f.) *(lee-breh-REE-ah)*
booth, phone cabina telefónica (f.) *(kah-BEE-nah teh-leh-FOH-nee-kah)*
born, to be nacer *(nah-SEHR)*
borrow pedir prestado *(peh-DEER prehs-TAH-doh)*
bother molestar *(moh-lehs-TAHR)*;
  don't bother no se moleste *(noh seh moh-LEHS-teh)*
bottle botella (f.) *(boh-TEH-yah)*
box caja (f.) *(KAH-hah)*
box office (theater) taquilla (f.) *(tah-KEE-yah)*

boy muchacho (m.), chico (m.) *(moo-CHAH-choh, CHEE-koh)*
bra; brassiere sostén (m.) *(sohs-TEHN)*
bracelet pulsera (f.) *(pool-SEH-rah)*
brakes (automobile) frenos (m.pl.) *(FREH-nohs)*
Brazilian brasileño(-a) *(brah-see-LEH-nyoh)(-nyah)*
bread pan (m.) *(pahn)*
break romper *(rrohm-PEHR)*
breakdown (car) avería (f.) *(ah-beh-REE-ah)*
breakfast desayuno (m.) *(deh-sah-YOO-noh)*
breathe respirar *(rrehs-pee-RAHR)*
bridge puente (m.) *(PWEHN-teh)*
bring traer *(trah-EHR)*
broiled a la parrilla *(ah lah pah-RREE-yah)*
broken roto, quebrado *(RROH-toh, keh-BRAH-doh)*
brother hermano *(ehr-MAH-noh)*
brown marrón, castaño *(mah-ROHN, kahs-TAH-nyoh)*
bruise (injury) contusión (f.) *(kohn-too-SYOHN)*
brush cepillo (m.) *(seh-PEE-yoh)*;
  shaving brush brocha de afeitar (f.) *(BROH-chah deh ah-fay-TAHR)*;
  to brush cepillar *(seh-pee-YAHR)*
building edificio (m.) *(eh-dee-FEE-syoh)*
bulb (electric) bombilla (f.), foco (m.) *(bohm-BEE-yah, FOH-koh)*
bullfight corrida de toros (f.) *(koh-RREE-dah deh TOH-rohs)*

bumper (automobile) para-choques (m.) *(pah-rah-CHOH-kehs)*

burn (injury) quemadura (f.) *(keh-mah-DOO-rah)*;
to burn quemar *(keh-MAHR)*

bus autobús (m.) *(ow-toh-BOOS)*

busy ocupado *(oh-koo-PAH-doh)*

but pero *(PEH-roh)*

butter mantequilla (f.) *(mahn-teh-KEE-yah)*

button botón (m.) *(boh-TOHN)*

buy comprar *(kohm-PRAHR)*

by de; por *(deh; pohr)*

C

cab taxi (m.) *(TAHK-see)*

cabaret cabaret (m.) *(kah-bah-REHT)*

cabbage col (f.), repollo (m./Mex.) *(kohl, rreh-POH-yoh)*

cable (telegram) cable-grama (m.) *(kah-bleh-GRAH-mah)*

cake torta (f.), pastel (m./Mex.) *(TOHR-tah, pahs-TEHL)*

call llamar *(yah-MAHR)*;
telephone call llamada telefónica (f.) *(yah-MAH-dah teh-leh-FOH-nee-kah)*

camera cámara (f.) *(KAH-mah-rah)*

can (container) lata (f.) *(LAH-tah)*;
can opener abrelatas (m.) *(ah-breh-LAH-tahs)*;
(to be able) poder *(poh-DEHR)*

Canadian canadiense *(kah-nah-DYEHN-seh)*

cancel cancelar *(kahn-seh-LAHR)*

candle vela (f.) *(BEH-lah)*

candy caramelo (m.s.) *(kah-rah-MEH-loh)*

cap gorra (f.) *(GOH-rrah)*

captain capitán (m./Sp.) *(kah-pee-TAHN)*

car (automobile) automóvil (m.), coche (m./Sp.) *(ow-toh-MOH-beel, KOH-cheh)*;
railroad car vagón (m.) *(bah-GOHN)*;
streetcar tranvía (m.) *(trahn-BEE-ah)*

carburetor carburador (m.) *(kahr-boo-rah-DOHR)*

card (playing) carta (f.), naipe (m.) *(KAHR-tah, NAH-ee-peh)*

care (caution) cuidado (m.) *(kwee-DAH-doh)*

careful, to be tener cuidado *(teh-NEHR kwee-DAH-doh)*

carefully con cuidado *(kohn kwee-DAH-doh)*

carrot zanahoria (f.) *(sah-nah-OH-ryah)*

carry llevar *(yeh-BAHR)*

carry-on luggage equipaje de mano (m.) *(eh-kee-PAH-heh deh MAH-noh)*

cash (money) dinero en efectivo (m.) *(dee-NEH-roh ehn eh-fehk-TEE-boh)*

cash cobrar *(koh-BRAHR)*

cashier cajero (-a) *(kah-HEH-roh)(-rah)*

castle castillo (m.) *(kahs-TEE-yoh)*

cat gato (m.) *(GAH-toh)*

catch coger, agarrar (Mex.) *(koh-HEHR, ah-gah-RRAHR)*

cathedral catedral (f.) *(kah-teh-DRAHL)*

Catholic católico(-a) *(kah-TOH-lee-koh)(-kah)*

cauliflower coliflor (f.) *(koh-lee-FLOHR)*

caution cuidado (m.), precaución (f.) *(kwee-DAH-doh, preh-kow-SYOHN)*

ceiling techo (m.) *(TEH-choh)*

celery apio (m.) *(AH-pyoh)*

center centro (m.) *(SEHN-troh)*

certainly ciertamente *(syehr-tah-MEHN-teh)*

certificate certificado (m.) *(sehr-tee-fee-KAH-doh)*

chain cadena (f.) *(kah-DEH-nah)*

chair silla (f.) *(SEE-yah)*

change (money) cambio (m.) *(KAHM-byoh)*

charge, cover cobro de entrada (m.) *(KOH-broh deh ehn-TRAH-dah);*
  minimum charge consumo mínimo (m.) *(kohn-SOO-moh MEE-nee-moh);*
  to charge cobrar *(koh-BRAHR)*

cheap barato *(bah-RAH-toh)*

check cheque (m.) *(CHEH-keh);*
  traveler's check cheque de viajero (m.) *(CHEH-keh deh byah-HEH-roh);*
  to check (luggage) facturar, revisar *(fahk-too-RAHR, rre-bee-SAHR)*

checkroom sala de equipaje (f.) *(SAH-lah deh eh-kee-PAH-heh)*

cheek mejilla (f.) *(meh-HEE-yah)*

cheese queso (m.) *(KEH-soh)*

cherry cereza (f.) *(seh-REH-sah)*

chest (body part) pecho (m.) *(PEH-choh)*

chestnut castaña (f.) *(kahs-TAH-nyah)*

chicken pollo (m.) *(POH-yoh)*

child niño(-a) *(NEE-nyoh) (-nyah)*

Chilean chileno(-a) *(chee-LEH-noh)(-nah)*

chill escalofrío (m.) *(ehs-kah-loh-FREE-oh)*

chin barba (f.) *(BAHR-bah)*

Chinese chino(-a) *(CHEE-noh)(-nah)*

chiropodist pedicuro *(peh-dee-KOO-roh)*

chocolate chocolate (m.) *(choh-koh-LAH-teh)*

choose escoger *(ehs-koh-HEHR)*

chop (cutlet) chuleta (f.) *(choo-LEH-tah)*

Christmas Navidad (f.) *(nah-bee-DAHD)*

church iglesia (f.) *(ee-GLEH-syah)*

cigar cigarro (m.), puro (m.) *(see-GAH-rroh, POO-roh)*

cigarette cigarrillo (m.) *(see-gah-RREE-yoh)*

cigar store tabaquería (f.) *(tah-bah-keh-REE-ah)*

city ciudad (f.) *(syoo-DAHD)*

class clase (f.) *(KLAH-seh)*

clean limpio *(LEEM-pyoh);*
  to clean limpiar *(leem-PYAHR)*

cleaner, dry tintorería (f.) *(teen-toh-reh-REE-ah)*

clear (transparent) claro *(KLAH-roh)*

climb trepar *(treh-PAHR)*

clock reloj (m.) *(rreh-LOH)*

close (near) cerca *(SEHR-kah);*
  to close cerrar *(seh-RRAHR);*
  closed cerrado *(seh-RRAH-doh)*

cloth tela (f.) *(TEH-lah)*

clothes ropa (f.) *(RROH-pah)*

cloud nube (f.) *(NOO-beh);*
  cloudy nublado *(noo-BLAH-doh)*

club, night cabaret (m.)
(kah-bah-REHT)

clutch (automobile) embrague (m.) *(ehm-BRAH-geh)*

coach (railroad) coche (m.), vagón (m.) *(KOH-cheh, bah-GOHN)*

coat saco (m.), abrigo (f.) *(SAH-koh, ah-BREE-goh)*

coat hanger colgador (m.) *(kohl-gah-DOHR)*

cocktail cóctel (m.) *(KOHK-tehl)*

coffee café (m.) *(kah-FEH)*

coin (money) moneda (f.) *(moh-NEH-dah)*

cold (temperature) frío *(FREE-oh)*;
  (illness) resfriado (m.) *(rehs-free-AH-doh)*

cold cuts fiambres (m.), carnes frías (f.) *(FYAHM-brehs, KAHR-nehs FREE-ahs)*

collar cuello (m.) *(KWEH-yoh)*

collect cobrar *(koh-BRAHR)*

cologne agua de colonia (f.) *(AH-gwah deh koh-LOH-nyah)*

color color (m.) *(koh-LOHR)*

color film película de color (f.) *(peh-LEE-koo-lah deh koh-LOHR)*

comb peine (m.) *(PAY-neh)*

come venir *(beh-NEER)*;
  to come in entrar *(ehn-TRAHR)*

comedy comedia (f.) *(koh-MEH-dyah)*

comfortable cómodo *(KOH-moh-doh)*

company compañía (f.) *(kohm-pah-NYEE-ah)*

compartment compartimiento (m.) *(kohm-pahr-tee-MYEHN-toh)*

complaint queja (f.) *(KEH-hah)*

computer computadora (f.) ordenador (m./Sp.) *(kohm-poo-tah-DOH-rah, or-deh-nah-DOHR)*

concert concierto (m.) *(kohn-SYEHR-toh)*

conductor (train) conductor (m.), revisor (m.) *(kohn-dook-TOHR, rreh-bee-SOHR)*

congratulations felicitaciones (f.pl.) *(feh-lee-see-tah-SYOH-nehs)*

consul cónsul (m.) *(KOHN-sool)*

consulate consulado (m.) *(kohn-soo-LAH-doh)*

continue continuar, seguir *(kohn-tee-NWAHR, seh-GEER)*

convent convento (m.) *(kohn-BEHN-toh)*

cooked cocido *(koh-SEE-doh)*

cool fresco *(FREHS-koh)*

corkscrew sacacorchos (m.) *(sah-kah-KOHR-chohs)*

corn maíz (m.) *(mah-EES)*

corner esquina (f.) *(ehs-KEE-nah)*

cost (amount) precio (m.) *(PREH-syoh)*;
  to cost costar *(kohs-TAHR)*

cotton algodón (m.) *(ahl-goh-DOHN)*

cough tos (f.) *(tohs)*;
  to cough toser *(toh-SEHR)*

count contar *(kohn-TAHR)*

country (nation) país (m.) *(pah-EES)*

countryside campo (m.) *(KAHM-poh)*

course (in meals) plato (m.) *(PLAH-toh)*

crazy loco *(LOH-koh)*

cream crema (f.) *(KREH-mah)*

crystal cristal (m.) *(krees-TAHL)*

Cuban cubano(-a) *(koo-BAH-noh)(-nah)*

cucumber pepino (m.) *(peh-PEE-noh)*

cup taza (f.) *(TAH-sah)*
curtain cortina (f.) *(kohr-TEE-nah)*;
  (stage) telón (m.) *(teh-LOHN)*
curve curva (f.) *(KOOR-bah)*
customs aduana (f.) *(ah-DWAH-nah)*
cut cortar *(kohr-TAHR)*;
  cut it out! ¡basta! *(BAHS-tah!)*
cutlet chuleta (f.) *(choo-LEH-tah)*
Czech checo(-a) *(CHEH-koh)(-kah)*

D

daily (by the day) por día, al día *(pohr DEE-ah, ahl DEE-ah)*
damp húmedo *(OO-meh-doh)*
dance baile (m.) *(BAHY-leh)*;
  to dance bailar *(bah-ee-LAHR)*
danger peligro (m.) *(peh-LEE-groh)*
dangerous peligroso *(peh-lee-GROH-soh)*
Danish danés(-esa) *(dah-NEHS)(-NEH-sah)*
dark oscuro *(ohs-KOO-roh)*
darn it! ¡caramba! *(kah-RAHM-bah!)*
date (calendar) fecha (f.) *(FEH-chah)*
daughter hija (f.) *(EE-hah)*
day día (m.) *(DEE-ah)*
dead muerto(-a) *(MWEHR-toh)(-tah)*
death muerte (f.) *(MWEHR-teh)*
December diciembre (m.) *(dee-SYEHM-breh)*
declaration declaración (f.) *(deh-klah-rah-SYOHN)*

declare declarar *(deh-klah-RHAR)*
deep profundo *(proh-FOON-doh)*
deliver entregar *(ehn-treh-GAHR)*
delivery entrega (f.) *(ehn-TREH-gah)*;
  special delivery entrega inmediata (f.) *(ehn-TREH-gah een-men-DYAH-tah)*
dental dental *(dehn-TAHL)*
dentist dentista (m./f.) *(dehn-TEES-tah)*
denture dentadura (f.) *(dehn-tah-DOO-rah)*
deodorant desodorante (m.) *(deh-soh-doh-RAHN-teh)*
department store almacén (m.) *(ahl-mah-SEHN)*
desk, information mostrador de información (m.) *(mohs-trah-DOHR deh een-fohr-mah-SYOHN)*
dessert postre (m.) *(POHS-treh)*
detour desvío (m.) *(dehs-BEE-oh)*
develop (film) revelar *(rreh-beh-LAHR)*
devil diablo (m.), demonio (m.) *(DYAH-bloh, deh-MOH-nyoh)*
diapers pañales (m.pl.) *(pah-NYAH-lehs)*
dictionary diccionario (m.) *(deek-syoh-NAH-ryoh)*
different diferente *(dee-feh-REHN-teh)*
difficult difícil *(dee-FEE-seel)*
difficulty dificultad (f.) *(dee-fee-kool-TAHD)*
dining car coche-comedor (m.) *(KOH-cheh koh-meh-DOHR)*
dining room comedor (m.) *(koh-meh-DOHR)*

dinner comida (f.) *(koh-MEE-dah)*

direct directo *(dee-REHK-toh)*;
to direct indicar, dirigir *(een-dee-KAHR, dee-ree-HEER)*

direction dirección (f.) *(dee-rehk-SYOHN)*

dirty sucio *(SOO-syoh)*

discount descuento (m.) *(dehs-KWEHN-toh)*

dish plato (m.) *(PLAH-toh)*

district barrio (m.) *(BAH-rryoh)*

disturb molestar *(moh-lehs-TAHR)*

dizzy, to feel estar mareado *(ehs-TAHR mah-reh-AH-doh)*

do hacer *(ah-SEHR)*

dock muelle (m.) *(MWEH-yeh)*

doctor médico(-a), doctor(-a) *(MEH-dee-koh[-kah], dohk-TOHR[-TOH-rah])*

document documento (m.) *(doh-koo-MEHN-toh)*

dog perro (m.) *(PEH-rroh)*

dollar dólar (m.) *(DOH-lahr)*

domestic nacional, doméstico *(nah-syoh-NAHL, doh-MEHS-tee-koh)*

door puerta (f.) *(PWEHR-tah)*

doorman portero (m.) *(pohr-TEH-roh)*

double room habitación para dos (f.) *(ah-bee-tah-SYOHN PAH-rah dohs)*

down abajo *(ah-BAH-hoh)*

dozen docena (f.) *(doh-SEH-nah)*

draw dibujar *(dee-boo-HAHR)*

drawer cajón (m.) *(kah-HOHN)*

dress (garment) vestido (m.) *(behs-TEE-doh)*;
to dress vestirse *(behs-TEER-seh)*

dressing gown bata (f.) *(BAH-tah)*

drink (beverage) bebida (f.) *(beh-BEE-dah)*;
to drink beber *(beh-BEHR)*

drinkable potable *(poh-TAH-bleh)*

drive (ride) paseo en coche (m.) *(pah-SEH-oh ehn KOH-cheh)*;
to drive conducir *(kohn-doo-SEER)*

driver chofer (m.) *(cho-FEHR)*

drugstore farmacia (f.) *(fahr-MAH-syah)*

drunk borracho *(boh-RRAH-choh)*

dry seco *(SEH-koh)*;
dry cleaning limpieza en seco (f.) *(leem-PYEH-sah ehn SEH-koh)*

duck pato (m.) *(PAH-toh)*

Dutch holandés(-esa) *(oh-lahn-DEHS)(-DEH-sah)*

dysentery disentería (f.) *(dee-sehn-teh-REE-ah)*

E

e-mail correo electrónico (m.) *(koh-REH-yoh eh-lek-TROH-nee-koh)*

each cada *(KAH-dah)*;
each one cada uno *(KAH-dah OO-noh)*

ear (outer) oreja (f.) *(oh-REH-hah)*;
(inner) ear oído (m.) *(oh-EE-doh)*;
earache dolor de oído (m.) *(doh-LOHR deh oh-EE-doh)*

early temprano *(tehm-PRAH-noh)*

easy fácil *(FAH-seel)*;
take it easy! ¡no se preocupe! *(noh seh preh-oh-KOO-peh!)*

Easter Pascua *(PAHS-kwah)*

eat comer *(koh-MEHR)*

egg huevo (m.) *(WEH-boh)*

eight ocho *(OH-choh)*

eighteen dieciocho *(dyeh-SYOH-choh)*

eighth octavo *(ohk-TAH-boh)*

eighty ochenta *(oh-CHEHN-tah)*

elbow codo (m.) *(KOH-doh)*

electric eléctrico *(eh-LEHK-tree-koh)*

elevator elevador (m.), ascensor (m.) *(eh-leh-bah-DOHR, ah-sehn-SOHR)*

eleven once *(OHN-seh)*

else, nothing nada más *(NAH-dah mahs)*;
  what else? ¿qué más? *(keh mahs?)*

empty vacío *(bah-SEE-oh)*

end (conclusion) fin (m.) *(feen)*;
  to end terminar *(tehr-mee-NAHR)*

endorse endosar *(ehn-doh-SAHR)*

engine motor (m.), máquina (f.) *(moh-TOHR, MAH-kee-nah)*

English inglés(-esa) *(een-GLEHS)(-GLEH-sah)*

enlargement ampliación (f.) *(ahm-plyah-SYOHN)*

enough bastante *(bahs-TAHN-teh)*

evening tarde (f.) *(TAHR-deh)*

every cada *(KAH-dah)*

everybody todo el mundo (m.), todos (m.pl.) *(TOH-doh ehl MOON-doh, TOH-dohs)*

everything todo *(TOH-doh)*

examine examinar *(ehk-sah-mee-NAHR)*

exchange cambiar *(kahm-BYAHR)*;
  exchange office casa de cambio (f.) *(KAH-sah deh KAHM-byoh)*

excursion excursión (f.) *(ehs-koor-SYOHN)*

excuse perdonar *(pehr-doh-NAHR)*

exhaust (automobile) escape (m.) *(ehs-KAH-peh)*

exit salida (f.) *(sah-LEE-dah)*

expect esperar *(ehs-peh-RAHR)*

expensive caro *(KAH-roh)*

express train expreso (m.) *(ehks-PREH-soh)*

extra extra *(EHKS-trah)*

extract (v.) sacar *(sah-KAHR)*

eye ojo (m.) *(OH-hoh)*

eyebrow ceja (f.) *(SEH-hah)*

eyeglasses gafas (f.pl.), anteojos (m.pl.) *(GAH-fahs, anh-teh-OH-hohs)*

eyelash pestaña (f.) *(pehs-TAH-nyah)*

eyelid párpado (m.) *(PAHR-pah-doh)*

F

face (body part) cara (f.) *(KAH-rah)*;
  face powder polvo para la cara (m.) *(POHL-boh PAH-rah lah KAH-rah)*

facial (massage) masaje facial (m.) *(mah-SAH-heh fah-SYAHL)*

fall (autumn) otoño (m.) *(oh-TOH-nyoh)*;
  (injury) caída (f.) *(kah-EE-dah)*;
  to fall caer *(kah-EHR)*

false falso *(FAHL-soh)*

family familia (f.) *(fah-MEE-lyah)*;
  family name (surname) apellido (m.) *(ah-peh-YEE-doh)*

fan (car or electric) ventilador (m.) *(behn-tee-lah-DOHR)*;
(hand) abanico (m.) *(ah-bah-NEE-koh)*
far lejos *(LEH-hohs)*
fare (fee) tarifa (f.) *(tah-REE-fah)*
fast de prisa, pronto *(deh PREE-sah, PROHN-toh)*
faster más de prisa, más rápido *(mahs deh PREE-sah, mahs RRAH-pee-doh)*
father padre (m.), papá (m.) *(PAH-dreh, pah-PAH)*
faucet grifo (m.) *(GREE-foh)*
fear miedo (m.) *(MYEH-doh)*;
to fear tener miedo *(teh-NEHR MYEH-doh)*
February febrero (m.) *(feh-BREH-roh)*
feel (sick, tired, happy, etc.) sentirse *(sehn-TEER-seh)*;
to feel like (doing something) tener ganas de *(teh-NEHR GAH-nahs deh)*
felt (cloth) fieltro (m.) *(FYEHL-troh)*
fender guardafango (m.), guardabarro (m.) *(gwahr-dah-FAHN-goh, gwahr-dah-BAH-rroh)*
festival fiesta (f.) *(FYEHS-tah)*
fever fiebre (f.) *(FYEH-breh)*
few pocos *(POH-kohs)*;
a few unos cuantos *(OO-nohs KWAHN-tohs)*
fifteen quince *(KEEN-seh)*
fifth quinto *(KEEN-toh)*
fig higo (m.) *(EE-goh)*
fill llenar *(yeh-NAHR)*;
(a tooth) empastar *(ehm-pahs-TAHR)*;
filling (tooth) empaste (m.), arreglo (m.) *(ehm-PAHS-teh, ah-RREH-gloh)*
film (movie) película (f.) *(peh-LEE-koo-lah)*

find encontrar, hallar *(ehn-kohn-TRAHR, ah-YAHR)*
fine (good quality) fino, bueno *(FEE-noh, BWEH-noh)*
fine (penalty) multa (f.) *(MOOL-tah)*
finger dedo (m.) *(DEH-doh)*
finish acabar, terminar *(ah-kah-BAHR, tehr-mee-NAHR)*
fire fuego (m.) *(FWEH-goh)*;
(destructive) incendio (m.) *(een-SEHN-dyoh)*
first primero *(pree-MEH-roh)*;
first aid primeros auxilios (m.pl.) *(pree-MEH-rohs owk-SEE-lyohs)*
fish (in water) pez (m.) *(pehs)*;
(when caught) pescado (m.) *(pehs-KAH-doh)*
fit (shoes) calzar *(kahl-SAHR)*;
(clothes) quedar *(KEH-dahr)*
fix componer, reparar, arreglar *(kohm-poh-NEHR, rreh-pah-RAHR, ah-rreh-GLAHR)*;
fixed price precio fijo (m.) *(PREH-syoh FEE-hoh)*
flashlight linterna (f.) *(leen-TEHR-nah)*
flat (level) llano *(YAH-noh)*;
flat tire neumático desinflado (m.), llanta reventada (f./Mex.) *(neoo-MAH-tee-koh deh-seen-FLAH-doh, YAHN-tah rreh-behn-TAH-dah)*
flight (plane) vuelo (m.) *(BWEH-loh)*
floor piso (m.), suelo (m.) *(PEE-soh, SWEH-loh)*
flower flor (f.) *(flohr)*
fog niebla (f.) *(NYEH-blah)*
follow seguir *(seh-GEER)*
foot pie (m.) *(pyeh)*
for (purpose, destination) para *(PAH-rah)*;
(exchange) por *(pohr)*

forbidden prohibido *(pro-ee-BEE-doh)*

forehead frente (f.) *(FREHN-teh)*

foreign extranjero (-a) (m.,f.) *(ehks-trahn-HEH-roh)*; **foreigner** extranjero (-a) (m.,f.) *(ehks-trahn-HEH-roh)(-rah)*

forget olvidar *(ohl-bee-DAHR)*

fork tenedor (m.) *(teh-neh-DOHR)*

form (document) formulario (m.) *(fohr-moo-LAH-ryoh)*

forty cuarenta *(kwah-REHN-tah)*

forward (direction) adelante *(ah-deh-LAHN-teh)*; **to forward (to a farther destination)** reexpedir *(rreh-ehks-peh-DEER)*

fountain fuente (f.) *(FWEHN-teh)*

fountain pen pluma de fuente *(ploo-mah deh FWEHN-teh)*

four cuatro *(KWAH-troh)*

fourteen catorce *(kah-TOHR-seh)*

fourth cuarto *(KWAHR-toh)*

fracture (injury) fractura (f.) *(frahk-TOO-rah)*

free (independent) libre *(LEE-breh)*; **(free of charge)** gratis *(GRAH-tees)*

French francés(-esa) *(frahn-SEHS)(-SEH-sah)*

Friday viernes (m.) *(BYEHR-nehs)*

fried frito *(FREE-toh)*

friend amigo(-a) *(ah-MEE-goh)(-gah)*

from de; desde *(deh; DEHS-deh)*

front (position) delantero *(deh-lahn-TEH-roh)*;

in front (facing the street) que dé a la calle *(keh dah ah lah KAH-yeh)*

fruit fruta (f.) *(FROO-tah)*

fuel pump bomba de combustible (f.) *(BOHM-bah deh kohm-boos-TEE-bleh)*

full lleno *(YEH-noh)*

furnished amueblado *(ah-mweh-BLAH-doh)*

G

game juego (m.) *(HWEH-goh)*; **(sports contest)** partido (m.) *(pahr-TEE-doh)*

garage garaje (m.) *(gah-RAH-heh)*

garden jardín (m.) *(hahr-DEEN)*

garlic ajo (m.) *(AH-hoh)*

garter liga (f.) *(LEE-gah)*

gas (fuel) gasolina (f.) *(gah-soh-LEE-nah)*; **gas station** gasolinera *(gah-soh-lee-NEH-rah)*

gate (railroad station) barrera (f.) *(bah-RREH-rah)*

gauze gasa (f.) *(GAH-sah)*

gear (car) engranaje (m.) *(ehn-grah-NAH-heh)*

gentleman caballero, señor *(kah-bah-YEH-roh, seh-NYOHR)*

German alemán(-ana) *(ah-leh-MAHN)(-MAH-nah)*

get (obtain) conseguir *(kohn-seh-GEER)*; **to get back (recover)** recobrar *(rreh-koh-BRAHR)*; **to get dressed** vestirse *(behs-TEER-se)*; **to get off** bajarse *(bah-HAHR-seh)*; **to get out** irse, salir *(EER-seh, sah-LEER)*; **to get up** levantarse *(leh-bahn-TAHR-seh)*

gift regalo (m.) *(rreh-GAH-loh)*

gin ginebra (f.) *(hee-NEH-brah)*

girl muchacha (f.), chica (f.) *(moo-CHAH-chah, CHEE-kah)*

give dar *(dahr)*;
to give back devolver *(deh-bohl-BEHR)*

glad contento *(kohn-TEHN-toh)*

gladly con mucho gusto *(kohn MOO-choh GOOS-toh)*

glass (drinking) vaso *(BAH-soh)*;
(material) vidrio *(BEE-dryoh)*

glasses (eye) gafas, anteojos *(GAH-fahs, ahn-teh-OH-hohs)*

glove guante *(GWAHN-teh)*

go ir*(eer)*;
to go away irse, marcharse *(EER-seh, mahr-CHAHR-seh)*;
to go shopping ir de compras *(eer deh KOHM-prahs)*;
to go down bajar *(bah-HAHR)*;
to go home ir a casa *(eer ah KAH-sah)*;
to go in entrar *(ehn-TRAHR)*;
to go out salir *(sah-LEER)*;
to go to bed acostarse *(ah-kohs-TAHR-seh)*;
to go up subir *(soo-BEER)*

gold oro *(OH-roh)*

good bueno *(BWEH-noh)*

good-bye! ¡hasta la vista! ¡adiós! *(AHS-tah lah BEES-tah!, ah-DYOHS!)*

goose ganso (m.) *(GAHN-soh)*

grade (on road) cuesta (f.) *(KWEHS-tah)*;
grade crossing paso a nivel (m.) *(PAH-soh ah nee-BEHL)*

gram gramo (m.) *(GRAH-moh)*

grapefruit toronja (f.), pomelo (m.) *(toh-ROHN-hah, poh-MEH-loh)*

grapes uvas (f.pl.) *(OO-bahs)*

grass hierba (f.), zacate (m.) (m./Mex.) *(YEHR-bah, sah-KAH-teh)*

grateful agradecido *(ah-grah-deh-SEE-doh)*

gravy (or sauce) salsa (f.) *(SAHL-sah)*

gray gris *(grees)*

grease (lubricate) engrasar *(ehn-grah-SAHR)*

Greek griego(-a) *(GRYEH-goh)(-gah)*

green verde *(BEHR-deh)*

greeting saludo (m.) *(sah-LOO-doh)*

guide guía (m./f.) *(GEE-ah)*;
guidebook guía (f.) *(GEE-ah)*

gum, chewing chicle (m.) *(CHEE-kleh)*

guy muchacho (m.) *(moo-CHAH-choh)*

H

hair pelo (m.), cabello (m.) *(PEH-loh, kah-BEH-yoh)*;
hair lotion loción para el cabello (f.) *(loh-SYOHN PAH-rah ehl kah-BEH-yoh)*;
hair rinse enjuague (m.) *(ehn-HWAH-geh)*

hairbrush cepillo (m.) *(seh-PEE-yoh)*

haircut corte de pelo (m.) *(KOHR-teh deh PEH-loh)*

hairnet redecilla (f.) *(rreh-deh-SEE-yah)*

hairpin gancho (m.), horquilla (f.) *(GAHN-choh, ohr-KEE-yah)*

half medio (adj.), mitad (f.) *(MEH-dyoh, mee-TAHD)*

halt! ¡alto! *(AHL-toh!)*

ham jamón (m.) *(hah-MOHN)*

hammer martillo (m.) *(mahr-TEE-yoh)*

hand mano (f.) *(MAH-noh)*

handbag cartera (f.), bolsa (f.) *(kahr-TEH-rah, BOHL-sah)*

handkerchief pañuelo (m.) *(pah-NYWEH-loh)*

handmade hecho a mano *(EH-choh ah MAH-noh)*

hanger (clothes) colgador (m.), gancho (m.) *(kohl-gah-DOHR, GAHN-choh)*

happen pasar, suceder, ocurrir, resultar *(pah-SAHR, soo-seh-DEHR, oh-koo-RREER, rreh-sool-TAHR)*

happy feliz *(feh-LEES)*

Happy New Year! ¡Feliz Año Nuevo! *(feh-LEES AH-nyoh NWEH-boh!)*

harbor puerto (m.) *(PWEHR-toh)*

hard (difficult) difícil *(dee-FEE-seel)*;
(tough) duro *(DOO-roh)*

hat sombrero (m.) *(sohm-BREH-roh)*

hat shop sombrerería (f.) *(sohm-breh-reh-REE-ah)*

have tener *(teh-NEHR)*;
to have to deber, tener que *(deh-BEHR, teh-NEHR keh)*

hazelnut avellana (f.) *(ah-beh-YAH-nah)*

he él *(ehl)*

head cabeza (f.) *(kah-BEH-sah)*;
headache dolor de cabeza (f.) *(doh-LOHR deh kah-BEH-sah)*

headlight luz delantera (f.) *(loos deh-lahn-TEH-rah)*

headwaiter jefe de comedor (m.) *(HEH-feh deh koh-meh-DOHR)*

health salud (f.) *(sah-LOOD)*;

health certificate certificado de salud (m.) *(sehr-tee-fee-KAH-doh deh sah-LOOD)*

hear oír *(oh-EER)*;
to hear from tener noticias de *(teh-NEHR noh-TEE-syahs deh)*

heart corazón (m.) *(koh-rah-SOHN)*

heat calor (m.) *(kah-LOHR)*

heaven cielo (m.) *(SYEH-loh)*

heavy pesado *(peh-SAH-doh)*

Hebrew hebreo (-a) *(eh-BREH-oh)(-ah)*

heel (of foot) talón (m.) *(tah-LOHN)*;
(of shoe) tacón (m.) *(tah-KOHN)*

hell infierno (m.) *(een-FYEHR-noh)*

hello! ¡hola! *(OH-lah!)*

help ayudar *(ah-yoo-DAHR)*

here aquí *(ah-KEE)*

high alto *(AHL-toh)*

highway carretera (f.) *(kah-rreh-TEH-rah)*

hip cadera (f.) *(kah-DEH-rah)*

hire contratar *(kohn-trah-TAHR)*

his su *(soo)*;
(w/pl.) sus *(soos)*;
(pron.) suyo *(SOO-yoh)*;
(w/pl.) suyos *(SOO-yohs)*

home casa (f.), hogar (m.) *(KAH-sah, oh-GAHR)*;
to go home ir a casa *(eer ah KAH-sah)*;
to be at home estar en casa *(ehs-TAHR ehn KAH-sah)*

hood (car) capó (m.) *(kah-POH)*

hook gancho (m.) *(GAHN-choh)*

hope esperar *(ehs-peh-RAHR)*

horn (car) bocina (f.) *(boh-SEE-nah)*

hors d'oeuvres entremeses (m.pl.), tapas (f.pl./Sp.), botanas (f.pl./Mex.) *(ehn-treh-MEH-sehs, TAH-pahs, boh-TAH-nahs)*

horse caballo (m.) *(kah-BAH-yoh)*

hospital hospital (m.) *(ohs-pee-TAHL)*

hostel, youth albergue de jóvenes *(ahl-BEHR-geh deh HOH-beh-nehs)*

hostess (plane) azafata (f.) *(ah-sah-FAH-tah)*; **(home)** anfitriona *(ahn-fee-TRYOH-nah)*

hot caliente *(kah-LYEHN-teh)*; **(piquant)** picante *(pee-KAHN-teh)*

hotel hotel (m.) *(oh-TEHL)*

hour hora (f.) *(OH-rah)*

house casa (f.) *(KAH-sah)*

how? ¿cómo? *(KOH-moh?)*; **how far?** ¿a qué distancia? *(ah keh dees-TAHN-syah?)*; **how long?** ¿cuánto tiempo?, ¿desde cuándo? *(KWAHN-toh TYEHM-poh?, DEHS-deh KWAHN-doh?)*; **how many?** ¿cuántos? *(KWAHN-tohs?)*; **how much?** ¿cuánto? *(KWAHN-toh?)*

hundred cien *(SYEHN)*; **a hundred and . . .** ciento . . . *(SYEHN-toh . . .)*

Hungarian húngaro(-a) *(OON-gah-roh)(-rah)*

hungry, to be tener hambre *(teh-NEHR AHM-breh)*

hurry (v.) darse prisa *(DAHR-seh PREE-sah)*; **to be in a hurry** tener prisa *(teh-NEHR PREE-sah)*

hurt (v.) lastimar *(lahs-tee-MAHR)*

husband esposo (m.) *(ehs-POH-soh)*

I

I yo *(yoh)*

ice hielo (m.) *(YEH-loh)*; **ice cream** helado (m.) *(eh-LAH-doh)*; **ice water** agua helada (f.) *(AH-gwah eh-LAH-dah)*

identification identificación (f.) *(ee-dehn-tee-fee-kah-SYOHN)*

if si *(see)*

ignition (car) encendido (m.) *(ehn-sehn-DEE-doh)*

ill enfermo *(ehn-FEHR-moh)*

illness enfermedad (f.) *(ehn-fehr-meh-DAHD)*

imported importado *(eem-pohr-TAH-doh)*

in en *(ehn)*

included incluido *(een-KLUEE-doh)*

indigestion indigestión (f.) *(een-dee-hehs-TYOHN)*

indisposed indispuesto *(een-dees-PWEHS-toh)*

information información (f.) *(een-fohr-mah-SYOHN)*; **information desk** mostrador de información (m.) *(mohs-trah-DOHR deh een-FOHR-mah-SYOHN)*

injection inyección (f.) *(een-yehk-SYOHN)*

ink tinta (f.) *(TEEN-tah)*

inner tube tubo interior (m.) *(TOO-boh een-teh-RYOHR)*

inquire preguntar, averiguar *(preh-goon-TAHR, ah-beh-ree-GWAHR)*

insect insecto (m.) *(een-SEHK-toh)*

insecticide insecticida (m.) *(een-sehk-tee-SEE-dah)*

inside dentro de *(DEHN-troh deh)*

instead of en vez de *(ehn behs deh)*

insurance seguro (m.) *(seh-GOO-roh)*

insure asegurar *(ah-seh-goo-RAHR)*

interest interés (m.) *(een-teh-REHS)*

interpreter intérprete (m./f.) *(een-TEHR-preh-teh)*

intersection intersección (f.) *(een-teer-sehk-SYOHN)*

into en; dentro de *(ehn; DEHN-troh deh)*

introduce presentar *(preh-sehn-TAHR)*

iodine yodo (m.) *(YOH-doh)*

iron (metal) hierro (m.) *(YEH-rroh)*;
(flatiron) plancha (f.) *(PLAHN-chah)*;
to iron planchar *(plahn-CHAHR)*

is es; está *(ehs; ehs-TAH)*

Italian italiano(-a) *(ee-tah-LYAH-noh) (-nah)*

J

jack (auto) gato (m.) *(GAH-toh)*;
to jack up (car) alzar (levantar) con el gato *(ahl-SAHR (leh-bahn-TAHR) kohn ehl GAH-toh)*

jam (fruit) mermelada (f.) *(mehr-meh-LAH-dah)*

January enero (m.) *(eh-NEH-roh)*

Japanese japonés(-esa) *(ha-poh-NEHS)(-NEH-sah)*

jaw quijada (f.) *(kee-HAH-dah)*

jeweler joyero (m.) *(hoh-YEH-roh)*

jewelry joyas (f.pl.) *(HOH-yahs)*;
jewelry store joyería (f.) *(hoh-yeh-REE-ah)*

Jewish judío(-a) *(joo-DEE-oh)(-ah)*

journey viaje (m.) *(BYAH-heh)*

juice jugo (m.), zumo (m./Sp.) *(HOO-goh, SOO-moh)*

July julio (m.) *(HOO-lyoh)*

June junio (m.) *(HOO-nyoh)*

K

keep guardar *(gwahr-DAHR)*;
(to hold on to) quedarse con *(keh-DAHR-seh kohn)*;
to keep right seguir a la derecha *(seh-GEER ah lah deh-REH-chah)*

key llave (f.) *(YAH-beh)*

kilogram kilogramo (m.) *(kee-loh-GRAH-moh)*

kilometer kilómetro (m.) *(kee-LOH-meh-troh)*

kind (nice) bueno, amable *(BWEH-noh, ah-mah-BLEH)*;
(type) clase (f.), género (m.) *(KLAH-seh, HEH-neh-roh)*

kiss beso (m.) *(BEH-soh)*;
to kiss besar *(beh-SAHR)*

kitchen cocina (f.) *(koh-SEE-nah)*

knee rodilla (f.) *(rroh-DEE-yah)*

knife cuchillo (m.) *(koo-CHEE-yoh)*

knock (v.) llamar *(yah-MAHR)*

know (a fact, how) saber *(sah-BEHR)*;
(a person or thing) conocer *(koh-noh-SEHR)*

L

label etiqueta (f.) *(eh-tee-KEH-tah)*

lace encaje (m.) *(ehn-KAH-heh)*

laces (shoe) cordones (m.pl.) *(kohr-DOH-nehs)*

ladies' room baño de señoras (m.) *(BAH-nyoh deh seh-NYOH-rahs)*

lady dama (f.), señora (f.) *(DAH-mah, seh-NYOH-rah)*

lamb cordero (m.) *(kohr-DEH-roh)*

lamp lámpara (f.) *(LAHM-pah-rah)*

land (ground) tierra (f.) *(TYEH-rrah)*;
   to land (by ship) desembarcar *(dehs-ehm-bahr-KAHR)*;
   to land (by plane) aterrizar *(ah-teh-rree-SAHR)*

language idioma (m.), lengua (f.) *(ee-DYOH-mah, LEHN-gwah)*

large grande *(GRAN-deh)*

last último *(OOL-tee-moh)*;
   (preceding) pasado *(pah-SAH-doh)*;
   to last durar *(doo-RAHR)*

late tarde *(TAHR-deh)*

latest, at the a más tardar *(ah mahs tahr-DAHR)*

laugh (v.) reír, reírse *(reh-EER, reh-EER-seh)*

laundry lavandería (f.) *(lah-bahn-deh-REE-ah)*

laundry woman lavandera (f.) *(lah-bahn-DEH-rah)*

lavatory lavabo (m.) *(lah-BAH-boh)*

laxative laxante (m.) *(lahk-SAHN-teh)*

leak escape (m.) *(ehs-KAH-peh)*;

to leak escapar *(ehs-KAH-pahr)*

lean on apoyarse en *(ah-poh-YAHR-seh ehn)*

learn aprender *(ah-prehn-DEHR)*

least, at al (por lo/a lo) menos *(ahl [pohr loh/ah loh] MEH-nos)*

leather cuero (m.) *(KWEH-roh)*

leave (behind) (v.) dejar *(deh-HAHR)*;
   (to depart) salir *(sah-LEER)*

left (direction) izquierda (f.) *(ees-KYEHR-dah)*

leg pierna (f.) *(PYEHR-nah)*

lemon limón (m.) *(lee-MOHN)*

lemonade limonada (f.) *(lee-moh-NAH-dah)*

lend prestar *(prehs-TAHR)*

length largo (m.) *(LAHR-goh)*

lens lente (m.) *(LEHN-teh)*

less menos *(MEH-nohs)*

let dejar, permitir *(deh-HAHR, pehr-mee-TEER)*

letter carta (f.) *(KAHR-tah)*;
   (of the alphabet) letra *(LEH-trah)*

letterbox buzón (m.) *(boo-SOHN)*

lettuce lechuga (f.) *(leh-CHOO-gah)*

library biblioteca (f.) *(bee-blyoh-TEH-kah)*

lie (down) acostarse *(ah-kohs-TAHR-seh)*

life vida (f.) *(BEE-dah)*;
   lifeboat bote salvavidas (m.) *(BOH-teh sahl-bah-BEE-dahs)*;
   lifeguard salvavidas (m./f.) *(sahl-bah-BEE-dahs)*;
   life preserver salvavidas (m.) *(sahl-bah-BEE-dahs)*

lift levantar *(leh-bahn-TAHR)*

light (color) claro *(KLAH-roh)*;
   (brightness) luz (f.) *(loos)*;

197

to light encender *(ehn-sehn-DEHR)*
lighter (cigarette) encendedor (m.) *(ehn-sehn-deh-DOHR)*
lightning relámpago (m.) *(rreh-LAHM-pah-goh)*
like (as) como *(KOH-moh)*;
  to like gustar *(goos-TAHR)*
limit, speed velocidad máxima (f.) *(beh-loh-see-DAHD MAHK-see-mah)*
line línea (f.) *(LEE-neh-ah)*
linen lino (m.); ropa blanca (f.) *(LEE-noh; RROH-pah BLAHN-kah)*
lip labio (m.) *(LAH-byoh)*
lipstick lápiz de labios (m.) *(LAH-pees deh LAH-byohs)*
liqueur licor (m.) *(lee-KOHR)*
liquor bebida alcohólica (f.) *(beh-BEE-dah ahl-KOH-lee-kah)*
list (wine, food) lista (f.) *(LEES-tah)*
listen (listen to) escuchar *(ehs-koo-CHAHR)*
liter litro (m.) *(LEE-troh)*
little pequeño *(peh-KEH-nyoh)*
live (v.) vivir *(bee-BEER)*
liver hígado (m.) *(EE-gah-doh)*
living room sala (f.) *(SAH-lah)*
lobby vestíbulo (m.) *(behs-TEE-boo-loh)*
lobster langosta (f.) *(lahn-GOHS-tah)*
local (train) el tren local (m.) *(ehl trehn loh-KAHL)*;
  local phone call llamada local (f.) *(yah-MAH-dah loh-KAHL)*
lock cerradura (f.) *(seh-rrah-DOO-rah)*
long largo *(LAHR-goh)*;
  how long? ¿cuánto tiempo? *(KWAHN-toh TYEHM-poh?)*

long-distance call llamada de larga distancia (f.) *(yah-MAH-dah deh LAHR-gah dees-TAHN-syah)*
look (look at) mirar *(mee-RAHR)*;
  to look for buscar *(boos-KAHR)*;
  to look out tener cuidado *(teh-NEHR kwee-DAH-doh)*
lose perder *(pehr-DEHR)*
lost-and-found objetos perdidos (m.pl.) *(ohb-HEH-tohs pehr-DEE-dohs)*
lotion loción (f.) *(loh-SYOHN)*
lots of (much) mucho *(MOO-choh)*;
  (many) muchos *(MOO-chohs)*
lounge salón (m.) *(sah-LOHN)*
low bajo *(BAH-hoh)*
lower berth litera baja (f.) *(lee-TEH-rah BAH-hah)*
luck suerte (f.) *(SWEHR-teh)*
lunch almuerzo (m.), comida (f.) *(ahl-MWEHR-soh, koh-MEE-dah)*;
  to lunch almorzar, comer *(ahl-mohr-SAHR, koh-MEHR)*
lung pulmón (m.) *(pool-MOHN)*

M

maid sirvienta (f.) *(seer-BYEHN-tah)*;
  chamber maid camarera (f.) *(kah-mah-REH-rah)*
mail correo (m.) *(koh-RREH-oh)*
mailbox buzón (m.) *(boo-SOHN)*
magazine revista (f.) *(rreh-BEES-tah)*
make hacer *(ah-SEHR)*
man hombre (m.) *(OHM-breh)*

manager director(-a), gerente (m./f.), administrador(-a) *(dee-rehk-TOHR)(-TOH-rah)*, *(heh-REHN-teh)*, *(-ahd-mee-nees-trah-DOHR)(-DOH-rah)*

manicure manicura (f.) *(mah-nee-KOO-rah)*

many muchos *(MOO-chohs)*

map (road) mapa (de carreteras) (m.) *(MAH-pah [deh kah-rreh-TEH-rahs])*

March marzo (m.) *(MAHR-soh)*

market mercado (m.) *(mehr-KAH-doh)*

mashed (food) puré de (m.) *(poo-REH deh)*

mass misa (f.) *(MEE-sah)*; **high mass** misa cantada (f.) *(MEE-sah kahn-TAH-dah)*

massage masaje (m.) *(mah-SAH-heh)*

match fósforo (m.), cerilla (m.) *(FOHS-foh-roh, seh-REE-yah)*

matter, it doesn't no importa *(noh eem-POHR-tah)*; **what's the matter?** ¿qué pasa? *(keh PAH-sah?)*

mattress colchón (m.) *(kohl-CHOHN)*

May mayo (m.) *(MAH-yoh)*

maybe quizás, tal vez *(kee-SAHS, tahl-BEHS)*

meal comida (f.) *(koh-MEE-dah)*

mean (v.) significar, querer decir *(seeg-nee-fee-KAHR, keh-REHR deh-SEER)*

measurement medida (f.) *(meh-DEE-dah)*

meat carne (f.) *(KAHR-neh)*

mechanic mecánico (m.) *(meh-KAH-nee-koh)*

medical médico (adj.) *(MEH-dee-koh)*

medicine medicina (f.) *(meh-dee-SEE-nah)*

meet encontrarse *(ehn-kohn-TRAHR-seh)*; **(for the first time)** conocer *(koh-noh-SEHR)*

melon melón (m.) *(meh-LOHN)*

mend remendar *(rreh-mehn-DAHR)*

men's room baño de señores (m.) *(BAH-nyoh deh seh-NYOH-rehs)*

menu menú (m.) *(meh-NOO)*

merry alegre *(ah-LEH-greh)*

Merry Christmas! ¡Feliz Navidad! *(feh-LEES nah-bee-DAHD!)*

message mensaje (m.) *(mehn-SAH-heh)*

meter (length) metro (m.) *(MEH-troh)*; **taxi meter** taxímetro (m.) *(tahk-SEE-meh-troh)*

Mexican mexicano(-a) *(meh-hee-KAH-noh)(-nah)*

middle (center) medio (m.); centro (m.) *(MEH-dyoh; SEHN-troh)*

midnight medianoche (f.) *(meh-dyah-NOH-cheh)*

mild ligero, suave *(lee-HEH-roh, SWAH-beh)*

milk leche (f.) *(LEH-cheh)*

million millón *(mee-YOHN)*

mind mente (f.) *(MEHN-teh)*; **never mind** no importa *(noh eem-POHR-tah)*

mine mío *(MEE-oh)*; **(w./pl)** míos *(MEE-ohs)*

mineral water agua mineral (f.) *(AH-gwah mee-neh-RAHL)*

minister ministro (m.) *(mee-NEES-troh)*

mirror espejo (m.) *(ehs-PEH-hoh)*

Miss señorita *(seh-nyoh-REE-tah)*

miss (a train, bus, etc.)
perder *(pehr-DEHR)*

missing, to be faltar *(fahl-TAHR)*

mistake error (m.) *(eh-RROHR)*

monastery monasterio (m.)
(moh-nahs-TEH-ryoh)

Monday lunes (m.) *(LOO-nehs)*

money dinero (m.) *(dee-NEH-roh)*;
money order giro (m.)
(HEE-roh)

month mes (m.) *(mehs)*

monument monumento (m.)
(moh-noo-MEHN-toh)

moon luna (f.) *(LOO-nah)*

more más *(mahs)*

morning mañana (f.) *(mah-NYAH-nah)*

mosquito mosquito (m.)
(mohs-KEE-toh)

mother madre (f.) *(MAH-dreh)*

motor motor (m.) *(moh-TOHR)*

mouth boca (f.) *(BOH-kah)*;
mouthwash enjuague
(m.) *(ehn-HWAH-geh)*

move mover *(moh-BEHR)*;
(to change residence) mu-
darse *(moo-DAHR-seh)*

movie película (f.) *(peh-LEE-koo-lah)*

Mr. (Mister) señor *(seh-NYOHR)*

Mrs. señora *(seh-NYOH-rah)*

much mucho *(MOO-choh)*

museum museo (m.) *(moo-SEH-oh)*

mushroom champiñón (m.)
(chahm-pee-NYOHN), seta
(f./Sp.), hongo (m./Mex.)
(SEH-tah, OHN-goh)

must deber, tener que *(deh-BEHR, teh-NEHR keh)*

my mi *(mee)*;
(w/pl.) mis *(mees)*

N

nail (finger, toe) uña (f.)
(OO-nyah)

name nombre (m.) *(NOHM-breh)*;
surname apellido (m.)
(ah-peh-YEE-doh)

napkin servilleta (f.) *(sehr-bee-YEH-tah)*

narrow estrecho, angosto
(ehs-TREH-choh, ahn-GOHS-toh)

nationality nacionalidad (f.)
(nah-syoh-nah-lee-DAHD)

nausea náusea (f.) *(NOW-seh-ah)*

near cerca *(SEHR-kah)*

nearly casi *(KAH-see)*

necessary necesario *(neh-seh-SAH-ryoh)*

neck cuello (m.) *(KWEH-yoh)*

necklace collar (m.) *(koh-YAHR)*

necktie corbata (f.) *(kohr-BAH-tah)*

need (v.) necesitar *(neh-seh-see-TAHR)*

needle aguja (f.) *(ah-GOO-hah)*

nerve nervio (m.) *(NEHR-byoh)*

net (hair) redecilla (f.) *(rreh-deh-SEE-yah)*

never nunca *(NOON-kah)*

new nuevo *(NWEH-boh)*

new year año nuevo (m.)
(AH-nyoh NWEH-boh)

newspaper periódico (m.)
(peh-RYOH-dee-koh)

newsstand quiosco (m.)
(KYOHS-koh)

next próximo, siguiente
(PROHK-see-moh, see-GYEHN-teh)

night noche (f.) *(NOH-cheh)*

night rate tarifa nocturna (f.) *(tah-REE-fah nohk-TOOR-nah)*

nightclub cabaret (m.) *(kah-bah-REHT)*

nightgown camisón (m.) *(kah-mee-SOHN)*

nightlife vida nocturna (f.) *(BEE-dah nohk-TOOR-nah)*

nine nueve *(NWEH-beh)*

nineteen diecinueve *(dyeh-see-NWEH-beh)*

ninety noventa *(no-BEHN-tah)*

ninth noveno *(noh-BEH-noh)*

no no *(noh)*;
  no one nadie, ninguno *(NAH-dyeh, neen-GOO-noh)*

noise ruido (m.) *(RRUEE-doh)*

noisy ruidoso *(rruee-DOH-soh)*

none ninguno *(neen-GOO-noh)*

noon mediodía (m.) *(meh-dyoh-DEE-ah)*

north norte (m.) *(NOHR-teh)*

Norwegian noruego(-a) *(noh-RWEH-goh)(-gah)*

nose nariz (f.) *(nah-REES)*

not no *(noh)*

nothing nada *(NAH-dah)*;
  nothing else nada más *(NAH-dah mahs)*

notice (announcement) aviso (m.) *(ah-BEE-soh)*

novel (book) novela (f.) *(noh-BEH-lah)*

November noviembre (m.) *(noh-BYEM-breh)*

now ahora *(ah-OH-rah)*

number número (m.) *(NOO-meh-roh)*

nurse enfermera (f.) *(ehn-fehr-MEH-rah)*

nut (food) nuez (f.) *(nwehs)*;
  (for a bolt or screw) tuerca (f.) *(TWEHR-kah)*

O

occupied ocupado *(oh-koo-PAH-doh)*

October octubre (m.) *(ohk-TOO-breh)*

oculist oculista (m./f.) *(oh-koo-LEES-tah)*

of de *(deh)*

of course naturalmente, desde luego, por supuesto *(nah-too-rahl-MEHN-teh, DEHS-deh LWEH-goh, pohr soo-PWEHS-toh)*

office oficina (f.) *(oh-fee-SEE-nah)*;
  box office taquilla (f.) *(tah-KEE-yah)*;
  post office correo (m.) *(koh-RREH-oh)*

often a menudo *(ah meh-NOO-doh)*

oil aceite (m.) *(ah-SAY-teh)*

okay, it's está bien. *(ehs-TAH byehn)*

old viejo, anciano *(BYEH-hoh, ahn-SYAH-noh)*;
  how old are you? ¿qué edad tiene? *(keh eh-DAHD TYEH-neh?)*

olive aceituna (f.) *(ah-say-TOO-nah)*

omelet tortilla de huevos (f.) *(tohr-TEE-yah deh WEH-bohs)*

on en, sobre *(ehn, SOH-breh)*

once (one time) una vez *(OO-nah behs)*;
  at once en seguida *(ehn seh-GEE-dah)*

one un (uno, una) *(oon [OO-noh, OO-nah])*;
  one-way (traffic) dirección única *(dee-rehk-SYOHN OO-nee-kah)*

onion cebolla (f.) *(seh-BOH-yah)*

only solamente, sólo *(soh-lah-MEHN-teh, SOH-loh)*

open abierto *(ah-BYEHR-toh)*;
  to open abrir *(ah-BREER)*

opera ópera (f.) *(OH-peh-rah)*

operator (phone) operadora (f.) *(oh-peh-rah-DOH-rah)*

optician óptico (-a) *(OHP-tee-koh)(-kah)*

orange naranja (f.) *(nah-RAHN-hah)*

orangeade naranjada (f.) *(nah-rahn-HAH-dah)*

orchestra (band) orquesta (f.) *(ohr-KEHS-tah)*

order pedido (m.) *(peh-DEE-doh)* encargo (m.) *(ehn-KAHR-goh)*;
  to order pedir *(peh-DEER)*, encargar *(ehn-kahr-GAHR)*

other otro *(OH-troh)*;
  (w/pl.) otros *(OH-trohs)*

ouch! ¡ay! *(ahy!)*

our, ours nuestro *(NWEHS-troh)*;
  (w/pl.) nuestros *(NWEHS-trohs)*

out afuera *(ah-FWEH-rah)*

outlet (electrical) toma de corriente (m.), enchufe (m.) *(toh-mah-koh-RRYEHN-teh, ehn-CHOO-feh)*

outside afuera *(ah-FWEH-rah)*

over (above) encima *(ehn-SEE-mah)*;
  (finished) terminado *(tehr-mee-NAH-doh)*;
  it's over ya terminó *(yah tehr-mee-NOH)*

overcoat abrigo (m.), sobretodo (m.) *(ah-BREE-goh, soh-breh-TOH-doh)*

overdone recocido, muy hecho *(reh-koh-SEE-doh, mwee EH-choh)*

overheat (motor) recalentar *(rreh-kah-lehn-TAHR)*

overnight por la noche *(pohr lah NOH-cheh)*

owe deber *(deh-BEHR)*

own (v.) poseer *(poh-seh-EHR)*

oyster ostra (f.) *(OHS-trah)*

P

pack (luggage) (v.) hacer las maletas *(ah-SEHR lahs mah-LEH-tahs)*

package paquete (m.), bulto (m.) *(pah-KEH-teh, BOOL-toh)*

packet paquete (m.) *(pah-KEH-teh)*

page (of book) página (f.) *(PAH-hee-nah)*;
  to page llamar *(yah-MAHR)*

pain dolor (m.) *(doh-LOHR)*

paint, wet pintura fresca (f.) *(peen-TOO-rah FREHS-kah)*

pair par (m.) *(pahr)*

pajamas pijama (f.) *(pee-HAH-mah)*

palace palacio (m.) *(pah-LAH-syoh)*

panties bragas (f.pl./Sp.), pantaletas (f.pl./Mex.) *(BRAH-gahs, pahn-tah-LEH-tahs)*

pants pantalones (m.pl.) *(pahn-tah-LOH-nehs)*

paper papel (m.) *(pah-PEHL)*;
  toilet paper papel higiénico *(pah-PEHL ee-HYEH-nee-koh)*;
  wrapping paper papel de regalo *(pah-PEHL deh rreh-GAH-loh)*

parcel paquete (m.) *(pah-KEH-teh)*

parcel post paquete postal (m.) *(pah-KEH-teh pohs-TAHL)*

pardon (v.) perdonar *(pehr-doh-NAHR)*

park (v.) estacionar *(ehs-tah-syoh-NAHR)*

parking, no prohibido estacionar *(proh-ee-BEE-doh ehstah-syoh-NAHR)*

part (section) parte (f.) *(PAHR-teh);*

to part hair hacer la raya *(ah-SEHR lah RRAH-yah);*

to separate separar, dividir *(seh-pah-RAHR, dee-bee-DEER)*

parts (spare) piezas de repuesto (f.pl.) *(PYEH-sahs deh rreh-PWEHS-toh)*

pass (permit) permiso (m.) *(pehr-MEE-soh);*

to pass pasar *(pah-SAHR)*

passenger pasajero (-a) (m.,f.) *(pah-sah-HEH-roh)(-rah)*

passport pasaporte (m.) *(pah-sah-POHR-teh)*

past pasado (m.) *(pah-SAH-doh)*

pastry masa (f.); pastel (m.) *(MAH-sah, pah-STEHL)*

pay (v.) pagar *(pah-GAHR)*

pea guisante (m.), chícharo (m.) *(gee-SAHN-teh, CHEE-chah-roh)*

peach melocotón (m.), durazno *(meh-loh-koh-TOHN, doo-RAHS-noh)*

pear pera (f.) *(PEH-rah)*

pedestrian peatón (m.) *(peh-ah-TOHN)*

pen pluma (f.) *(PLOO-mah)*

pencil lápiz (m.) *(LAH-pees)*

people gente (f.) *(HEHN-teh)*

pepper, black pimienta negra (f.) *(pee-MYEHN-tah NEH-grah)*

peppers pimientos (m.pl.), chiles (m.pl./Mex.) *(pee-MYEHN-tohs, CHEE-lehs)*

performance función (m.) *(foon-SYOHN)*

perfume perfume (m.) *(pehr-FOO-meh)*

perhaps quizás, tal vez *(kee-SAHS, tahl BEHS)*

permanent (wave) permanente (f.) *(pehr-mah-NEHN-teh)*

permit (pass) permiso (m.) *(pehr-MEE-soh);*

to permit permitir *(pehr-mee-TEER)*

Persian persa (m./f.) *(PEHR-sah)*

personal personal *(pehr-soh-NAHL)*

phone teléfono (m.) *(teh-LEH-foh-noh);*

to phone telefonear *(teh-leh-foh-neh-AHR)*

photograph fotografía (f.) *(foh-toh-grah-FEE-ah);*

to take a photo tomar una foto *(toh-MAHR OO-nah FOH-toh)*

pickle encurtido (m.) *(ehn-koor-TEE-doh)*

picnic picnic (m.) *(HEE-rah, PEEK-neek)*

picture (art) cuadro (m.), pintura (f.) *(KWAH-droh, peen-TOO-rah);*

motion picture película (f.) *(peh-LEE-koo-lah)*

pie tarta (f.), pastel (m.) *(TAHR-tah, pahs-TEHL)*

piece pedazo (m.) *(peh-DAH-soh)*

pier muelle (f.) *(MWEH-yeh)*

pill píldora (f.) *(PEEL-doh-rah)*

pillow almohada (f.) *(ahl-moh-AH-dah)*

pillowcase funda (f.) *(FOON-dah)*

pilot piloto (m.) *(pee-LOH-toh)*

pin alfiler (m.) *(ahl-fee-LEHR);*

safety pin imperdible (m.) *(eem-pehr-DEE-bleh)*

pineapple piña (f.), ananá (m.) *(PEE-nyah, ah-nah-NAH)*

pink rosado *(rroh-SAH-doh)*

pipe (smoking) pipa (f.)
(PEE-pah)

pitcher jarro (m.), cántaro
(m.) *(HAH-rroh, KAHN-tah-roh)*

pity!, what a ¡qué lástima!
(keh-LAHS-tee-mah!)

place (site) sitio (m.) *(SEE-tyoh)*;
to place colocar *(koh-loh-KAHR)*

plane (air) avión (m.) *(ah-BYOHN)*

plate plato (m.) *(PLAH-toh)*

platform andén (m.),
plataforma (f.) *(ahn-DEHN, plah-tah-FOHR-mah)*

play drama (m.) *(DRAH-mah)*;
to play (a game) jugar
(hoo-GAHR);
to play (an instrument)
tocar *(toh-KAHR)*

playing cards naipes (m.pl.)
(NAH-ee-pehs)

pleasant agradable *(ah-grah-DAH-bleh)*;
(person) simpático *(seem-PAH-tee-koh)*

please por favor, haga el
favor de *(pohr fah-BOHR, AH-gah ehl fah-BOHR deh)*

pleasure gusto (m.), placer
(m.) *(GOOS-toh, plah-SEHR)*

pliers alicates (m.pl.) *(ah-lee-KAH-tehs)*

plug (spark) bujía (f.) *(boo-HEE-ah)*

plum ciruela (f.) *(see-RWEH-lah)*

p.m. de la tarde, de la
noche *(deh lah TAHR-deh, deh lah NOH-cheh)*

pocket bolsillo (m.) *(bohl-SEE-yoh)*

pocketbook bolso (f.), bi-
lletero(-a), cartera *(BOHL-soh, bee-yeh-TEH-roh[-rah], kahr-TEH-rah)*

point (place) punto (m.)
(POON-toh)

poison veneno (m.) *(beh-NEH-noh)*

police policía (f.) *(poh-lee-SEE-ah)*

policeman policía (m.),
agente de policía (m.)
(poh-lee-SEE-ah, ah-HEHN-teh deh poh-lee-SEE-ah)

Polish polaco(-a) *(poh-LAH-koh)(-kah)*

polish (nail) esmalte (m.)
(ehs-MAHL-teh);
polish remover acetona
(f.) *(ah-seh-TOH-nah)*

polite cortés *(kohr-TEHS)*

politeness cortesía (f.) *(kohr-teh-SEE-ah)*

poor pobre *(POH-breh)*

pork carne de cerdo (f.)
(KAHR-neh deh SEHR-doh)

port (harbor) puerto (m.)
(PWEHR-toh)

porter mozo (m.) *(MOH-soh)*

portion porción (f.), ración
(f.) *(pohr-SYOHN, rrah-SYOHN)*

Portuguese portugués(-esa)
(pohr-too-GEHS)(-GEH-sah)

possible posible *(poh-SEE-bleh)*

postcard tarjeta postal (f.)
(tar-HEH-tah pohs-TAHL)

postage porte (m.), franqueo (m.) *(POHR-teh, frahn-KEH-oh)*

potato papa (f.), patata
(f./Sp.) *(PAH-pah, pah-TAH-tah)*

pour (rain) llover a cántaros
(yoh-BEHR ah KAHN-tah-rohs)

powder polvo (m.) *(POHL-boh)*;
face powder polvo para
la cara (m.) *(POHL-boh PAH-rah lah KAH-rah)*

prefer preferir *(pre-feh-REER)*

204

prepare preparar *(preh-pah-RAHR)*

prescription receta (f.) *(rreh-SEH-tah)*

press (iron) planchar *(plahn-CHAHR)*

pretty bonito, lindo *(boh-NEE-toh, LEEN-doh)*

price precio (m.) *(PREH-syoh)*

priest cura (m.), sacerdote (m.) *(KOO-rah, sah-sehr-DOH-teh)*

print (photo) copia (f.) *(KOH-pyah)*

program programa (m.) *(proh-GRAH-mah)*

promise (v.) prometer *(proh-meh-TEHR)*

Protestant protestante (m./f.) *(proh-tehs-TAHN-teh)*

prune ciruela pasa (f.) *(see-RWEH-lah PAH-sah)*

pudding budín (m.) *(boo-DEEN)*

pump (fuel) bomba de combustible (f.) *(BOHM-bah deh kohm-boos-TEE-bleh)*

puncture (tire) pinchazo (m.) *(peen-CHAH-soh)*

purchase (item) compra (f.) *(KOHM-prah)*

purple morado *(moh-RAH-doh)*

purse bolso (m.), cartera (f.) *(BOHL-soh, kahr-TEH-rah)*

purser contador de barco *(kohn-tah-DOHR deh BAHR-koh)*

push (v.) empujar *(ehm-poo-HAHR)*

put poner *(poh-NEHR)*;
put in meter en *(meh-TEHR ehn)*;
put (clothes) on ponerse *(poh-NEHR-seh)*

Q

quarter (fraction) cuarto (m.) *(KWAHR-toh)*

quick; quickly pronto *(PROHN-toh)*

quiet quieto, tranquilo *(KYEH-toh, trahn-KEE-loh)*

quinine quinina (f.) *(kee-NEE-nah)*

quite bastante *(bahs-TAHN-teh)*

R

rabbi rabino (m.) *(rrah-BEE-noh)*

rabbit conejo (m.) *(koh-NEH-hoh)*

rack (train or bus) rejilla (f.) *(rreh-HEE-yah)*

radiator radiador (m.) *(rrah-dyah-DOHR)*

radio radio (m.) *(RRAH-dyoh)*

radish rábano (m.) *(RRAH-bah-noh)*

railroad ferrocarril (m.) *(feh-rroh-kah-RREEL)*

rain lluvia (f.) *(YOO-byah)*

raincoat impermeable (m.) *(eem-pehr-meh-AH-bleh)*

rare (meat) poco asada *(POH-koh ah-SAH-dah)*

rate of exchange tipo de cambio *(TEE-poh deh KAHM-byoh)*

rather (prefer) preferir *(preh-feh-REER)*

razor navaja de afeitar (f.) *(nah-BAH-hah deh ah-fay-TAHR)*

razor blade hoja de afeitar (f.) *(oh-HA-yah deh ah-fay-TAHR)*

read leer *(leh-EHR)*

ready, to be estar listo *(ehs-TAHR LEES-toh)*

ENGLISH–SPANISH

real verdadero *(behr-dah-DEH-roh)*
really de veras, de verdad *(deh BEH-rahs, deh behr-DAHD)*
reasonable razonable *(rrah-soh-NAH-bleh)*
receipt recibo (m.) *(rreh-SEE-boh)*
receiver (on package) destinatario (m.) *(dehs-tee-nah-TAH-ryoh)*
recommend recomendar *(rreh-koh-mehn-DAHR)*
record (phonograph) disco (m.) *(DEES-koh)*
recover (get back) recobrar *(rreh-koh-BRAHR);*
(health) reponerse *(rreh-poh-NEHR-seh)*
red rojo *(RROH-hoh)*
refund (payment) reembolso (m.) *(rreh-ehm-BOHL-soh);*
to refund reembolsar *(rreh-ehm-bohl-SAHR)*
refuse (v.) rehusar, rechazar *(rreh-oo-SAHR, rreh-chah-SAHR)*
regards recuerdos (m.pl.), saludos (m.pl.) *(rreh-KWEHR-dohs, sah-LOO-dohs)*
registered (mail) certificado *(sehr-tee-fee-KAH-doh)*
registry window ventanilla de los certificados (f.) *(behn-tah-NEE-yah deh lohs sehr-tee-fee-KAH-dohs)*
regular (ordinary) ordinario *(ohr-dee-NAH-ryoh)*
remedy remedio (m.) *(rreh-MEH-dyoh)*
remember recordar, acordarse de *(rreh-kohr-DAHR, ah-kohr-DAHR-seh deh)*
rent alquiler (m.) *(ahl-kee-LEHR);*
to rent alquilar *(ahl-kee-LAHR)*

repair reparación (f.) *(rreh-pah-rah-SYOHN)*
repeat repetir *(rreh-peh-TEER)*
reply (v.) responder *(rrehs-pohn-DEHR)*
reservation reservación (f.), reserva (f./Sp.) *(rreh-sehr-bah-SYOHN, rreh-SEHR-bah)*
reserve reservar *(rreh-sehr-BAHR)*
reserved seat asiento reservado (m.) *(ah-SYEHN-toh rreh-sehr-BAH-doh)*
rest (v.) descansar *(dehs-kahn-SAHR)*
restroom lavabo (m.), retrete (m.) *(lah-BAH-boh, rreh-TREH-teh)*
restaurant restaurante (m.) *(rrehs-tow-RAHN-teh)*
return (give back) devolver *(deh-bohl-BEHR);*
(go back) volver *(bohl-BEHR)*
rib costilla (f.) *(kohs-TEE-yah)*
ribbon cinta (f.) *(SEEN-tah)*
rice arroz (m.) *(ah-RROHS)*
rich rico *(RREE-koh)*
ride paseo (m.) *(pah-SEH-oh);*
to ride (on a car, train, etc.) pasear en, ir en *(pah-seh-AHR ehn, EER ehn)*
right (direction) derecha (f.) *(deh-REH-chah);*
to be right tener razón *(teh-NEHR rrah-SOHN);*
all right está bien *(ehs-TAH byehn);*
right now ahora mismo *(ah-OH-rah MEES-moh)*
ring (on finger) anillo, sortija *(ah-NEE-yoh, sohr-TEE-hah)*
rinse enjuague (m.) *(ehn-HWAH-geh)*
river río (m.) *(RREE-oh)*
road camino (m.) *(kah-MEE-noh);*

206

(highway) carretera (f.)
(kah-rreh-TEH-rah);
road map mapa de ca-
rreteras (m.) *(MAH-pah de
kah-rreh-TEH-rahs)*
roast asado (m.) *(ah-SAH-
doh);*
roast beef rosbif (m.)
(rohs-BEEF)
rob robar *(rroh-BAHR)*
robe bata (f.) *(BAH-tah)*
roll (bread) panecillo (m.),
bolillo (m./Mex.) *(pah-neh-
SEE-yoh, boh-LEE-yoh);*
(film) rollo (m.) *(RROH-yoh)*
room cuarto (m.), alcoba
(f.), habitación (f.)
*(KWAHR-toh, ahl-KOH-bah, ah-
bee-tah-SYOHN)*
root raíz (f.) *(rrah-EES)*
rope cuerda (f.) *(KWER-dah)*
rouge colorete (m.) *(koh-loh-
REH-teh)*
round redondo *(rreh-DOHN-
doh);*
round trip viaje de ida y
vuelta (m.) *(BYAH-heh deh EE-
dah ee BWEHL-tah)*
row (theatre) fila (f.) *(FEE-
lah)*
rubber caucho (m.) *(KOW-
choh);*
rubber eraser goma de
borrar (f.) *(GOH-mah deh
boh-RRAHR);*
rubber band elástico (m.)
(eh-LAHS-tee-koh)
rug alfombra (f.) *(ahl-FOHM-
brah)*
Rumanian rumano(-a) *(rroo-
MAH-noh)(-nah)*
rum ron (m.) *(rrohn)*
run correr *(koh-RREHR)*
running water agua corriente (f.) *(AH-gwah koh-
RRYEHN-teh)*
runway (plane) pista (f.)
(PEES-tah)

Russian ruso(-a) *(RROO-soh)(-
sah)*

S

salad ensalada (f.) *(ehn-sah-
LAH-dah)*
sale venta (f.), oferta
(f./Mex.) *(BEHN-tah, oh-
FEHR-tah)*
salon (beauty) salón de
belleza (m.) *(sah-LOHN deh
beh-YEH-sah)*
saloon cantina (f.) *(kahn-TEE-
nah)*
salt sal (f.) *(sahl)*
same mismo *(MEES-moh)*
sand arena (f.) *(ah-REH-nah)*
sandwich bocadillo (m.)
(boh-kah-DEE-yoh);
(in a roll) torta (f./Mex.)
(TOHR-tah)
sardine sardina (f.) *(sahr-
DEE-nah)*
Saturday sábado (m.) *(SAH-
bah-doh)*
sauce salsa (f.) *(SAHL-sah)*
saucer platillo (m.) *(plah-TEE-
yoh)*
sausage salchicha (f.),
chorizo (m.) *(sahl-CHEE-
chah, choh-REE-soh)*
say decir *(deh-SEER)*
scarf bufanda (f.) *(boo-
FAHN-dah)*
school escuela (f.) *(ehs-
KWEH-lah)*
scissors tijeras (f.pl.) *(tee-
HEH-rahs)*
screwdriver destornillador
(m.) *(dehs-tohr-nee-yah-DOHR)*
sea mar (m.) *(mahr)*
seafood mariscos (m.pl.)
(mah-REES-kohs)
seasickness mareo (m.)
(mah-REH-oh)

season estación (f.) *(ehs-tah-SYOHN)*

seasoned sazonado *(sah-soh-NAH-doh)*

seat asiento (m.) *(ah-SYEHN-toh)*

seat (v.) sentarse *(sehn-TAHR-seh)*

second segundo *(seh-GOON-doh)*

secretary secretario(-a) *(seh-kreh-TAH-ryoh)(-ryah)*

see ver *(behr)*

seem parecer *(pah-reh-SEHR)*

select escoger *(ehs-koh-HEHR)*

sell vender *(behn-DEHR)*

send mandar, enviar *(mahn-DAHR, ehn-BYAHR)*

sender (on mail) remitente (m.) *(rreh-mee-TEHN-teh)*

September septiembre (m.) *(sehp-TYEHM-breh)*

serve servir *(sehr-BEER)*

service servicio (m.) *(sehr-BEE-syoh)*;
  at your service a sus órdenes *(ah soos OHR-deh-nehs)*

set (hair) (v.) arreglarse *(ah-rreh-GLAHR-seh)*

seven siete *(SYEH-teh)*

seventeen diecisiete *(dye-see-SYEH-teh)*

seventh séptimo *(SEPH-tee-moh)*

seventy setenta *(seh-TEHN-tah)*

several varios *(BAH-ryohs)*

shade, in the en la sombra *(ehn lah SOHM-brah)*

shampoo champú (m.) *(chahm-POO)*

shave (v.) afeitar *(ah-fay-TAHR)*

shawl chal (m.) *(chahl)*

she ella *(EH-yah)*

sheet sábana (f.) *(SAH-bah-nah)*

shine (v.) (shoes) lustrar *(loos-TRAHR)*;
  (stars) brillar *(bree-YAHR)*

ship buque (m.) *(BOO-keh)*;
  to ship enviar *(ehn-BYAHR)*

shirt camisa (f.) *(kah-MEE-sah)*

shoe zapato (m.) *(sah-PAH-toh)*

shoelaces cordones de zapato (m.pl.) *(kohr-DOH-nehs deh sah-PAH-tohs)*

shop tienda (f.) *(TYEHN-dah)*

shopping, to go ir de compras *(eer deh KOHM-prahs)*

short corto *(KOHR-toh)*

shorts (underwear) calzoncillos (m.pl.) *(kahl-sohn-SEE-yohs)*

shoulder hombro (m.) *(OHM-broh)*;
  (on road) borde (m.) *(BOHR-deh)*

show (art) exposición (f.) *(ehks-poh-see-SYOHN)*;
  (performance) función (f.) *(foon-SYOHN)*;
  to show mostrar *(mohs-TRAHR)*

shower ducha (f.), regadera (f./Mex.) *(DOO-cha, rreh-gah-DEH-rah)*

shrimp gamba (f./Sp.), camarón (m.) *(GAHM-bah, kah-mah-ROHN)*

shrine santuario (m.) *(sahn-TWAH-ryah)*

shut (v.) cerrar *(seh-RRAHR)*

sick enfermo *(ehn-FEHR-moh)*

sickness enfermedad (f.) *(ehn-fehr-meh-DAHD)*

side lado (m.) *(LAH-doh)*

sidewalk acera (f.) *(ah-SEH-rah)*

sight-see hacer turismo, visitar *(ah-SEHR too-REES-moh, bee-see-TAHR)*

sign (display) letrero (m.) *(leh-TREH-roh)*;
  to sign firmar *(feer-MAHR)*
silk seda (f.) *(SEH-dah)*
silver plata (f.) *(PLAH-tah)*
since desde *(DEHS-deh)*
sing cantar *(kahn-TAHR)*
single room habitación para uno (f.) *(ah-bee-tah-SYOHN PAH-rah OO-noh)*
sink (basin) lavabo (m.) *(lah-BAH-boh)*
sir señor (m.) *(seh-NYOHR)*
sister hermana (f.) *(ehr-MAH-nah)*
sit (down) (v.) sentarse *(sehn-TAHR-seh)*
sixteen dieciséis *(dyeh-see-SAYS)*
sixth sexto *(SEHKS-toh)*
sixty sesenta *(seh-SEHN-tah)*
size tamaño (m.) *(tah-MAH-nyoh)*
skin piel (f.) *(pyehl)*
skirt falda (f.) *(FAHL-dah)*
sky cielo (m.) *(SYEH-loh)*
sleep (v.) dormir *(dohr-MEER)*
sleeping car coche-cama (m.) *(KOH-chech KAH-mah)*
sleepy, to be tener sueño *(teh-NEHR SWEH-nyoh)*
slip (garment) combinación (f.) *(kohm-bee-nah-SYOHN)*
slippers zapatillas (f.pl.) *(sah-pah-TEE-yahs)*
slow lento *(LEHN-toh)*;
  the watch is slow el reloj está atrasado *(ehl rreh-LOH ehs-TAH ah-trah-SAH-doh)*
slowly despacio, lentamente *(dehs-PAH-syoh, lehn-tah-MEHN-teh)*
small pequeño *(peh-KEH-nyoh)*
smoke (v.) fumar *(foo-MAHR)*
smoking car coche fumador (m.) *(KOH-cheh foo-mah-DOHR)*

snow nieve (f.) *(NYEH-beh)*;
  to snow nevar *(neh-BAHR)*
so así *(ah-SEE)*
soap jabón (m.) *(hah-BOHN)*
soccer fútbol (m.) *(FOOT-bohl)*
socks calcetines (m.pl.) *(kahl-seh-TEE-nehs)*
sofa sofá (m.) *(soh-FAH)*
soft blando, suave *(BLAHN-doh, SWAH-beh)*
soft drink refresco (m.) *(rreh-FREHS-koh)*
sole (shoe) suela (f.) *(SWEH-lah)*
some algún *(ahl-GOON)*;
  (w/pl.) algunos *(ahl-GOO-nohs)*
someone alguien *(AHL-gyehn)*
something algo *(AHL-goh)*
sometimes a veces, algunas veces *(ah BEH-sehs, ahl-GOO-nahs BEH-sehs)*
son hijo (m.) *(EE-hoh)*
song canción (f.) *(kahn-SYOHN)*
soon pronto *(PROHN-toh)*
sore throat dolor de garganta (m.) *(doh-LOHR deh gohr-GAHN-tah)*
sorry, to be sentirlo *(sehn-TEER-loh)*;
  I am sorry lo siento *(loh SYEHN-toh)*
soup sopa (f.) *(SOH-pah)*
sour agrio *(AH-gryoh)*
south sur (m.), sud (m.) *(soor, sood)*
souvenir recuerdo (m.) *(rreh-KWEHR-doh)*
Spanish español(-a) *(ehs-pah-NYOHL)(-NYOH-lah)*
spare tire neumático de repuesto (m.) *(neoo-MAH-tee-koh deh rreh-PWEHS-toh)*
spark plug bujía (f.) *(boo-HEE-ah)*

sparkling wine vino espumante (m.) *(BEE-noh ehs-poo-MAHN-teh)*

speak hablar *(ah-BLAHR)*

special especial *(ehs-peh-SYAHL)*

speed limit velocidad máxima (f.) *(beh-loh-see-DAHD MAHK-see-mah)*

spend (money) gastar *(gahs-TAHR);*
  spend time pasar tiempo *(pah-SAHR TYEHM-poh)*

spinach espinaca (f.) *(ehs-pee-NAH-kah)*

spoon cuchara (f.) *(koo-CHAH-rah)*

sprain torcedura (f.) *(tohr-seh-DOO-rah)*

spring (mechanical) resorte (m.) *(rreh-SOHR-teh);*
  (season) primavera (f.) *(pree-mah-BEH-rah)*

square (adj.) cuadrado *(kwah-DRAH-doh);*
  main square plaza principal (f.), zócalo (m./Mex.) *(PLAH-sah preen-see-PAHL, SOH-kah-loh)*

stairs escalera (f.) *(ehs-kah-LEH-rah)*

stamp (postage) sello (m.), estampilla (f./Mex.) *(SEH-yoh, ehs-tahm-PEE-yah)*

stand (v.) estar de pie *(ehs-TAHR deh pyeh);*
  stand up ponerse de pie *(poh-NEHR-seh deh pyeh);*
  stand in line hacer cola *(ha-SEHR KOH-lah)*

star estrella (f.) *(ehs-TREH-yah)*

starch (laundry) almidón (m.) *(ahl-mee-DOHN)*

start (v.) empezar, comenzar, principiar *(ehm-peh-SAHR, koh-mehn-SAHR, preen-see-PYAHR)*

stateroom camarote (m.) *(kah-mah-ROH-teh)*

station (gasoline) gasolinera (f.) *(gah-soh-lee-NEH-rah);*
  (railroad) estación de tren (f.) *(ehs-tah-SYOHN deh trehn);*
  (bus) terminal de autobúses (f.) *(tehr-mee-NAHL deh ow-toh-BOO-sehs)*

stay (a visit) estancia (f.) *(ehs-TAHN-syah);*
  to stay quedarse *(keh-DAHR-seh)*

steak bistec (m.) *(bees-TEHK)*

steal (v.) robar *(rroh-BAHR)*

steel acero (m.) *(ah-SEH-roh)*

steering wheel volante (m.) *(boh-LAHN-teh)*

stew guiso (m.) *(gee-SOH)*

stewardess (airplane) azafata (f.) *(ah-sah-FAH-tah)*

stockings medias (f.pl.) *(MEH-dyahs)*

stomach estómago (m.) *(ehs-TOH-mah-goh);*
  stomachache dolor de estómago (m.) *(doh-LOHR deh ehs-TOH-mah-goh)*

stop (bus) parada (f.) *(pah-RAH-dah)*

stoplight semáforo (m.) *(seh-MAH-foh-roh)*

store tienda (f.) *(TYEHN-dah)*

straight derecho *(deh-REH-choh)*

strap correa (f.) *(koh-RREH-ah)*

straw paja (f.) *(PAH-hah)*

strawberry fresa (f.) *(FREH-sah)*

street calle (f.) *(KAH-yeh)*

streetcar tranvía (m.) *(trahn-BEE-ah)*

string cuerda (f.) *(KWEHR-dah)*

string (green) beans judías verdes (f.), ejotes (m./Mex.) *(hoo-DEE-ahs BEHR-dehs, eh-HOH-tehs)*

strong fuerte *(FWEHR-teh)*

style estilo (m.) *(ehs-TEE-loh)*; **(fashion)** moda (f.) *(MOH-dah)*

sudden repentino *(rreh-pehn-TEE-noh)*

suddenly de repente *(deh rreh-PEHN-teh)*

sugar azúcar (m.) *(ah-SOO-kahr)*

suit traje (m.) *(TRAH-heh)*

suitcase maleta (f.), valija (f.) *(mah-LEH-tah, bah-LEE-hah)*

summer verano (m.) *(beh-RAH-noh)*

sun sol (m.) *(sohl)*

sunglasses gafas (para sol) (f.pl.) *(GAH-fahs (PAH-rah sohl))*

Sunday domingo (m.) *(doh-MEEN-goh)*

sunny soleado *(soh-leh-AH-doh)*

supper cena (f.) *(SEH-nah)*

surgeon cirujano (m.) *(see-roo-HAN-noh)*

sweater suéter (m.) *(SWEH-tehr)*

Swedish sueco(-a) *(SWEH-koh)(-kah)*

sweet dulce *(DOOL-seh)*

swell (v.) hinchar *(een-CHAHR)*

swim nadar *(nah-DAHR)*

swimming pool piscina (f.), alberca (f./Mex.) *(pees-SEE-nah, ahl-BEHR-kah)*

Swiss suizo(-a) *(SUEE-soh) (-sah)*

switch (electric) interruptor (m.) *(een-teh-rroop-TOHR)*

swollen hinchado, infla-mado *(een-CHAH-doh, een-flah-MAH-doh)*

synagogue sinagoga (f.) *(see-nah-GOH-gah)*

syrup (cough) jarabe para la tos (m.) *(hah-RAH-beh PAH-rah lah tohs)*

T

table mesa (f.) *(MEH-sah)*

tablecloth mantel (m.) *(mahn-TEHL)*

tablespoon cuchara (f.) *(koo-CHAH-rah)*

tablespoonful cucharada (f.) *(koo-chah-RAH-dah)*

tablet pastilla (f.), compri-mido (m.) *(pahs-TEE-yah)(kohm-pree-MEE-doh)*

taillight (car) luz trasera (f.) *(loos trah-SEH-rah)*

tailor sastre (m.) *(SAHS-treh)*

take (carry) llevar *(yeh-BAHR)*; **(a person)** conducir *(kohn-doo-SEER)*; **(a thing)** tomar *(toh-MAHR)*; **takes time** toma tiempo *(TOH-mah TYEHM-poh)*

take off (a garment) quitarse *(kee-TAHR-seh)*

taken (occupied) ocupado *(oh-koo-PAH-doh)*

talcum powder talco (m.) *(TAHl-koh)*

tall alto *(AHL-toh)*

tan (color) color canela (m.) *(koh-LOHR kah-NEH-lah)*

tangerine mandarina (f.) *(mahn-dah-REE-nah)*

tank tanque (m.) *(TAHN-keh)*

tap grifo (m.) *(GREE-foh)*

tape (adhesive) es-paradrapo (m.) *(ehs-pah-rah-DRAH-poh)*

tasty sabroso, rico *(sah-BROH-soh, RREE-koh)*

tax impuesto (m.) *(eem-PWEHS-toh)*

tea té (m.) *(teh)*

teaspoon cucharita (f.), cucharilla (f.) *(koo-chah-REE-tah, koo-chah-REE-yah)*

teaspoonful cucharadita (f.) *(koo-char-rah-DEE-tah)*

telegram telegrama (m.) *(teh-leh-GRAH-mah)*

telegraph (v.) telegrafiar *(tel-leh-GRAH-mah)*

telegraph (n.) telégrafo *(teh-LEH-grah-foh)*

telephone teléfono (m.) *(teh-LEH-foh-noh)*;

    to telephone telefonear *(teh-leh-foh-neh-AHR)*

tell decir *(deh-SEER)*

teller (bank) cajero (-a) *(kah-HEH-roh)(-rah)*

temporarily temporalmente *(tehm-poh-rahl-MEHN-teh)*

ten diez *(dyehs)*

tenth décimo *(deh-see-moh)*

terminal terminal (f.) *(tehr-mee-NAHL)*

thank agradecer, dar las gracias *(ah-grah-deh-SEHR, dahr lahs GRAH-syahs)*

thank you! ¡gracias! *(GRAH-syahs!)*

that (adj.) ese (esa), aquel (aquella) *(EH-seh [EH-sah], ah-KEHL [ah-KEH-yah])*;
    (pron.) eso *(EH-soh)*;
    (conj.) que *(keh)*

the el (la); los (las) *(ehl [lah], lohs [lahs])*

theater teatro (m.) *(teh-AH-troh)*

their su *(soo)*;
    (w/pl.) sus *(soos)*

there ahí, allí *(ah-EE, ah-YEE)*;
    there is; there are hay (AHY)

thermometer termómetro (m.) *(tehr-MOH-meh-troh)*

these estos (estas) *(EHS-tohs [EHS-tahs])*

they ellos (ellas) *(EH-yohs [EH-yahs])*

thick espeso, denso, grueso *(ehs-PEH-soh, DEHN-soh, GRWEH-soh)*

thief ladrón (m.) *(lah-DROHN)*

thigh muslo (m.) *(MOOS-loh)*

thing cosa (f.) *(KOH-sah)*

think pensar *(pehn-SAHR)*

third tercero *(tehr-SEH-roh)*

thirsty, to be tener sed *(teh-NEHR sehd)*

thirteen trece *(TREH-seh)*

thirty treinta *(TRAYN-tah)*

this este (esta, esto) *(EHS-teh [EHS-tah, EHS-toh])*

those esos (esas), aquellos (aquellas) *(EH-sohs [EH-sahs], ah-KEH-yohs [ah-KEH-yahs])*

thousand mil *(meel)*

thread hilo (m.) *(EE-loh)*

three tres *(trehs)*

throat garganta (f.) *(gahr-GAHN-tah)*

through por, a través de *(pohr, a trah-BEHS deh)*

thumb pulgar (m.) *(pool-GAHR)*

thunder trueno (m.) *(TRWEH-noh)*;
    to thunder tronar *(troh-NAHR)*

Thursday jueves (m.) *(HWEH-behs)*

ticket billete (m.), entrada (f.) *(bee-YEH-teh, ehn-TRAH-dah)*
    ticket window ventanilla (f.) *(behn-tah-NEE-yah)*

tie (neck-) corbata (f.) *(kohr-BAH-tah)*

tighten apretar *(ah-preh-TAHR)*

till hasta (que) *(ahs-tah [keh])*

time tiempo (m.) *(TYEHM-poh)*;
  on time a tiempo *(ah TYEHM-poh)*;
  at what time? ¿a qué hora? *(ah keh OH-rah?)*
timetable horario (m.) *(oh-RAH-ryoh)*
tint (hair) (v.) teñir *(teh-NYEER)*
tip (gratuity) propina (f.) *(proh-PEE-nah)*
tire (car) llanta (f.), neumático (m.) *(YAYH-tah, neoo-MAH-tee-koh)*
tired, to be cansado (estar) *(kahn-SAH-doh [ehs-TAHR])*
tissue paper papel de seda (m.) *(pah-PEHL deh SEH-doh)*
to a; por; para *(ah; pohr; PAH-rah)*
toast (bread) tostada (f.) *(tohs-TAH-dah)*;
  (drink) brindis (m.) *(BREEN-dees)*
tobacco tabaco (m.) *(tah-BAH-koh)*
today hoy *(ohy)*
toe dedo (del pie) *(DEH-doh [dehl pyeh])*
together juntos *(HOON-tohs)*
toilet retrete (m.) *(rreh-TREh-teh)*;
  toilet paper papel higiénico (m.) *(pah-PEHL ee-HYEH-nee-koh)*
tomato tomate (m.) *(toh-MAH-teh)*
tomorrow mañana (f.) *(mah-NYAH-nah)*
tongue lengua (f.) *(LEHN-gwah)*
tonic (hair) tónico para el cabello (m.) *(TOH-nee-koh PAH-rah ehl kah-BEH-yoh)*
tonight esta noche *(EHS-tah NOH-cheh)*

too (also) también *(tahm-BYEHN)*;
  too bad ¡qué lástima! *(keh LAHS-tee-mah!)*;
  too much demasiado *(deh-mah-SYAH-doh)*
tooth diente (m.) *(DHYEN-teh)*;
  toothache dolor de muelas (m.) *(doh-LOHR deh MWEH-lahs)*
toothbrush cepillo de dientes (m.) *(seh-PEE-yoh deh DYEHN-tehs)*
top cima (f.) *(SEE-mah)*
touch (v.) tocar *(toh-KAHR)*
tough duro *(DOO-roh)*
tourist turista (m./f.) *(too-REES-tah)*
tow (car) remolcar *(rreh-MOHL-kahr)*
toward hacia *(AH-syah)*
towel toalla (f.) *(toh-AH-yah)*
town pueblo (m.) *(PWEH-bloh)*
track (railroad) vía (f.) *(BEE-yah)*, riel (f.s.) *(RRYEHL)*
traffic light semáforo (m.) *(seh-MAH-foh-roh)*
train tren (m.) *(trehn)*
transfer (ticket) transbordo *(trahns-BOHR-doh)*;
  to transfer transbordar *(trahns-bohr-DAHR)*
translate traducir *(trah-doo-SEER)*
travel viajar *(byah-HAHR)*;
  travel insurance seguro de viaje (m.) *(seh-GOO-roh deh BYAH-heh)*
traveler viajero (-a) *(byah-HEH-roh)(-rah)*;
  traveler's check cheque de viajero (m.) *(CHEH-keh deh byah-HEH-roh)*
tree árbol (m.) *(AHR-bohl)*
trip (voyage) viaje (m.) *(BYAH-heh)*

trolley car tranvía (m.) *(trahn-BEE-ah)*

trouble, to be in tener dificultades *(teh-NEHR dee-fee-kool-TAH-desh)*

trousers pantalones (m.pl.) *(pahn-tah-LOH-nehs)*

truck camión (m.) *(kah-MYOHN)*

true verdadero *(behr-dah-DEH-roh)*

trunk (car) cajuela (f./Mex.), maletero (m.) *(kah-HWEH-lah, mah-leh-TEH-rah)*

try tratar *(trah-TAR);*
try on probarse *(proh-BAHR-seh);*
try to tratar de *(trah-TAHR-deh)*

tube (inner) cámara de aire (f.) *(KAH-mah-rah deh AH-ee-reh)*

Tuesday martes (m.) *(MAHR-tehs)*

Turkish turco(-a) *(TOOR-koh) (-kah)*

turn vuelta (f.) *(BWEHL-tah);*
to turn doblar *(doh-BLAHR)*

tuxedo esmoquin (m.), traje de etiqueta (m.) *(ehs-MOH-keeng, TRAH-heh deh eh-tee-KEH-tah)*

twelve doce *(DOH-seh)*

twenty veinte *(BAYN-teh)*

twice dos veces *(dohs BEH-sehs)*

twin beds camas gemelas (f.pl.) *(KAH-mahs heh-MEH-lahs)*

two dos *(dohs)*

U

ugly feo *(FEH-oh)*

umbrella paraguas (m.) *(pah-RAH-gwahs)*

uncle tío (m.) *(TEE-oh)*

uncomfortable incómodo *(een-KOH-moh-doh)*

under debajo de *(deh-BAH-hoh deh)*

undershirt camiseta (f.) *(kah-mee-SEH-tah)*

understand comprender, entender *(kohm-prehn-DEHR, ehn-tehn-DEHR)*

underwear ropa interior (f.) *(RROH-pah een-teh-RYOHR)*

United States (of America) Estados Unidos (de América) (m.pl.) *(ehs-TAH-dohs oo-NEE-dohs [deh ah-MEH-ree-kah])*

university universidad (f.) *(oo-nee-behr-see-DAHD)*

until hasta *(AHS-tah)*

up arriba *(ah-RREE-bah)*

upon sobre, encima de *(SOH-breh, ehn-SEE-mah deh)*

upper alto *(AHL-toh)*

upstairs arriba *(ah-RREE-bah)*

use (purpose) uso, empleo *(OO-soh, ehm-PLEH-oh);*
to use usar *(oo-SAHR)*

V

valise valija (f.), maleta (f.) *(bah-LEE-hah, mah-LEH-tah)*

veal ternera (f.) *(tehr-NEH-rah)*

vegetables legumbres (m.) *(leh-GOOM-brehs);*
(greens) verduras (f.pl.) *(behr-DOO-rahs)*

velvet terciopelo (m.) *(tehr-syoh-PEH-loh)*

very muy *(mwee)*

vest chaleco (m.) *(chah-LEH-koh)*

veterinarian veterinario (m.) *(beh-teh-ree-NAH-ryoh)*

view vista (f.) *(BEES-tah)*

vinegar vinagre (m.) *(bee-NAH-greh)*

visit visita (f.) *(bee-SEE-tah*

W

waist cintura (f.) *(seen-TOO-rah)*

wait (for) esperar*(ehs-peh-RAHR)*

waiter mozo (m.), camarero (m.), mesero (m./Mexico) *(MOH-soh, kah-mah-REH-roh, meh-SEH-roh);*
headwaiter jefe de comedor *(HEH-feh deh koh-meh-DOHR)*

waiting room sala de espera (f.) *(SAH-lah deh ehs-PEH-rah)*

waitress camarera (f.) *(kah-mah-REH-rah)*

wake up despertarse *(dehs-pehr-TAHR-seh)*

walk, take a dar un paseo *(dahr oon pah-SEH-oh)*

wall (interior) pared (f.) *(pah-REHD);*
(exterior) muro (m.) *(MOO-roh)*

wallet billetera (f.), cartera (f.) *(bee-yeh-TEH-rah, kahr-TEH-rah)*

want (v.) querer *(keh-REHR)*

warm caliente *(kah-LYEHN-teh)*

was era; estaba *(EH-rah; ehs-TAH-bah)*

wash (v.) lavar *(lah-BAHR);*
(oneself) lavarse *(lah-BAHR-seh)*

washroom lavabo (m.) *(lah-BAH-boh)*

watch (timepiece) reloj (m.) *(rreh-LOH);*

to watch mirar *(mee-RAHR);*
watch out! ¡cuidado! *(kwee-DAH-dohl)*

water agua (f.) *(AH-gwah)*

watermelon sandía (m.) *(sahn-DEE-ah)*

way (path) vía (f.) *(BEE-ah);*
(manner) manera (f.), modo (m.) *(mah-NEH-rah, MOH-doh);*
by way of por vía de *(pohr BEE-ah deh)*
one-way dirección única *(dee-rehk-SYOHN OO-nee-kah);*
which way? ¿por dónde? *(pohr DOHN-deh?)*

we nosotros (-as) *(noh-SOH-trohs) (-trahs)*

weak débil *(DEH-beel)*

wear llevar *(yeh-BAHR)*

weather tiempo (m.) *(TYEHM-poh)*

Web site página web (f.) *(PAH-hee-nah web)*

Wednesday miércoles (m.) *(MYEHR-koh-lehs)*

week semana (f.) *(seh-MAH-nah)*

weight peso (m.) *(PEH-soh)*

welcome, you're de nada *(deh NAH-dah)*

well bien *(byehn);*
well-done (meat) bien cocido *(byehn koh-SEE-doh)*

west oeste (m.) *(oh-EHS-teh)*

wet mojado *(moh-HAH-doh);*
wet paint pintura fresca *(peen-TOO-rah FREHS-kah)*

what? ¿qué? *(keh?)*

wheel rueda (f.) *(RRWEH-dah);*
steering wheel volante (m.) *(boh-LAHN-teh)*

when? ¿cuándo? *(KWAHN-doh?)*

where? ¿dónde? *(DOHN-deh?)*

which? ¿cuál? *(kwahl?)*

whiskey whisky (m.) *(WEES-kee)*

white blanco *(BLAHN-koh)*

who? ¿quién? *(kyehn?)*;
(pl.) ¿quiénes? *(KYEH-nehs?)*;
why? ¿por qué? *(pohr KEH?)*

wide ancho *(AHN-choh)*

width anchura *(ahn-CHOO-rah)*

wife esposa (f.) *(ehs-POH-sah)*

wind viento (m.) *(BYEHN-toh)*

window ventana (f.) *(behn-TAH-nah)*;
display window escaparate (m.) *(ehs-kah-pah-RAH-teh)*;
(of a train station, post office, bank, etc.) ventanilla (f.) *(behn-tah-NEE-yah)*

windshield parabrisas (m.pl.) *(pah-rah-BREE-sahs)*

windy ventoso *(behn-TOH-soh)*;
it's windy hace viento *(AH-seh BYEHN-toh)*

wine vino (m.) *(BEE-noh)*;
wine list lista de vinos (f.) *(LEES-tah deh BEE-nohs)*

winter invierno (m.) *(een-BYEHR-noh)*

wish (v.) querer, desear *(keh-REHR, deh-seh-AHR)*;
best wishes saludos (m.pl.) *(sah-LOO-dohs)*

with con *(kohn)*

without sin *(seen)*

woman mujer (f.) *(moo-HEHR)*

wood madera (f.) *(mah-DEH-rah)*

wool lana (f.) *(LAH-nah)*

word palabra (f.) *(pah-LAH-brah)*

work trabajo (m.) *(trah-BAH-hoh)*;

(piece of work) obra (f.) *(OH-brah)*;
to work trabajar *(trah-bah-HAHR)*

worry (v.) preocuparse *(preh-oh-koo-PAHR-seh)*;
don't worry no se preocupe *(noh seh preh-oh-KOO-peh)*

worse peor *(peh-OHR)*

worst el peor *(ehl peh-OHR)*

worth, to be valer *(bah-LEHR)*

wound (injury) herida (f.) *(eh-REE-dah)*

wounded herido *(eh-REE-doh)*

wrap (up) envolver *(ehn-BOHL-behr)*

wrapping paper papel de envolver (m.) *(pah-PEHL deh ehn-bohl-BEHR)*

wrench (tool) llave inglesa (f.) *(YAH-beh een-GLEH-sah)*

wrist muñeca (f.) *(moo-NYEH-kah)*;
wristwatch reloj pulsera (f.) *(rreh-LOH pool-SEH-rah)*

write escribir *(ehs-kree-BEER)*

writing paper papel de carta (m.) *(pah-PEHL deh KAHR-tah)*

wrong, to be equivocarse, no tener razón *(eh-kee-boh-KAHR-seh, noh teh-NEHR RRAH-sohn)*

X

X-ray radiografía (f.) *(rrah-dyoh-grah-FEE-ah)*

Y

year año (m.) *(AH-nyoh)*

yellow amarillo *(ah-mah-REE-yoh)*

yes sí *(see)*

yesterday ayer *(ah-YEHR)*

yet todavía *(toh-dah-BEE-ah);*
  not yet todavía no *(toh-dah-BEE-ah noh)*
you tú (familiar); usted
  (formal); ustedes (pl.) *(too; oos-TEHD; oos-TEH-dehs)*
young joven *(HOH-behn)*
your (sing./familiar) tu *(too);*
  (w/pl.) tus *(toos);*
  (sing./formal) su *(soo);*
  (w/pl.) sus *(soos);*
  your (pl.) su *(soo);*
  (w/pl.) sus *(soos)*
yours (sing./familiar) tuyo
  (TOO-yoh);
  (w/pl.) tuyos *(TOO-yohs);*

(sing./formal) suyo *(SOO-yoh);*
  (w/pl.) suyos *(SOO-yohs);*
  yours (pl.) suyo *(SOO-yoh);*
  (w/pl.) suyos *(SOO-yohs)*
youth hostel albergue juvenil (m.) *(ahl-BEHR-geh hoo-beh-NEEL)*
Yugoslav yugoslavo(-a)
  (yoo-gohs-LAH-boh)(-bah)

Z

zipper cierre (m.) *(SYEH-rreh)*
zoo zoológico (m.) *(soh-oh-LOH-hee-koh)*

SPANISH-ENGLISH DICTIONARY

A

a *(ah)* to; in; on; by
abajo *(ah-BAH-hoh)* below; down
abierto *(ah-BYEHR-toh)* open
abrigo (m.) *(ah-BREE-goh)* coat
abril (m.) *(ah-BREEL)* April
abrir *(ah-BREER)* to open
acabar *(ah-kah-BAHR)* to finish
aceite (m.) *(ah-SAY-teh)* oil
aceituna (f.) *(ah-say-TOO-nah)* olive
acero (m.) *(ah-SEH-roh)* steel
acetona (f.) *(ah-seh-TOH-nah)* nail polish remover
aclarar *(ah-klah-RAHR)* to clear up (weather); to clarify
acordarse *(ah-kohr-DAHR-seh)* to remember
acostarse *(ah-kohs-TAHR-seh)* to lie down, to go to bed
acuerdo (m.) *(ah-KWEHR-doh)* agreement
acumulador (m.) *(ah-koo-moo-lah-DOHR)* car battery
adelante *(ah-deh-LAHN-teh)* ahead, forward; come in
adiós *(ah-DYOHS)* goodbye, farewell
aduana (f.) *(ah-DWAH-nah)* customs
afuera *(ah-FWEH-rah)* out, outside
agosto (m.) *(ah-GOHS-toh)* August
agradable *(ah-grah-DAH-bleh)* pleasant

agradecido *(ah-grah-deh-SEE-doh)* grateful, thankful
agrio *(AH-gryoh)* sour
agua (m.) *(AH-gwah)* water;
  agua corriente *(. . . koh-RRYEHN-teh)* running water;
  agua potable *(. . . poh-TAH-bleh)* drinking water;
  agua mineral *(. . . mee-neh-RAHL)* mineral water
aguardar *(ah-gwahr-DAHR)* to expect, to wait for
aguja (f.) *(ah-GOO-hah)* needle
agujero (m.) *(ah-goo-HEH-roh)* hole
ahí *(ah-EE)* there
ahora *(ah-OH-rah)* now;
  ahora mismo *(ah-OH-rah MEES-moh)* right now
ajo (m.) *(AH-ho)* garlic
ajustar *(ah-hoos-TAHR)* to adjust
albaricoque (m.) *(ahl-bah-ree-KOH-keh)* apricot
alcachofa (f.) *(ahl-kah-CHOH-fah)* artichoke
alcoba (f.) *(ahl-KOH-bah)* bedroom
alegrarse *(ah-leh-GRAHR-seh)* to be glad, to rejoice
alegre *(ah-LEH-greh)* glad, merry, jolly
alemán (-ana) *(ah-leh-MAHN) (-MAH-nah)* German
alfiler (m.) *(ahl-fee-LEHR)* pin
alfombra (f.) *(ahl-FOHM-brah)* rug
algo *(AHL-goh)* something; anything

antigua = older

algodón (m.) *(ahl-goh-DOHN)* cotton

alguien *(AHL-gyehn)* someone, somebody; anyone, anybody

algún *(ahl-GOON)* some; any;
  algunas veces *(ahl-GOO-nahs BEH-sehs)* sometimes

alicates (m.pl.) *(ah-lee-KAH-tehs)* pliers

almacén (m.) *(ahl-mah-SEHN)* store, warehouse

almendra (f.) *(ahl-MEHN-drah)* almond

almidón (m.) *(ahl-mee-DOHN)* starch

almidonar *(ahl-mee-doh-NAHR)* to starch

almohada (f.) *(ahl-moh-AH-dah)* pillow

almorzar *(ahl-mohr-SAHR)* to have lunch; to have breakfast (Mex.)

almuerzo (m.) *(ahl-MWEHR-soh)* lunch; breakfast (Mex.)

alquilar *(ahl-kee-LAHR)* to rent

alquiler (m.) *(ahl-kee-LEHR)* rent

alrededor de *(ahl-reh-deh-DOHR deh)* around

alto *(AHL-toh)* tall

¡alto! *(AHL-toh!)* halt, stop

allá *(ah-YAH)* there (over there)

allí *(ah-YEE)* there (right there)

amargo *(ah-MAHR-goh)* bitter

amarillo *(ah-mah-REE-yoh)* yellow

amigo(-a) (m.,f.) *(ah-MEE-goh) (-gah)* friend

amueblado *(ah-mweh-BLAH-doh)* furnished

ancho *(AHN-choh)* wide

anchura (f.) *(ahn-CHOO-rah)* width

andén (m.) *(ahn-DEHN)* platform

angosto *(ahn-GOHS-toh)* narrow

anillo (m.) *(ah-NEE-yoh)* ring

anteojos (m.pl.) *(ahn-teh-OH-hos)* eyeglasses

antes de *(AHN-tehs-deh)* before

antipático *(ahn-tee-PAH-tee-koh)* unpleasant, not likable

año *(AN-nyoh)* year

apellido (m.) *(ah-peh-YEE-doh)* family name, surname

apio (m.) *(AH-pyoh)* celery

aprender *(ah-prehn-DEHR)* to learn

apretar *(ah-preh-TAHR)* to tighten

apuro (m.) *(ah-POO-roh)* trouble, difficulty; hurry, haste

aquel *(ah-KEHL)* that

aquí *(ah-KEE)* here

árabe *(AH-rah-beh)* Arab

árbol (m.) *(AHR-bohl)* tree

arena (f.) *(ah-REH-nah)* sand

arete (m.) *(ah-REH-teh)* earring

argentino(-a) *(ahr-hehn-TEE-noh) (-nah)* Argentine

armario (m.) *(ahr-MAH-ryoh)* closet

arreglar *(ah-rreh-GLAHR)* to fix, to repair

arroz (m.) *(ah-RROHS)* rice

asado (m.) *(ah-SAH-doh)* roast

asar *(ah-SAHR)* to roast

ascensor (m.) *(ah-sehn-SOHR)* elevator

asegurar *(ah-seh-goo-RAHR)* to insure; to ensure

así *(ah-SEE)* so, thus

asiento (m.) *(ah-SYEHN-toh)* seat;

asiento reservado *(. . . rreh-sehr-BAH-doh)* reserved seat

aterrizar *(ah-teh-rree-SAHR)* to land (by plane)

atrás *(ah-TRAHS)* back, behind

austríaco(-a) *(ows-TREE-ah-koh) (-kah)* Austrian

avellana (f.) *(ah-beh-YAH-nah)* hazelnut

avería (f.) *(ah-beh-REE-ah)* breakdown (car)

avión (m.) *(ah-BYOHN)* airplane

aviso (m.) *(ah-BEE-soh)* notice; sign; warning

ayer *(ah-YEHR)* yesterday

ayudar *(ah-yoo-DAHR)* to help

ayuntamiento (m.) *(ah-yoon-tah-MYEHN-toh)* city hall

azafata (f.) *(ah-sah-FAH-tah)* stewardess

azúcar (f.) *(ah-SOO-kahr)* sugar

azul *(ah-SOOL)* blue

B

bailar *(bahy-LAHR)* to dance

bajada (f.) *(bah-HAH-dah)* descent, path down; **de bajada** *(deh . . .)* downhill

bajar *(bah-HAHR)* to go down, to come down, to step down

bajo *(BAH-hoh)* low

banderilla (f.) *(bahn-deh-REE-yah)* banderilla (long dart used to prick the bull)

bañarse *(bah-NYAHR-seh)* to bathe, to take a bath

barato *(bah-RAH-toh)* cheap

barba (f.) *(BAHR-bah)* beard, chin

barco (m.) *(BAHR-koh)* boat

barrio (m.) *(BAH-rryoh)* district, suburb

¡basta! *(BAHS-tah!)* enough!, cut it out!, stop!

bata (f.) *(BAH-tah)* robe

baúl (m.) *(bah-OOL)* trunk

beber *(beh-BEHR)* to drink

bebida (f.) *(beh-BEE-dah)* drink

belga *(BEHL-gah)* Belgian

bello *(BEH-yoh)* beautiful

besar *(beh-SAHR)* to kiss

beso (m.) *(BEH-soh)* kiss

biblioteca (f.) *(bee-blyoh-TEH-kah)* library

bien *(byehn)* well

billete (m.) *(bee-YEH-teh)* ticket

billetera (f.) *(bee-yeh-TEH-rah)* wallet

billón (m.) *(bee-YOHN)* trillion (U.S.); billion (Great Britain)

blanco *(BLAHN-koh)* white

blando *(BLAHN-doh)* soft

boca (f.) *(BOH-kah)* mouth

bocacalle (f.) *(boh-kah-KAH-yeh)* side street

bocadillo (m.) *(boh-kah-DEE-yoh)* sandwich

bocina (f.) *(boh-SEE-nah)* car horn

bolso (f.) *(BOHL-soh)* purse; bag

bolsillo (m.) *(bohl-SEE-yoh)* pocket

bolillo (m.) *(boh-LEE-yoh)* roll (bread) (Mex.)

bombilla(-o) (m.,f.) *(bohm-BEE-yah) (-yah)* electric bulb

bonito *(boh-NEE-toh)* pretty

borracho *(boh-RRAH-choh)* drunk

bote (m.) *(BOH-teh)* boat

botón (m.) *(boh-TOHN)* button

botones (m.) *(boh-TOH-nehs)* bellboy, bellhop

bragas (f.) *(BRAH-gahs)* panties

brasileño(-a) *(brah-see-LEH-nyoh) (-nah)* Brazilian

brazo (m.) *(BRAH-soh)* arm

brillar *(bree-YHAR)* to shine

brindis (m.) *(BREEHN-dees)* toast (as in "to drink to")

brocha de afeitar (f.) *(BROH-chah deh ah-fay-TAHR)* shaving brush

bueno *(BWEH-noh)* good

bufanda (f.) *(boo-FAHN-dah)* scarf

bujía (f.) *(boo-HEE-ah)* spark plug

buscar *(boos-KAHR)* to look for, to search

buzón (m.) *(boo-SOHN)* mailbox

C

caballero (m.) *(kah-bah-YEH-roh)* gentleman

caballo (m.) *(kah-BAH-yoh)* horse

cabello (m.) *(kah-BEH-yoh)* hair (on head)

cabeza (f.) *(kah-BEH-sah)* head

cabina (f.) *(kah-BEE-nah)* phone booth

cada *(KAH-dah)* each; **cada uno** *(. . . OO-noh)* each one

cadena (f.) *(kah-DEH-nah)* chain

cadera (f.) *(kah-DEH-rah)* hip

caer *(kah-EHR)* to fall

café (m.) *(kah-FEH)* coffee

caja (f.) *(KAH-hah)* box, case; cashier, cashbox

caja fuerte (f.) *(KAH-hah-FWEHR-teh)* safe

cajero (-a) *(kah-HEH-roh) (-rah)* cashier, teller

caliente *(kah-LYEHN-teh)* hot

calor (m.) *(kah-LOHR)* heat, warmth

calzoncillos (m.pl.) *(kahl-sohn-SEE-yohs)* drawers, undershorts

calle (f.) *(KAH-yeh)* street

cama (f.) *(KAH-mah)* bed

cámara fotográfica (f.) *(KAH-mah-rah foh-toh-GRAH-fee-kah)* camera

camarero (-a) *(kah-mah-REH-roh) (-rah)* waiter, waitress

camarón (m.) *(kah-mah-ROHN)* shrimp

camarote (m.) *(kah-mah-ROH-teh)* stateroom

camas gemelas (f.) *(KAH-mahs heh-MEH-lahs)* twin beds

cambiar *(kahm-BYAHR)* to change

cambio (m.) *(KAHM-byoh)* change

camino (m.) *(kah-MEE-noh)* road

camión (m.) *(kah-MYOHN)* truck

camisa (f.) *(kah-MEE-sah)* shirt

camiseta (f.) *(kah-mee-SEH-tah)* undershirt

camisón (m.) *(kah-mee-SOHN)* nightgown, nightshirt

campo (m.) *(KAHM-poh)* countryside

canadiense *(kah-nah-DYEHN-seh)* Canadian

canción (f.) *(kahn-SYOHN)* song

cansado *(kahn-SAH-doh)* tired

cantar *(kahn-TAHR)* to sing

cantina (f.) *(kahn-TEE-nah)* saloon

cara (f.) *(KAH-rah)* face

caro *(KAH-roh)* expensive

¡caramba! *(kah-RAHM-bah!)* darn it!

carne (f.) *(KAHR-neh)* meat

carta (f.) *(KAHR-tah)* letter; playing card

cartera (f.) *(kahr-TEH-rah)* pocketbook, wallet

carretera (f.) *(kah-rreh-TEH-rah)* highway

casa (f.) *(KAH-sah)* house, home

casi *(KAH-see)* almost

caso (m.) *(KAH-soh)* case (as in, "in case of")

castaña (f.) *(kahs-TAH-nyah)* chestnut

castillo (m.) *(kahs-TEE-yoh)* castle

catarro (m.) *(kah-TAH-rroh)* (common) cold

catorce *(kah-TOHR-seh)* fourteen

caucho (m.) *(KOW-choh)* rubber

cebolla (f.) *(seh-BOH-yah)* onion

ceja (f.) *(SEH-hah)* eyebrow

cena (f.) *(SEH-nah)* dinner, supper

cenicero (m.) *(seh-nee-SEH-roh)* ashtray

cepillar *(seh-pee-YAHR)* to brush

cepillo (m.) *(seh-PEE-yoh)* brush

cerca de *(SEHR-kah deh)* near, close to

cerdo (m.) *(SEHR-doh)* pig, hog

cereza (f.) *(seh-REH-sah)* cherry

cerilla (m.) *(seh-REE-yah)* match

certificado *(sehr-tee-fee-KAH-doh)* registered (mail)

cerveza (f.) *(sehr-BEH-sah)* beer

cerrado *(seh-RRAH-doh)* closed

cerradura (f.) *(seh-rrah-DOO-rah)* lock

cerrajero (m.) *(seh-rrah-HEH-roh)* locksmith

cerrar *(seh-RRAHR)* to close

cesta (f.) *(SEHS-tah)* basket

chal (m.) *(chahl)* shawl

chaleco (m.) *(chah-LEH-koh)* vest

checo(-a) *(CHEH-koh) (-kah)* Czech

cheque (m.) *(CHEH-keh)* check

chileno(-a) *(chee-LEH-noh)(-nah)* Chilean

chino(-a) *(CHEE-noh) (-nah)* Chinese

chorizo (m.) *(choh-REE-soh)* sausage

chuleta (f.) *(choo-LEH-tah)* chop, cutlet

cielo (m.) *(SYEH-loh)* sky; heaven

cien; ciento *(syehn; SYEHN-toh)* hundred

cima (f.) *(SEE-mah)* top

cincuenta *(seen-KWEHN-tah)* fifty

cine (m.) *(SEE-neh)* movie theater; movie

cinta (f.) *(SEEN-tah)* ribbon; (audio, video) tape

cintura (f.) *(seen-TOO-rah)* waist

cinturón (m.) *(seen-too-ROHN)* belt

ciruela (f.) *(see-RWEH-lah)* plum

ciruela pasa (f.) *(. . . PAH-sah)* prune

cirujano (-a) *(see-roo-HAH-noh) (-nah)* surgeon

ciudad (f.) *(syoo-DAHD)* city

claro *(KLAH-roh)* clear

cobrar *(koh-BRAHR)* to collect

cocido *(koh-SEE-doh)* cooked; stew

cocina (f.) *(koh-SEE-nah)* kitchen

cocinar *(koo-see-NAHR)* to cook

coche (m.) *(KOH-cheh)* car

codo (m.) *(KOH-doh)* elbow

coger *(koh-HEHR)* to catch, to take

colchón (m.) *(kohl-CHOHN)* mattress

col (f.) *(kohl)* cabbage

colgador (m.) *(kohl-gah-DOHR)* coat hanger

color (m.) *(koh-LOHR)* color

combinación (f.) *(kohm-bee-nah-SYOHN)* slip (garment)

comenzar *(koh-mehn-SAHR)* to begin

comer *(koh-MEHR)* to eat

comida (f.) *(koh-MEE-dah)* meal;
  comida corrida(. . . koh-RREE-dah) a fixed menu (Mex.)

comisaría (f.) *(koh-mee-SAH-REE-ah)* police station

como *(KOH-moh)* as, like

cómo *(KOH-moh)* how

cómodo *(KOH-moh-doh)* comfortable

compañía (f.) *(kohm-pah-NYEE-ah)* company

compra (f.) *(KOHM-prah)* buy

comprar *(kohm-PRAHR)* to buy

comprender *(kohm-prehn-DEHR)* to understand

computadora (f.) *(kohm-poo-tah-DOH-rah)* computer

con *(kohn)* with

conducir *(kohn-doo-SEER)* to drive

conductor (m.) *(kohn-dook-TOHR)* conductor

conferencia (f.) *(kohn-feh-REHN-syah)* conference

conocer *(koh-noh-SEHR)* to know; to make the acquaintance of

conseguir *(kohn-seh-GEER)* to get, to obtain

contar *(kohn-TAHR)* to count; to tell (narrate)

contestar *(kohn-tehs-TAHR)* to answer, to reply

contra *(KOHN-trah)* against

contusión (f.) *(kohn-too-SYOHN)* bruise

copia (f.) *(KOH-pyah)* copy

corazón (m.) *(koh-rah-SOHN)* heart

corbata (f.) *(kohr-BAH-tah)* necktie

cortar *(kohr-TAHR)* to cut

corte de pelo (m.) *(KOHR-teh deh PEH-loh)* haircut

cortés *(kohr-TEHS)* polite

cortesía (f.) *(kohr-teh-SEE-ah)* politeness, courtesy

corto *(KOHR-toh)* short (length, distance, or time)

correo (m.) *(koh-RREH-oh)* mail; post office;
  correo aéreo (. . . ah-EH-reh-oh) air mail
  correo electrónico (. . . eh-lehk-TROH-nee-koh) e-mail

correr *(koh-RREHR)* to run

cosa (f.) *(KOH-sah)* thing

costilla (f.) *(kohs-TEE-yah)* rib

creer *(kreh-EHR)* to believe

crema (f.) *(KREH-mah)* cream

cruce (m.) *(KROO-seh)* crossroad

cuadra (f.) *(KWAH-drah)* city block

cuadrado (m.) *(kwah-DRAH-doh)* square (shape)

cuadrilla (f.) *(kwah-DREE-yah)* cuadrilla (the team of assistants to a matador)

cuadro (m.) *(KWAH-droh)* picture, printing

¿cuál? *(kwahl?)* which?, which one?

cualquier; cualquiera *(kwahl-KYEHR; kwahl-KYEH-rah)* any

¿cuándo? *(KWAHN-doh?)* when?

¿cuánto? *(KWAHN-toh?)* how much?

¿cuántos? *(KWAHN-tohs?)* how many?

cuarenta *(kwah-REHN-tah)* forty

cuarto (m.) *(KWAHR-toh)* room; fourth

cuatro *(KWAH-troh)* four

cubano (-a) *(koo-BAH-noh)(-nah)* Cuban

cuchara (f.) *(koo-CHAH-rah)* spoon

cucharada (f.) *(koo-chah-RAH-dah)* (table) spoonful

cucharadita (f.) *(koo-chah-rah-DEE-tah)* teaspoonful

cucharilla (f.) *(koo-chah-REE-yah)* teaspoon

cuchillo (m.) *(koo-CHEE-yoh)* knife

cuello (m.) *(KWEH-yoh)* neck

cuenta (f.) *(KWEHN-tah)* bill (restaurant); count, calculation

cuerda (f.) *(KWEHR-dah)* rope, cord, string

cuero (m.) *(KWEH-roh)* leather, hide

cuerpo (m.) *(KWEHR-poh)* body

cuidado (m.) *(kwee-DAH-doh)* care;
con cuidado *(kohn . . .)* carefully;
tener cuidado *(teh-NEHR . . .)* to be careful;
¡cuidado! *(kwee-DAH-doh)* be careful, watch out!

cura (m.) *(KOO-rah)* priest

D

danés(-esa) *(dah-NEHS)(-NEH-sah)* Danish

dar *(dahr)* to give;

dar las gracias *(. . . lahs GRAH-syahs)* to thank;
dar un paseo *(. . . oon pah-SEH-oh)* to take a walk

darse prisa *(DAHR-seh PREE-sah)* to hurry

de *(deh)* from, of

debajo de *(deh-BAH-hoh deh)* under, beneath

deber *(deh-BEHR)* to have to; to owe

deber (m.) *(deh-BEHR)* duty, obligation

débil *(DEH-beel)* weak

décimo *(DEH-see-moh)* tenth

decir *(deh-SEER)* to say, to tell

dedo (m.) *(DEH-doh)* finger

dejar *(deh-HAHR)* to leave behind; to let, to permit

demasiado *(deh-mah-SYAH-doh)* too much

dentadura (f.) *(dehn-tah-DOO-rah)* dentures

dentro *(DEHN-troh)* inside, within

depósito (m.) *(deh-POH-see-toh)* deposit; tank (car)

derecha (f.) *(deh-REH-chah)* right (direction)

derecho *(deh-REH-choh)* straight ahead

desayunar *(deh-sah-yoo-NAHR)* to have breakfast

desayuno (m.) *(deh-sah-YOO-noh)* breakfast

descansar *(dehs-kahn-SAHR)* to rest

descuento (m.) *(dehs-KWEHN-toh)* discount

desde *(DEHS-deh)* since; from

desear *(deh-seh-AHR)* to wish

desembarcar *(deh-sehm-bahr-KAHR)* to disembark, to land (by ship)

desodorante (m.) *(deh-soh-doh-RAHN-teh)* deodorant

despacio *(des-PAH-syoh)* slow; slowly

despejar *(dehs-peh-HAR)* to clear up (sky)

despertador (m.) *(dehs-pehr-tah-DOHR)* alarm clock

despertar *(dehs-pehr-TAHR)* to wake up

después (de) *(dehs-PWEHS [deh])* after, afterward, later

destinatario (m.) *(dehs-tee-nah-TAH-ryoh)* addressee (on mail)

destornillador (m.) *(dehs-tohr-nee-yah-DOHR)* screwdriver

desvío (f.) *(dehs-BEE-oh)* detour

detrás de *(deh-TRAHS deh)* in back of, behind

devolver *(deh-bohl-BEHR)* to return

día (m.) *(DEE-ah)* day;
   por día (m.) *(pohr . . .)* by the day;
   buenos días *(BWEH-nohs DEE-ahs)* good morning, good day

diciembre (m.) *(dee-SYEHM-breh)* December

diecinueve *(dyeh-see-NWEH-beh)* nineteen

dieciocho *(dyeh-SYOH-choh)* eighteen

dieciséis *(dyeh-see-SAYS)* sixteen

diecisiete *(dyeh-see-SYEH-teh)* seventeen

diente (m.) *(DYEHN-teh)* tooth

diez *(dyehs)* ten

difícil *(dee-FEE-seel)* difficult

dinero (m.) *(dee-NEH-roh)* money;
   dinero al contado *(. . . ahl kohn-TAH-doh)* cash

dirección (f.) *(dee-rehk-SYOHN)* address; direction;
   dirección única *(. . . OO-nee-kah)* one-way (traffic)

dirigir *(dee-ree-HEER)* to direct

disco (m.) *(DEES-koh)* (phonograph) record

disparate (m.) *(dees-pah-RAH-teh)* nonsense

dispensar *(dees-pehn-SAHR)* to excuse, to pardon

distancia (f.) *(dees-TAHN-syah)* distance

doblar *(doh-BLAHR)* to fold; to turn

doce *(DOH-seh)* twelve

docena *(doh-SEH-nah)* dozen

dolor (m.) *(doh-LOHR)* pain

domingo (m.) *(doh-MEEN-goh)* Sunday

donde *(DOHN-deh)* where

dormir *(dohr-MEER)* to sleep

dormitorio (m.) *(dohr-mee-TOH-ryoh)* bedroom

dos *(dohs)* two

ducha (f.) *(DOO-chah)* shower

dulce (m.) *(DOOL-seh)* candy

dulce *(DOOL-seh)* sweet

durar *(doo-RAHR)* to last

durazno (m.) *(doo-RAHS-noh)* peach

duro *(DOO-roh)* hard, tough

E

elástico (m.) *(eh-LAHS-tee-koh)* rubber band

el *(ehl)* the

él *(ehl)* he

ella *(EH-yah)* she

ellas *(EH-yahs)* they (f.)

ellos *(EH-yohs)* they (m.)

embrague (m.) *(ehm-BRAH-geh)* (car) clutch

empastar *(ehm-pahs-TAHR)* to fill (a tooth)

empezar *(ehm-peh-SAHR)* to begin, to start

emplear *(ehm-pleh-AHR)* to use; to hire

empleo (m.) *(ehm-PLEH-oh)* use, purpose; job

empujar *(ehm-poo-HAHR)* to push

en *(ehn)* at, in, on;
  en casa *(. . . KAH-sah)* at home;
  en seguida *(. . . seh-GEE-dah)* at once, right away

encendedor (m.) *(ehn-sehn-deh-DOHR)* cigarette lighter

encender *(ehn-sehn-DEHR)* to light

encendido (m.) *(ehn-sehn-DEE-doh)* (car) ignition

encías (f.pl.) *(ehn-SEE-ahs)* gums (in mouth)

encima (de) *(ehn-SEE-mah [deh])* on top (of), above

encontrar *(ehn-kohn-TRAHR)* to find, to meet

encurtidos (m.pl.) *(ehn-koor-TEE-dohs)* pickles

enchufe (m.) *(ehn-CHOO-feh)* (electrical) outlet

enero (m.) *(eh-NEH-roh)* January

enfermedad (f.) *(ehn-fehr-meh-DAHD)* illness

enfermera (f.) *(ehn-fehr-MEH-rah)* nurse

enfermo *(ehn-FEHR-moh)* sick, ill

engranaje (m.) *(ehn-grah-NAH-heh)* (car) gears

engrasar *(ehn-grah-SAHR)* to grease, to lubricate

enjuague (m.) *(ehn-HWAH-geh)* rinse

ensalada (f.) *(ehn-sah-LAH-dah)* salad

enseñar *(ehn-seh-NYAHR)* to teach; to show

entender *(ehn-tehn-DEHR)* to understand

entrar *(ehn-TRAHR)* to enter, to come in

entre *(EHN-treh)* between, among

entrega (f.) *(ehn-treh-gah)* delivery

entregar *(ehn-treh-GAHR)* to deliver, to hand over

entremés (m.) *(ehn-treh-MEHS)* appetizer, hors d'oeuvre

enviar *(ehn-BYAHR)* to send

envolver *(ehn-bohl-BEHR)* to wrap

equipaje (m.) *(eh-kee-PAH-heh)* luggage

equivocarse *(eh-kee-boh-KAHR-seh)* to be mistaken

escalera (f.) *(ehs-kah-LEH-rah)* stairs

escalofrío (m.) *(ehs-kah-loh-FREE-oh)* chill

escaparate (m.) *(ehs-kah-pah-RAH-teh)* display window

escape (m.) *(ehs-KAH-peh)* exhaust (car); leak

escoger *(ehs-koh-HEHR)* to choose, to select

escribir *(ehs-kree-BEER)* to write

escuchar *(ehs-koo-CHAHR)* to listen (to)

escuela (f.) *(ehs-KWEH-lah)* school

escupir *(ehs-koo-PEER)* to spit

ese (esa, eso) *(EH-seh [EH-sah, EH-soh])* that

esmalte (m.) *(ehs-MAHL-teh)* nail polish

esmoquin (m.) *(ehs-MOH-keeng)* tuxedo

esos (esas) *(EH-sohs [EH-sahs])* those

espalda (f.) *(ehs-PAHL-dah)* back (body part)

español(-a) *(ehs-pah-NYOHL) (-NYOH-lah)* Spanish

esparadrapo (m.) *(ehs-pah-rah-DRAH-poh)* adhesive tape; bandage

espejo (m.) *(ehs-PEH-hoh)* mirror

esperar *(ehs-peh-RAHR)* to hope; to expect; to wait

espeso *(ehs-PEH-soh)* thick (consistency of liquid)

espinaca (f.) *(ehs-pee-NAH-kah)* spinach

esposa (f.) *(ehs-POH-sah)* wife

esposo (m.) *(ehs-POH-soh)* husband

está bien *(ehs-TAH byehn)* all right, okay

estación (f.) *(ehs-tah-SYOHN)* station; season

estacionar *(ehs-tah-syoh-NAHR)* to park

Estados Unidos de América (EE.UU.) (m.pl.) *(ehs-TAH-dohs oo-NEE-dohs deh ah-MEH-ree-kah)* United States of America

estanco (m.) *(ehs-TAHN-koh)* cigar store

estar *(ehs-TAHR)* to be

este (m.) *(EHS-teh)* east

este (esta, esto) *(EHS-teh [EHS-tah, EHS-toh])* this

estancia (f.) *(ehs-TAHN-syah)* stay

estofado (m.) *(ehs-toh-FAH-doh)* stew

estómago (m.) *(ehs-TOH-mah-goh)* stomach

estos (estas) *(ESH-tohs [EHS-tahs])* these

estrecho *(ehs-TREH-choh)* narrow; strait

estrella (f.) *(ehs-TREH-yah)* star

esquina (f.) *(ehs-KEE-nah)* corner

etiqueta (f.) *(eh-tee-KEH-tah)* label; etiquette;

traje de etiqueta *(TRAH-heh deh . . .)* evening gown; tuxedo

evitar *(eh-bee-TAHR)* to avoid

extranjero (m.) *(eks-trahn-HEH-roh)* foreigner

F

facturar *(fahk-too-RAHR)* to check (baggage)

faja (f.) *(FAH-hah)* girdle

falda (f.) *(FAHL-dah)* skirt

faro (f.) *(FAH-roh)* headlight

farol (m.) *(fah-ROHL)* street lamp

favor (m.) *(fah-BOHR)* favor; **por favor** *(pohr . . .)* please; **haga el favor** *(AH-gah ehl . . .)* please

febrero (m.) *(feh-BREH-roh)* February

fecha (f.) *(FEH-chah)* date

¡Feliz Navidad! *(feh-LEES nah-bee-DAHD!)* Merry Christmas!

felicitaciones (f.pl.) *(feh-lee-see-tah-SYOH-nehs)* congratulations

feliz *(feh-LEES)* happy; **¡feliz cumpleaños!** *(. . . koom-pleh-AH-nyohs!)* happy birthday!; **¡feliz Año Nuevo!** *(. . . AH-nyoh NWEH-boh!)* Happy New Year!; **¡feliz Navidad!** *(. . . nah-bee-DAHD!)* Merry Christmas!

feo *(FEH-oh)* ugly

ferrocarril (m.) *(feh-rroh-kah-RREEL)* railroad

fiambre (m.) *(FYAHM-breh)* cold cut

ficha (f.) *(FEE-chah)* token (bus or phone)

fiebre (f.) *(FYEH-breh)* fever

227

fila (f.) *(FEE-lah)* row, queue, line

fin (m.) *(feen)* end

flor (f.) *(flohr)* flower

fósforo (m.) *(FOHS-foh-roh)* match

francés(-esa) *(frahn-SEHS)* *(-SEH-sah)* French

franqueo (m.) *(frahn-KEH-oh)* postage

frenos (m.pl.) *(FREH-nohs)* brakes

frente (m.) *(FREHN-teh)* front; forehead

fresa (f.) *(FREH-sah)* strawberry

fresco *(FREHS-koh)* fresh, cool

frijol (m.) *(free-HOHL)* bean (Mex.)

frío (m.) *(FREE-oh)* cold; **hacer frío** *(ah-SEHR . . .)* to be cold (weather); **tener frío** *(teh-NEHR . . .)* to be cold (person)

frito *(FREE-toh)* fried

fuego (m.) *(FWEH-goh)* fire

fuente (f.) *(FWEHN-teh)* fountain

fuera *(FWEH-rah)* outside; out

fuerte *(FWEHR-teh)* strong

fumador (-a) *(foo-mah-DOHR)* *(-DOH-rah)* smoker

fumar *(foo-MAHR)* to smoke

función (f.) *(foon-SYOHN)* performance, show; ceremony, function

funda (f.) *(FOON-dah)* pillowcase

G

gafas (f.pl.) *(GAH-fahs)* eyeglasses

gana (f.) *(GAH-nah)* desire; **tener ganas de** *(teh-NEHR GAH-nahs deh)* to feel like

ganado (m.) *(gah-NAH-doh)* cattle

gancho (m.) *(GAHN-choh)* hook; clothes hanger

ganga (f.) *(GAHN-gah)* bargain, sale

ganso (m.) *(GAHN-soh)* goose

garganta (f.) *(gahr-GAHN-tah)* throat

gasa (f.) *(GAH-sah)* gauze

gastar *(gahs-TAHR)* to spend; to waste

gasto (m.) *(GAHS-toh)* expense

gato (m.) *(GAH-toh)* cat

gemelos (m.pl.) *(heh-MEH-lohs)* twins; cuff links; binoculars

gente (f.) *(HEHN-teh)* people

gerente (m.) *(he-REHN-teh)* manager

ginebra (f.) *(hee-NEH-brah)* gin

gira (f.) *(HEE-rah)* tour

giro postal (m.) *(HEE-roh pohs-TAHL)* money order

gorra (f.) *(GOH-rrah)* cap

gracias (f.pl.) *(GRAH-syahs)* thanks

gracias *(GRAH-syahs)* thank you

grande *(GRAHN-deh)* large, big

granizar *(grah-nee-SAHR)* to hail (precipitation)

griego(-a) (m.) *(GRYEH-goh)* *(-gah)* Greek

grifo (m.) *(GREE-foh)* tap, faucet

gris *(grees)* gray

grueso *(GRWEH-soh)* thick, stout

guante (m.) *(GWAHN-teh)* glove

guardar *(gwahr-DAHR)* to keep, to look after; to put away; to guard

guardafangos (m.) *(gwahr-dah-FAHN-gohs)* fender

guía (m./f.) *(GEE-ah)* guide; guidebook

guiar *(gee-AHR)* to guide; to drive

guisante (m.) *(gee-SAHN-teh)* pea (Sp.)

guiso (m.) *(gee-SOH)* stew

gustar *(goos-TAHR)* to like

gusto (m.) *(GOOS-toh)* pleasure, taste;
  con mucho gusto *(kohn MOO-choh . . .)* gladly

H

habichuela (f.) *(ah-bee-CHWEH-lah)* bean

habitación (f.) *(ah-bee-tah-SYOHN)* room

hablar *(ah-BLAHR)* to speak

hace *(AH-seh)* ago

hacer *(ah-SEHR)* to do, to make

hacerse *(ah-SEHR-seh)* to become

hacia *(AH-syah)* toward

hallar *(ah-YAHR)* to find

hasta *(AHS-tah)* until;
  hasta mañana *(. . . mah-NYAH-nah)* until tomorrow;
  hasta la vista *(. . . lah BEES-tah)* till we meet again

hay *(AHY)* there is, there are

hebreo(-a) *(eh-BREH-oh)* (-ah) Hebrew

hecho a mano *(EH-choh ah MAH-noh)* handmade

helado (m.) *(eh-LAH-doh)* ice cream; cold (temperature)

herida (f.) *(eh-REE-dah)* wound

herido *(eh-REE-doh)* wounded

herir *(eh-REER)* to wound

hermana (f.) *(ehr-MAH-nah)* sister

hermano (m.) *(ehr-MAH-noh)* brother

hermoso *(ehr-MOH-soh)* beautiful

hervido *(ehr-BEE-doh)* boiled

hielo (m.) *(YEH-loh)* ice

hierro (m.) *(YEH-rroh)* iron

hígado (m.) *(EE-gah-doh)* liver

higo (m.) *(EE-goh)* fig

hierba (f.) *(YEHR-bah)* grass

hilo (m.) *(EE-loh)* thread

hinchado *(een-CHAH-doh)* swollen

hinchar *(een-CHAHR)* to swell

holandés(-esa) *(oh-lahn-DEHS)* (-DEH-sah)* Dutch

hombre (m.) *(OHM-breh)* man

hombro (m.) *(OHM-broh)* shoulder

hongo (m.) *(OHN-goh)* mushroom

hora (f.) *(OH-rah)* hour

horario (m.) *(oh-RAH-ryoh)* schedule, timetable

horno (m.) *(OHR-noh)* oven

horquilla (f.) *(ohr-KEE-yah)* hairpin

hoy *(ohy)* today

hueso (m.) *(WEH-soh)* bone

huevo (m.) *(WEH-boh)* egg

húngaro(-a) *(OON-gah-roh)* (-rah)* Hungarian

I

idioma (m.) *(ee-DYOH-mah)* language

iglesia (f.) *(ee-GLEH-syah)* church

impermeable (m.) *(eem-pehr-meh-AH-bleh)* raincoat

importar *(eem-pohr-TAHR)* to be important; to import

impuesto (m.) *(eem-PWEHS-toh)* tax

incómodo *(een-KOH-moh-doh)* uncomfortable

infierno (m.) *(een-FYEHR-noh)* hell

informes (m.pl.) *(een-FOHR-mehs)* information

inglés(-esa) *(een-GLES)(-GLEH-sah)* English

interruptor (m.) *(een-teh-rroop-TOHR)* electric switch

invierno (m.) *(een-BYEHR-noh)* winter

ir *(eer)* to go

irse *(EER-seh)* to go away, to leave

italiano(-a) *(ee-tah-LYAH-noh)(-nah)* Italian

izquierda (f.) *(ees-KYEHR-dah)* left

J

jabón (m.) *(hah-BOHN)* soap

jamás *(hah-MAHS)* never

jamón (m.) *(hah-MOHN)* ham

jaqueca (f.) *(hah-KEH-kah)* headache

japonés(-esa) *(hah-poh-NEHS)(-NEH-sah)* Japanese

jarabe (m.) *(hah-RAH-beh)* syrup

jardín (m.) *(hahr-DEEN)* garden

jarra (f.) *(HAH-rrah)* pitcher

jarro (m.) *(HAH-rroh)* mug

jefe (m./f.) *(HEH-feh)* chief, leader, boss

joven *(HOH-behn)* young

joven (m./f.) *(HOH-behn)* youngster

joya (f.) *(HOH-yah)* jewel

joyería (f.) *(hoh-yeh-REE-ah)* jewelry; jewelry store

joyero (m.) *(hoh-YEH-roh)* jeweler

judías (f.pl.) *(hoo-DEE-ahs)* green beans (Sp.)

judío(-a) *(hoo-DEE-oh) (-ah)* Jewish

juego (m.) *(HWEH-goh)* game

jueves (m.) *(HWEH-behs)* Thursday

jugar *(hoo-GAHR)* to play (a game)

jugo (m.) *(HOO-goh)* juice

julio (m.) *(HOO-lyoh)* July

junio (m.) *(HOO-nyoh)* June

L

la *(lah)* the

labio (m.) *(LAH-byoh)* lip

lado (m.) *(LAH-doh)* side

ladrón (m.) *(lah-DROHN)* thief

lámpara (f.) *(LAHM-pah-rah)* lamp

langosta (f.) *(lahn-GOHS-tah)* lobster

lápiz (m.) *(LAH-pees)* pencil

largo *(LAHR-goh)* long

lástima (f.) *(LAHS-tee-mah)* pity

lastimar *(lahs-tee-MAHR)* to hurt, to injure, to bruise

lata (f.) *(LAH-tah)* can; tin

lavabo (m.) *(lah-BAH-boh)* sink

lavandera (f.) *(lah-bahn-DEH-rah)* laundress

lavandería (f.) *(lah-bahn-deh-REE-ah)* laundry

lavar *(lah-BAHR)* to wash

lavarse *(lah-BAHR-seh)* to wash (oneself)

laxante (m.) *(lahk-SAHN-teh)* laxative

leche (f.) *(LEH-cheh)* milk

lechuga (f.) *(leh-CHOO-gah)* lettuce

leer *(leh-EHR)* to read

legumbres (f.pl.) *(leh-GOOM-brehs)* vegetables

lejos *(LEH-hohs)* far, distant

lengua (f.) *(LEHN-gwah)* tongue; language

lentamente *(lehn-tah-MEHN-teh)* slowly

lento *(LEHN-toh)* slow

letra (f.) *(LEH-trah)* letter (in alphabet); bank draft

letrero (m.) *(leh-TREH-roh)* sign, poster

levantar *(leh-BAHN-tahr)* to lift

levantarse *(leh-BAHN-tahr-seh)* to get up, to stand up

libre *(LEE-breh)* independent; free; at liberty

librería (f.) *(lee-breh-REE-ah)* bookstore

libro (m.) *(LEE-broh)* book

liga (f.) *(LEE-gah)* garter;
  liga de goma *(. . . deh GOH-mah)* rubber band

ligero *(lee-HEH-roh)* light; agile

lima de uñas (f.) *(LEE-mah deh OO-nyahs)* nail file

limpiar *(leem-PYAHR)* to clean

limpieza en seco *(leem-PYEH-sah ehn SEH-koh)* dry cleaning

limpio *(LEEM-pyoh)* clean

lindo *(LEEN-doh)* pretty

línea aérea (f.) *(LEE-neh-ah ah-EH-reh-ah)* airline

lino (m.) *(LEE-noh)* linen

linterna (f.) *(leen-TEHR-nah)* flashlight

lista (f.) *(LEES-tah)* list;
  lista de correo *(. . . deh koh-RREH-oh)* general delivery;
  lista de vinos *(. . . deh BEE-nohs)* wine list

litera (f.) *(lee-TEH-rah)* berth

llamada (f.) *(yah-MAH-dah)* call (telephone)

llamar *(yah-MAHR)* to call

llamarse *(yah-MAHR-seh)* to call oneself, to be named

llanta (f.) *(YAHN-tah)* tire

llave (f.) *(YAH-beh)* key

llegada (f.) *(yeh-GAH-dah)* arrival

llegar *(yeh-GAHR)* to arrive

llenar *(yeh-NAHR)* to fill

lleno (m.) *(YEH-noh)* full

llevar *(yeh-BAHR)* to take

llover *(yoh-BEHR)* to rain

lluvia (f.) *(YOO-byah)* rain

loco *(LOH-koh)* crazy

los (las) *(lohs (lahs))* the (pl.)

lograr *(loh-GRAHR)* to obtain, to get

luego *(LWEH-goh)* then, afterwards; later;
  desde luego *(DEHS-deh . . .)* of course;
  hasta luego *(AHS-tah . . .)* until later

lugar (m.) *(loo-GAHR)* place, spot

luna (f.) *(LOO-nah)* moon

lunes (m.) *(LOO-nehs)* Monday

luz (f.) *(loos)* light;
  luz delantera *(. . . deh-lahn-TEH-rah)* headlight;
  luz trasera *(. . . trah-SEH-rah)* taillight

M

madera (f.) *(mah-DEH-rah)* wood

madre (f.) *(MAH-dreh)* mother

maíz (m.) *(mah-EES)* corn

mal *(mahl)* bad

maleta (f.) *(mah-LEH-tah)* suitcase

mandar *(mahn-DAHR)* to send; to command

mandarina (f.) *(mahn-dah-REE-nah)* tangerine

manga (f.) *(MAHN-gah)* sleeve

231

mango (m.) *(MAHN-goh)* mango (tropical fruit)

mano (f.) *(MAH-noh)* hand

manteca (f.) *(mahn-TEH-kah)* lard

mantel (m.) *(mahn-TEHL)* tablecloth

mantequilla (f.) *(mahn-teh-KEE-yah)* butter

manzana (f.) *(mahn-SAH-nah)* apple

mañana *(mah-NYAH-nah)* morning; tomorrow; **hasta mañana** *(AHS-tah . . .)* until tomorrow; **pasado mañana** *(pah-SAH-doh . . .)* day after tomorrow

mapa (m.) *(MAH-pah)* map

mar (m.)-*(mahr)* sea

mareado *(mah-reh-AH-doh)* seasick, dizzy

mareo (m.) *(mah-REH-oh)* seasickness

marido (m.) *(mah-REE-doh)* husband

mariscos (m.) *(mah-REES-kohs)* seafood

martes (m.) *(MAHR-tehs)* Tuesday

martillo (m.) *(mahr-TEE-yoh)* hammer

marzo (m.) *(MAHR-soh)* March

más *(mahs)* more

masaje (m.) *(mah-SAH-heh)* massage

matador (m.) *(mah-tah-DOHR)* matador (principal bull-fighter)

mayo (m.) *(MAH-yoh)* May

medianoche (f.) *(meh-dyah-NOH-cheh)* midnight

medias (f.pl) *(MEH-dyahs)* stockings

médico (m.) *(MEH-dee-koh)* (medical) doctor

medidas (f.pl) *(meh-DEE-d ahs)* measurements; measures

medio *(MEH-dyoh)* half (adj.)

mediodía (m.) *(meh-dyoh-DEE-ah)* noon

mejilla (f.) *(meh-HEE-yah)* cheek

mejillón (m.) *(meh-hee-YOHN)* mussel

mejor *(meh-HOHR)* better

melocotón (m.) *(meh-loh-koh-TOHN)* peach

menos *(MEH-nohs)* less

menudo *(meh-NOO-doh)* small, minute; **a menudo** *(ah . . .)* often

mercado (m.) *(mehr-KAH-doh)* market

mes (m.) *(mehs)* month

mesa (f.) *(MEH-sah)* table

meter *(meh-TEHR)* to put in, to insert

mexicano(-a) *(meh-hee-KAH-noh)(-nah)* Mexican

miedo (m.) *(MYEH-doh)* fear; **tener miedo** *(teh-NEHR . . .)* to be afraid

miércoles (m.) *(MYEHR-koh-lehs)* Wednesday

mil *(meel)* thousand

millón *(mee-YOHN)* million

mirar *(mee-RAHR)* to look, to look at

misa (f.) *(MEE-sah)* mass

mismo *(MEES-moh)* same

mitad (f.) *(mee-TAHD)* half

moda (f.) *(MOH-dah)* fashion

mojado *(moh-HAH-doh)* wet

mojarse *(moh-HAHR-seh)* to get wet

molestar *(moh-lehs-TAHR)* to bother, to annoy

moneda (f.) *(moh-NEH-dah)* coin

monosabio (m.) *(moh-noh-SAH-byoh)* bullring attendant

morado *(moh-RAH-doh)* purple

moreno *(moh-REH-noh).* dark-complexioned; brunette

mosquitero (m.) *(mohs-kee-TEH-roh)* mosquito net

mostaza (f.) *(mohs-TAH-sah)* mustard

mostrar *(mohs-TRAHR)* to show

mozo (m.) *(MOH-soh)* waiter, porter

muchacho (-a) *(moo-CHAH-cho) (-cha)* boy, girl

mucho *(MOO-choh);* much; **mucho gusto** *(. . . GOOS-toh)* it's a pleasure (to meet you)

muchos *(MOO-chohs)* many, lots of

muelle (m.) *(MWEH-yeh)* dock, pier, wharf

muerte (f.) *(MWEHR-teh)* death

muerto *(MWEHR-toh)* dead

mujer (f.) *(moo-HEHR)* woman

multa (f.) *(MOOL-tah)* fine (penalty)

muñeca (f.) *(moo-NYEH-kah)* doll; wrist

muro (m.) *(MOO-roh)* (exterior) wall

museo (m.) *(moo-SEH-oh)* museum

muslo (m.) *(MOOS-loh)* thigh

muy *(mwee)* very

N

nacer *(nah-SEHR)* to be born

nada *(NAH-dah)* nothing; **de nada** *(deh . . .)* you're welcome (it's nothing)

nadar *(nah-DAHR)* to swim

nadie *(NAH-dyeh)* nobody, no one

naranja (f.) *(nah-RAHN-hah)* orange

nariz (f.) *(nah-REES)* nose

navaja (f.) *(nah-BAH-hah)* razor; pocket knife

Navidad (f.) *(nah-bee-DAHD)* Christmas

necesitar *(neh-seh-see-TAHR)* to need

neumático (m.) *(neoo-MAH-tee-koh)* tire

nevar *(neh-BAHR)* to snow

niebla (f.) *(NYEH-blah)* fog

nieve (f.) *(NYEH-beh)* snow

ninguno (-a) *(neen-GOO-noh) (-nah)* none

niño(-a) *(NEE-nyoh)(-nyah)* boy, girl

noche (f.) *(NOH-cheh)* night; **buenas noches** *(BWEH-nahs NOH-ches)* good evening; good night

nombre (m.) *(NOHM-breh)* name

norte (m.) *(NOHR-teh)* north

norteamericano(-a) *(nohr-teh-ah-meh-ree-KAH-noh)(-nah)* (North) American

noruego(-a) *(noh-RWEH-goh) (-gah)* Norwegian

nos *(nohs)* us, ourselves

nosotros *(noh-SOH-trohs)* we; us

novela (f.) *(noh-BEH-lah)* novel

noveno *(noh-BEH-noh)* ninth

noventa *(noh-BEHN-tah)* ninety

noviembre (m.) *(noh-BYEHM-breh)* November

nube (f.) *(NOO-beh)* cloud

nublado *(noo-BLAH-doh)* cloudy

nuestro *(NWEHS-troh)* our; ours

nueve *(NWEH-beh)* nine

nuevo *(NWEH-boh)* new; **de nuevo** *(deh . . .)* again, anew

nuez (f.) *(nwehs)* nut (food)

número (m.) *(NOO-meh-roh)* number

nunca *(NOON-kah)* never

O

occidente (m.) *(ohk-see-DEHN-teh)* West, Western world

octavo *(ohk-TAH-boh)* eighth

octubre (m.) *(ohk-TOO-breh)* October

ocupado *(oh-koo-PAH-doh)* occupied, busy; occupied, taken

ocurrir *(oh-koo-RREER)* to happen

ochenta *(oh-CHEN-tah)* eighty

ocho *(OH-choh)* eight

oeste (m.) *(oh-EHS-teh)* west

oficina (f.) *(oh-fee-SEE-nah)* office;
oficina de cambio *(. . . deh KAHM-byoh)* money exchange;
oficina de información *(. . . deh een-fohr-mah-SYOHN)* information bureau;
oficina de objetos perdidos *(. . . deh ohb-HEH-tohs per-DEE-dohs)* lost-and-found

oído (m.) *(oh-EE-doh)* (inner) ear

oír *(oh-EER)* to hear

ojo (m.) *(OH-hoh)* eye

olvidar; olvidarse de *(ohl-bee-DAHR; ohl-bee-DAHR-seh deh)* to forget

once *(OHN-seh)* eleven

óptico (m.) *(OHP-tee-koh)* optician

oreja (f.) *(oh-REH-hah)* (outer) ear

oro (m.) *(OH-roh)* gold

ostra (f.); **ostión** (m.) *(OHS-trah; ohs-TYOHN)* oyster

otoño (m.) *(oh-TOH-nyoh)* autumn, fall

otra vez *(OH-trah-behs)* again

otro *(OH-troh)* other, another

P

padre (m.) *(PAH-dreh)* father

pagar *(pah-GAHR)* to pay

página (f.) *(PAH-hee-nah)* page

página web (f.) *(. . . web)* Web site

país (m.) *(pah-EES)* country, nation

paja (f.) *(PAH-hah)* straw

pájaro (m.) *(PAH-hah-roh)* bird

palabra (f.) *(pah-LAH-brah)* word

pan (m.) *(pahn)* bread

panecillo (m.) *(pah-neh-SEE-yoh)* roll (bread)

pantalones (m.pl.) *(pahn-tah-LOH-nehs)* pants, trousers

pañales (m.pl.) *(pah-NYAH-lehs)* diapers

paño (m.) *(PAH-nyoh)* cloth

pañuelo (m.) *(pah-NYWEH-loh)* handkerchief

papa (f.) *(PAH-pah)* potato (Mex.)

papel (m.) *(pah-PEHL)* paper;
papel de cartas; papel de escribir *(. . . deh KAHR-tahs; . . . deh ehs-kree-BEER)* stationery, writing paper;
papel de envolver *(. . . deh ehn-bohl-BEHR)* wrapping paper;
papel higiénico *(. . . ee-HYEH-nee-koh)* toilet paper

papelería (f.) *(pah-peh-leh-REE-ah)* stationer's

paquete (m.) *(pah-KEH-teh)* package, parcel, packet;
paquete postal *(. . . pohs-TAHL)* parcel post

par (m.) *(pahr)* pair

para *(PAH-rah)* for (purpose or destination)

parabrisas (m.) *(pah-rah-BREE-sahs)* windshield

parachoques (m.) *(pah-rah-CHOH-kehs)* bumper (car)

parada (f.) *(pah-RAH-dah)* (bus) stop

paraguas (m.) *(pah-RAH-gwahs)* umbrella

parar *(pah-RAHR)* to stop

pardo *(PAHR-doh)* brown

parecer *(pah-reh-SEHR)* to seem, to appear

pared (f.) *(pah-REHD)* (interior) wall

párpado (m.) *(PAHR-pah-doh)* eyelid

partida (f.) *(pahr-TEE-dah)* game (contest)

parrilla (f.) *(pah-RREE-yah)* grill;
a la parrilla *(ah lah . . .)* broiled, grilled

pasado *(pah-SAH-doh)* last, past;
el año pasado *(ehl AH-nyoh . . .)* last year

pasajero(-a) *(pah-sah-HEH-roh) (-rah)* passenger

pasar *(pah-SAHR)* to pass; to happen; to spend (time)

pasear; pasearse *(pah-seh-AHR; pah-seh-AHR-seh)* to take a walk

paseo (m.) *(pah-SEH-oh)* walk;
paseo en coche *(. . . ehn KOH-cheh)* ride

pastel (m.) *(pahs-TEHL)* pie, cake

pastilla (f.) *(pahs-TEE-yah)* pill, tablet

pato (m.) *(PAH-toh)* duck

peatón (m.) *(peh-ah-TOHN)* pedestrian

pecho (m.) *(PEH-choh)* chest (body part)

pedazo (m.) *(peh-DAH-soh)* piece

pedir *(peh-DEER)* to ask for;
pedir prestado *(. . . prehs-TAH-doh)* to borrow

peinar *(pay-NAHR)* to comb

peine (m.) *(PAY-neh)* comb

película (f.) *(peh-LEE-koo-lah)* movie; (photographic) film;
película de color *(. . . deh koh-LOHR)* color film

peligro (m.) *(peh-LEE-groh)* danger

peligroso *(peh-lee-GROH-soh)* dangerous

pelo (m.) *(PEH-loh)* hair

pelota (m.) *(peh-LOH-tah)* ball (sports)

peluquería (f.) *(peh-loo-keh-REE-ah)* hairdresser shop, barbershop

peluquero (m.) *(peh-loo-KEH-roh)* hairdresser, barber

pendiente (m.) *(pehn-DYEHN-teh)* earring

pensar *(pehn-SAHR)* to think; to intend

pensión (f.) *(pehn-SYOHN)* pension, inn

peor *(peh-OHR)* worse; worst

pepino (m.) *(peh-PEE-noh)* cucumber

pequeño *(peh-KEH-nyoh)* small

pera (f.) *(PEH-rah)* pear

perder *(pehr-DEHR)* to lose; to miss (a bus or train)

¡perdón! *(pehr-DOHN)* excuse me!; pardon me!

perdonar *(pehr-don-NAHR)* to excuse; to pardon

perfumería (f.) *(pehr-foo-meh-REE-ah)* perfumery

periódico (m.) *(peh-RYOH-dee-koh)* newspaper

permiso (m.) *(pehr-MEE-soh)* pass, permit

SPANISH–ENGLISH

permitir *(pehr-mee-TEER)* to permit, to allow
perno (m.) *(PEHR-noh)* bolt
pero *(PEH-roh)* but
perro (m.) *(PEH-rroh)* dog
pertenecer *(pehr-teh-neh-SEHR)* to belong (to)
pesado *(peh-SAH-doh)* heavy
pesar *(peh-SAHR)* to weigh
pescado (m.) *(pehs-KAH-doh)* fish (caught)
peso (m.) *(PEH-soh)* weight; monetary unit (Mex.)
pestaña (f.) *(pehs-TAH-nyah)* eyelash
pez (m.) *(pehs)* fish (in water)
picador (m.) *(pee-kah-DOHR)* assistant (on horseback) to matador
pie (m.) *(pyeh)* foot;
a pie *(ah . . .)* on foot
piel (f.) *(pyehl)* skin; leather, fur
pierna (f.) *(PYEHR-nah)* leg (body part)
pieza (f.) *(PYEH-sah)* piece; play (theater)
píldora (f.) *(PEEL-doh-rah)* pill
pimienta (f.) *(pee-MYEHN-tah)* black pepper
pimientos (m.pl.) *(pee-NYEHN-tohs)* peppers
pinacoteca (f.) *(pee-nah-koh-TEH-kah)* art gallery
pinchazo (m.) *(peen-CHAH-soh)* puncture (tire)
piña (f.) *(PEE-nyah)* pineapple
piscina (f.) *(pees-SEE-nah)* swimming pool
piso (m.) *(PEE-soh)* floor; apartment
pista (f.) *(PEES-tah)* trail; (airport) runway
placer (m.) *(plah-SEHR)* pleasure

plancha (f.) *(PLAHN-chah)* (flat) iron; grill surface
planchar *(plan-CHAHR)* to iron, to press
planilla (f.) *(plah-NEE-yah)* form, document
plata (f.) *(PLAH-tah)* silver
plátano (m.) *(PLAH-tah-noh)* banana
platillo (m.) *(plah-TEE-yoh)* saucer
plato (m.) *(PLAH-toh)* plate; course (meal);
plato del día *(. . . dehl DEE-ah)* daily special (restaurant)
playa (f.) *(PLAH-yah)* beach
plaza (f.) *(PLAH-sah)* square;
plaza de toros *(. . . deh TOH-rohs)* bullring
pluma (f.) *(PLOO-mah)* pen; feather
poblado (m.) *(poh-BLAH-doh)* village
pobre *(POH-breh)* poor
poco *(POH-koh)* little;
un poco *(oon. . . .)* a little
pocos *(POH-kohs)* few, a few
poder *(poh-DEHR)* to be able
polaco(-a) *(poh-LAH-koh)(-kah)* Polish
polvo (m.) *(POHL-boh)* powder, dust
pollo (m.) *(POH-yoh)* chicken
poner *(poh-NEHR)* to place, to put
ponerse *(poh-NEHR-seh)* to put on; to become
por *(pohr)* by, for
porque *(POHR-keh)* because
¿por qué? *(pohr-KEH?)* why?
porte (m.) *(pohr-TEH)* postage
portero (m.) *(pohr-TEH-roh)* porter
portugués(-esa) *(pohr-too-GEHS)(-GEH-sah)* Portuguese

poseer *(poh-seh-EHR)* to possess, to own

postre (m.) *(POHS-treh)* dessert

precio (m.) *(PREH-syoh)* price

pregunta (f.) *(preh-GOON-tah)* question

preguntar *(preh-goon-TAHR)* to ask

preocuparse *(preh-oh-koo-PAHR-seh)* to worry;

no se preocupe *(noh seh preh-oh-KOO-peh)* don't worry

presentar *(preh-sehn-TAHR)* to present

prestar *(prehs-TAHR)* to lend

primavera (f.) *(pree-mah-BEH-rah)* spring (season)

primer(-a) *(pree-MEHR)(-MEH-rah)* first

prisa (f.) *(PREE-sah)* hurry, haste

probarse *(proh-BAHR-seh)* to try on

prohibido *(proh-ee-BEE-doh)* prohibited, forbidden

prohibir *(proh-ee-BEER)* to forbid

prometer *(proh-meh-TEHR)* to promise

pronto *(PROHN-toh)* quick, quickly, soon

propina (f.) *(proh-PEE-nah)* tip

próximo(-a) *(PROHK-see-moh)(-mah)* next

puede ser *(PWEH-deh sehr)* could be, maybe

puente (m.) *(PWEHN-teh)* bridge (span); bridge (dental)

puerta (f.) *(PWEHR-tah)* door

puerto (m.) *(PWEHR-toh)* port

pulgada (f.) *(pool-GAH-dah)* inch

pulgar (m.) *(pool-GAHR)* thumb

pulsera (f.) *(pool-SEH-rah)* bracelet;

reloj pulsera *(reh-LOH . . .)* wristwatch

puro *(POO-roh)* pure

puro (m.) *(POO-roh)* cigar

Q

que *(keh)* that, which, who

¿qué? *(keh?)* what?

quebrado *(keh-BRAH-doh)* broken

quedarse *(keh-DAHR-seh)* to remain, to stay

queja (f.) *(KEH-hah)* complaint

quejarse *(keh-HAHR-seh)* to complain

quemadura (f.) *(keh-mah-DOO-rah)* burn

quemar *(keh-MAHR)* to burn

querer *(keh-REHR)* to desire, to want, to wish

queso (m.) *(KEH-soh)* cheese

quien *(kyehn)* who

¿quién? *(kyehn?)* who?

quijada (f.) *(kee-HAH-dah)* jaw

quince *(KEEN-seh)* fifteen

quinto *(KEEN-toh)* fifth

quitarse *(kee-TAHR-seh)* to take off

quitasol (m.) *(kee-tah-SOHL)* parasol

quizá *(kee-SAH)* maybe, perhaps

quizás *(kee-SAHS)* maybe, perhaps

R

rábano (m.) *(RRAH-bah-noh)* radish

rabino (m.) *(rrah-BEE-noh)* rabbi

radiografía (f.) *(rrah-dyoh-grah-FEE-ah)* X-ray

raíz (f.) *(rrah-EES)* root

237

raya (f.) *(RRAH-yah)* line; part (of hair)

razón (f.) *(rrah-SOHN)* reason

real *(rreh-AHL)* real; royal

recado (m.) *(rre-KAH-doh)* message

recalentar *(rreh-kah-lehn-TAHR)* to overheat; to reheat

receta (f.) *(rre-SEH-tah)* prescription; recipe

recibir *(rreh-see-BEER)* to receive

recibo (m.) *(rre-SEE-boh)* receipt

recobrar *(rreh-koh-BRAHR)* to recover, to get back

recomendar *(rreh-koh-mehn-DAHR)* to recommend

reconocer *(rreh-koh-noh-SEHR)* to recognize

recordar *(rreh-kohr-DAHR)* to remind, to remember

recuerdos (m.pl.) *(rreh-KWEHR-dohs)* regards; memories

rechazar *(rreh-chah-SAHR)* to refuse; to reject

red (f.) *(rred)* net; network

redondo *(rreh-DOHN-doh)* round

refresco (m.) *(rreh-FREHS-koh)* refreshment, soft drink

regalo (m.) *(rreh-GAH-lah)* gift

rehusar *(rreh-oo-SAHR)* to refuse

reírse *(rreh-EER-seh)* to laugh

rejilla (f.) *(rreh-HEE-yah)* (overhead) rack (in trains and buses)

relámpago (m.) *(rreh-LAHM-pah-goh)* lightning

reloj (m.) *(rreh-LOH)* clock, watch

remendar *(rreh-mehn-DAHR)* to mend

remitente *(rreh-mee-TEHN-teh)* sender

remolacha (f.) *(rreh-moh-LAH-chah)* beet

remolcar *(rreh-mahl-KAHR)* to tow

repentino *(rreh-pehn-TEE-nah)* sudden

repetir *(rreh-peh-TEER)* to repeat

reponerse *(rreh-poh-NEHR-se)* to recover (health)

resfriado *(rrehs-FRYAH-doh)* (common) cold

resorte (m.) *(rreh-SOHR-teh)* spring (mechanical)

respirar *(rrehs-pee-RAHR)* to breathe

responder *(rrehs-pahn-DEHR)* to answer, to respond

respuesta (f.) *(rrehs-PWEHS-tah)* answer

resultar *(rreh-sool-TAHR)* to result

retrete (m.) *(rreh-TREH-teh)* rest room, toilet

revelar *(rreh-beh-LAHR)* to develop (film)

revisar *(rreh-bee-SAHR)* to check

revista (f.) *(rreh-BEES-tah)* magazine

rico *(RREE-kah)* rich

rieles (m.pl.) *(RRYEH-lehs)* train tracks

río (m.) *(RREE-oh)* river

robar *(rroh-BAHR)* to steal, to rob

rodilla (f.) *(rroh-DEE-yah)* knee

rojo *(RROH-hah)* red

rollo (m.) *(RROH-yoh)* roll (film)

romper *(rrohm-PEHR)* to break, to tear

ropa (f.) *(RROH-pah)* clothes;
   ropa blanca *(. . . BLAHN-kah)* linen;
   ropa interior *(. . . een-teh-RYOHR))* underwear

rosado *(rroh-SAH-doh)* pink

roto *(RROH-toh)* broken; torn

rueda (f.) *(RRWEH-dah)* wheel

ruido (m.) *(RRUEE-doh)* noise

ruidoso *(rruee-DOH-soh)* noisy

rumano(-a) *(roo-MAH-noh) (-nah)* Rumanian

ruso(-a) *(ROO-soh)(-sah)* Russian

S

sábana (f.) *(SAH-bah-nah)* bedsheet

sábado (m.) *(SAH-bah-doh)* Saturday

saber *(sah-BEHR)* to know (a fact), to know (how)

sabroso *(sah-BROH-soh)* tasty

sacacorchos (m.) *(sah-kah-KOHR-chohs)* corkscrew

sacar *(sah-KAHR)* to take out, to extract

sacerdote *(sah-serh-DOH-teh)* priest

saco (m.) *(SAH-koh)* coat

sal (f.) *(sahl)* salt

sala (f.) *(SAH-lah)* living room

salado *(sah-LAH-doh)* salty

salchicha (f.) *(sahl-CHEE-chah)* hot dog, sausage

salchichón (m.) *(sahl-chee-CHOHN)* salami, bologna

salida (f.) *(sah-LEE-dah)* exit

salir *(sah-LEER)* to leave, to go out, to depart

salón (m.) *(sah-LOHN)* lounge;
salón de belleza *(. . . deh beh-YEH-sah)* beauty parlor

salsa (f.) *(SAHL-sah)* sauce, gravy

salud (f.) *(sah-LOOD)* health;
¡salud! *(sah-LOOD!)* (to your) health! (toast)

saludo (m.) *(sah-LOO-doh)* greeting

saludos (m.pl.) *(sah-LOO-dohs)* greetings, regards

salvavidas (m.) *(sahl-bah-BEE-dahs)* life preserver, life-guard

sandalia (f.) *(sahn-DAH-lyah)* sandal

sandía (f.) *(sahn-DEE-ah)* watermelon

sangre (f.) *(SAHN-greh)* blood

sanidad (f.) *(sah-nee-DAHD)* health

santuario (m.) *(sahn-TWAH-ryoh)* sanctuary, shrine

sastre (m.) *(SAHS-treh)* tailor

sazonado *(sah-soh-NAH-doh)* seasoned (food)

se *(seh)* self, himself, herself, itself, themselves

seco *(SEH-koh)* dry;
limpieza en seco *(leem-PYEH-sah ehn . . .)* dry cleaning

sed (f.) *(sehd)* thirst;
tener sed *(teh-NEHR . . .)* to be thirsty

seda (f.) *(SEH-dah)* silk

seguir *(seh-GEEHR)* to follow; to continue

segundo *(seh-GOON-doh)* second

segundo (m.) *(seh-GOON-doh)* second (unit of time)

seguro *(seh-GOO-roh)* sure, certain;
seguro (m.) *(seh-GOO-roh)* insurance;
seguro de viaje *(. . . deh BYAH-heh)* travel insurance

seis *(says)* six

sellar *(seh-YAHR)* to seal

sello (m.) *(SEH-yoh)* seal; postage stamp

semana (f.) *(seh-MAH-nah)* week

semáforo (m.) *(seh-MAH-foh-roh)* traffic light

sentar *(sehn-TAHR)* to seat

sentarse *(sehn-TAHR-seh)* to sit down

sentir *(sehn-TEER)* to be sorry; to feel

sentirse *(sehn-TEER-seh)* to feel (sick, tired, happy, etc.)

señor (m.) *(seh-NYOHR)* Mr., sir; gentleman

señora (f.) *(seh-NYOH-rah)* Mrs., madam; lady

señorita (f.) *(seh-nyoh-REE-tah)* Miss, Ms.; young lady

septiembre (m.) *(sehp-TYEHM-breh)* September

séptimo *(SEHP-tee-moh)* seventh

ser *(sehr)* to be

servicio (m.) *(sehr-BEE-syoh)* service

servilleta (f.) *(sehr-bee-YEH-tah)* napkin

servir *(sehr-BEER)* to serve

servirse *(sehr-BEER-seh)* to help (serve) oneself

sesenta *(seh-SEHN-tah)* sixty

setenta *(seh-TEHN-tah)* seventy

sexto *(SEHKS-toh)* sixth

si *(see)* if

sí *(see)* yes

siempre *(SYEHM-preh)* always

siete *(SYEH-teh)* seven

significar *(seeg-nee-fee-KAHR)* to signify; to mean

silla (f.) *(SEE-yah)* chair

sillón (m.) *(see-YOHN)* armchair

simpático *(seem-PAH-tee-koh)* pleasant, likable (person)

sin *(seen)* without

sinagoga (f.) *(see-nah-GOH-gah)* synagogue

sitio (m.) *(SEE-tyoh)* place, spot

sobre (m.) *(SOH-breh)* envelope

sobre *(SOH-breh)* on, upon; **sobre todo** *(. . . TOH-doh)* above all, especially

sobretodo (m.) *(soh-breh-TOH-doh)* overcoat

sol (m.) *(sohl)* sun

solamente *(soh-lah-MEHN-teh)* only, solely

soleado *(ah-soh-LEH-ah-doh)* sunny

solo *(SOH-loh)* alone

sólo *(SOH-loh)* only, solely

sombra (f.) *(SOHM-brah)* shadow

sombrerería (f.) *(sohm-breh-reh-REE-ah)* hat shop

sombrero (m.) *(sohm-BREH-roh)* hat

sortija (f.) *(sohr-TEE-hah)* ring

sostén (m.) *(sohs-TEHN)* bra, brassiere

su; sus (w/pl.) *(soo; soos)* his, her, its, their, your

suave *(SWAH-beh)* soft, mild

subir *(soo-BEER)* to go up, to climb

suceder *(soo-seh-DEHR)* to happen

sucio *(SOO-syoh)* dirty, soiled

sueco(-a) *(SWEH-koh)(-kah)* Swedish

suela (f.) *(SWEH-lah)* (shoe) sole

suelo (m.) *(SWEH-loh)* floor, ground

suelto *(SWEHL-toh)* loose

suelto (m.) *(SWEHL-toh)* small change

sueño (m.) *(SWEH-nyoh)* dream; sleep; **tener sueño** *(teh-NEHR . . .)* to be sleepy

suerte (f.) *(SWEHR-teh)* luck; **¡buena suerte!** *(BWEH-nah . . . !)* good luck!

suizo(-a) *(SUEE-soh)(-sah)*
Swiss

supuesto *(soo-PWEHS-toh)*
supposed;
por supuesto *(pohr . . .)* of
course

sur (m.) *(soor)* south

suyo; suyos (w/pl.) *(SOO-yoh;
SOO-yohs)* his, hers,
yours, theirs, one's, its

T

taberna (f.) *(tah-BEHR-nah)*
tavern

tacón (m.) *(tah-KOHN)* (shoe)
heel

talón (m.) *(tah-LOHN)* baggage claim check; heel
(foot)

tal vez *(tahl behs)* perhaps,
maybe

talle (m.) *(TAH-yeh)* size
(clothing)

también *(tahm-BYEHN)* also,
too

tapa (f.) *(TAH-pah)* lid

taquilla (f.) *(tah-KEE-yah)*
ticket office

tarde *(TAHR-deh)* late

tarde (f.) *(TAHR-deh)* afternoon;
¡buenas tardes! *(BWEH-nahs
TAHR-dehs!)* good after-
noon!

tarifa (f.) *(tah-REE-fah)* fare,
rate

tarjeta postal (f.) *(tahr-HEH-tah
pohs-TAHL)* postcard

taza (f.) *(TAH-sah)* cup

té (m.) *(teh)* tea

techo (m.) *(TEH-choh)* roof

tela (f.) *(TEH-lah)* cloth

telefonista (m./f.) *(teh-leh-foh-
NEES-tah)* telephone oper-
ator

temporalmente *(tehm-poh-rahl-
MEHN-teh)* temporarily

temprano *(tehm-PRAH-noh)*
early

tenazas (f.pl.) *(teh-NAH-sahs)*
pliers

tenedor (m.) *(teh-neh-DOHR)*
fork

tener *(teh-NEHR)* to have;
tener que *(. . . keh)* to have
to;
tener prisa *(. . . PREE-sah)*
to be in a hurry

teñir *(teh-NYEER)* to dye, to
tint

tercero *(tehr-SEH-roh)* third

terciopelo (m.) *(tehr-syoh-PEH-
loh)* velvet

ternera (f.) *(tehr-NEH-rah)*
veal

tía (f.) *(TEE-ah)* aunt

tiempo (m.) *(TYEHM-poh)*
time; weather

tienda (f.) *(TYEHN-dah)* store,
shop

tierra (f.) *(TYEH-rrah)* dirt;
soil; land; earth

tijeras (f.pl.) *(tee-HEH-rahs)*
scissors

timbre (m.) *(TEEM-breh)* bell

tinta (f.) *(TEEN-tah)* ink

tintorería *(teen-toh-reh-REE-ah)*
dry cleaner's

tío (m.) *(TEE-oh)* uncle

toalla (f.) *(toh-AH-yah)* towel

tobillo (m.) *(toh-BEE-yoh)*
ankle

tocar *(toh-KAHR)* to touch; to
play (an instrument)

tocino (m.) *(toh-SEE-noh)*
bacon

todavía *(toh-dah-BEE-ah)* still,
yet;
todavía no *(. . . noh)* not
yet

todo *(TOH-doh)* all, everything, every, each;

todo el mundo *(. . . ehl MOON-doh)* everybody, everyone

todos *(TOH-dohs)* everybody, everyone, all

tomacorriente (m.) *(toh-mah-koh-RRYEHN-teh)* (electrical) outlet

tomar *(toh-MAHR)* to take; to drink

tontería (f.) *(tohn-teh-REE-ah)* nonsense

torcedura (f.) *(tohr-seh-DOO-rah)* sprain

toro (m.) *(TOH-roh)* bull
  corrida de toros (f.) *(koh-RREE-dah deh. . . .)* bullfight

toronja (f.) *(toh-ROHN-hah)* grapefruit

torta (f.) *(TOHR-tah)* cake

tortilla (f.) *(TOHR-tee-yah)* omelet (Sp.); tortilla (a flat cornmeal cake/Mex.)

tos (f.) *(tohs)* cough

toser *(toh-SEHR)* to cough

tostada (f.) *(tohs-TAH-dah)* toast; tostada (a type of Mexican food)

trabajar *(trah-bah-HAHR)* to work

traducir *(trah-doo-SEER)* to translate

traer *(trah-EHR)* to bring

traje (m.) *(TRAH-heh)* suit;
  traje de baño *(. . . deh BAH-nyoh)* bathing suit

transbordar *(trahns-bohr-DAHR)* to transfer

transbordo (m.) *(trahns-BOHR-doh)* transfer (pass)

tranquilo *(trahn-KEE-loh)* quiet; tranquil

tranvía (m.) *(trahn-BEE-ah)* trolley, streetcar

trece *(TREH-seh)* thirteen

treinta *(TRAYN-tah)* thirty

trepar *(treh-PAHR)* to climb

tres *(trehs)* three

tronar *(troh-NAHR)* to thunder

trueno (m.) *(TRWEH-noh)* thunder

tú *(too)* you (familiar)

tuerca (f.) *(TWEHR-kah)* nut (for a bolt or screw)

turco(-a) *(TOOR-koh)(-kah)* Turkish

turismo (m.) *(too-REES-moh)* tourism

U

un (una) *(oon (OO-nah)* a/an;
  una vez *(OO-nah behs)* once (one time)

uno(-a) *(OO-noh)(-nah)* one (person), someone

uña (f.) *(OO-nyah)* nail (finger, toe)

usar *(oo-SAHR)* to use

uso (m.) *(OO-soh)* use, purpose

usted (abbr.: Ud.) *(oos-TEHD)* you (formal)

ustedes (abbr.: Uds.) *(oos-TEH-dehs)* you (pl.)

uvas (f.pl.) *(OO-bahs)* grapes

V

vacío *(bah-SEE-oh)* empty

valer *(bah-LEHR)* to be worth

válido *(BAH-lee-doh)* valid, good

variedades (f.pl.) *(bah-ryeh-DAH-dehs)* vaudeville

varios *(BAH-ryohs)* several, various

vaso (m.) *(BAH-soh)* drinking glass

¡váyase! *(BAH-yah-seh!)* go away! scram!

veinte *(BAYN-teh)* twenty

velocidad máxima (f.) *(beh-loh-see-DAHD MAHK-see-mah)* speed limit

venda (f.) *(BEHN-dah)* bandage

vendar *(behn-DAHR)* to bandage

vender *(behn-DEHR)* to sell

veneno (m.) *(beh-NEH-noh)* poison

venir *(beh-NEER)* to come

venta (f.) *(BEHN-tah)* sale

ventana (f.) *(behn-TAH-nah)* window

ventanilla (f.) *(behn-tah-NEE-yah)* window (train, airplane); ticket window

ventilador (m.) *(behn-tee-lah-DOHR)* (electric) fan

ver *(behr)* to see

verano (m.) *(beh-RAH-noh)* summer

verdad (f.) *(behr-DAHD)* truth

verdaderamente *(behr-dah-deh-rah-MEHN-teh)* really, truly

verdadero *(behr-dah-DEH-roh)* true

verde *(BEHR-deh)* green

verduras (f.) *(behr-DOO-rahs)* vegetables; greens

vestido (m.) *(behs-TEE-doh)* dress

vestirse *(behs-TEER-seh)* to get dressed

vez (f.) *(behs)* time (occasion); **una vez** *(OO-nah . . .)* once; **en vez de** *(ehn . . . deh)* instead of, in place of

viajar *(bee-ah-HAR)* to travel

viaje (m.) *(BYAH-heh)* trip, journey; **¡buen viaje!** *(bwehn . . .)* bon voyage!

viajero (-a) *(byah-HEH-roh) (-rah)* traveler

vida (f.) *(BEE-dah)* life

vidrio (m.) *(BEE-dryoh)* glass (material)

viejo *(BYEH-hoh)* old

viento (m.) *(BYEHN-toh)* wind; **hace viento** *(ah-seh . . .)* it's windy

viernes (m.) *(BYEHR-nehs)* Friday

vino (m.) *(BEE-noh)* wine

vista (f.) *(BEES-tah)* view

vitrina (f.) *(bee-TREE-nah)* showcase, store window

vivir *(bee-BEER)* to live

volante (m.) *(boh-LAHN-teh)* steering wheel

volver *(bohl-BEHR)* to return

vuelo (m.) *(BWEH-loh)* flight

vuelta (f.) *(BWEHL-tah)* turn

Y

y *(ee)* and

ya *(yah)* already

yo *(yoh)* I

yodo (m.) *(YOH-doh)* iodine

yugoslavo(-a) *(yoo-gohs-LAH-boh)(-bah)* Yugoslav

Z

zanahoria (f.) *(sah-nah-OH-ryah)* carrot

zapatería (f.) *(sah-pah-teh-REE-ah)* shoe store

zapatillas (f.pl.) *(sah-pah-TEE-yahs)* slippers

zapato (m.) *(sah-PAH-toh)* shoe

zarpar *(sahr-PAHR)* to sail

zarzuela (f.) *(sahr-SWEH-lah)* operetta (Sp.)

zumo (m.) *(SOO-moh)* juice (Sp.)

243